HaynesXtreme
Customiz

D0129204

Sport Utility Vehicle
Customizing

3 1336 07108 5790

Haynes Publishing Group
Sparkford Nr Yeovil
Somerset BA22 7JJ
England

Haynes North America, Inc
861 Lawrence Drive
Newbury Park
California 91320 USA

ABCDE
FGHIJ
KLMNO
PQRST

Acknowledgements

Photos on front cover: Main SUV, owned by Don Boehm. Suspension parts, courtesy of RCD suspension.
SUV shown in inset photo, courtesy of Warn Industries, Inc.

Our sincere thanks to the following SUV owners who allowed us to photograph their outstanding vehicles for use throughout this book:

Jeri and Rex Bartle, Wendy Henderson and Robert Maddox.

Various photographs of vehicles throughout the book used with permission of RCD Suspensions, ATS Design, Warn Industries, Inc., Universal Products, Edelbrock, Smittybilt, Grillcraft Custom Products, Street Scene Equipment, and Lund, a brand of Lund International.

ISBN 1 56392 545 1
Library of Congress Control Number 2004111808

Printed in the U.S.A.

While every attempt is made to ensure that the information in this manual is correct, no liability can be accepted by the authors or publishers for loss, damage, or injury caused by any errors in, or omissions from, the information given.

04-208

Be **careful** and know the **law**!

1 Advice on safety procedures and precautions is contained throughout this manual, and more specifically within the Safety section towards the back of this book. You are strongly recommended to note these comments, and to pay close attention to any instructions that may be given by the parts supplier.

2 Haynes recommends that vehicle modification should only be undertaken by individuals with experience of vehicle mechanics; if you are unsure as to how to go about the modification, advice should be sought from a competent and experienced individual. Any questions regarding modification should be addressed to the product manufacturer concerned, and not to Haynes, nor the vehicle manufacturer.

3 The instructions in this manual are followed at the risk of the reader who remains fully and solely responsible for the safety, roadworthiness and legality of his/her vehicle. Thus Haynes is giving only non-specific advice in this respect.

4 When modifying a SUV it is important to bear in mind the legal responsibilities placed on the owners, drivers and modifiers of vehicles. If you or others modify the SUV you drive, you and they can be held legally liable for damages or injuries that may occur as a result of the modifications.

5 The safety of any alteration and its compliance with construction and use regulations should be checked before a modified vehicle is sold as it may be an offense to sell a vehicle which is not roadworthy.

6 Any advice provided is correct to the best of our knowledge at the time of publication, but the reader should pay particular attention to any changes of specification to the vehicles, or parts, which can occur without notice.

7 Alterations to a vehicle should be disclosed to insurers and licensing authorities, and legal advice taken from the police, vehicle testing centers, or appropriate regulatory bodies.

8 Some of the procedures shown in this manual will vary from model to model; not all procedures are applicable to all models. Readers should not assume that the vehicle manufacturer has given their approval to the modifications.

9 Neither Haynes nor the manufacturer give any warranty as to the safety of a vehicle after alterations, such as those contained in this book, have been made. Haynes will not accept liability for any economic loss, damage to property or death and personal injury other than in respect to injury or death resulting directly from Haynes' negligence.

Contents

1

2

7

8

9

10

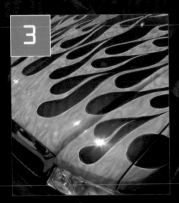

Painting and graphics

Interiors

Wheels & tires

Suspension

In-car entertainment

Accessories

From here . . .

We've all seen them on the road; those tricked-out SUVs that make us feel inadequate in our stock rides. Some are raised up so high there's almost enough room for another vehicle beneath, while others are dropped so low they practically touch the ground. They've been debaged, painted and chromed and when they roar past, it's enough to make any enthusiast's mouth water. But, the best thing about these modified SUVs is just that - they're modified, so they stand out from all the others that rolled off the line.

. . . to **there**

There's no question you'll want to personalize your SUV, adding the options the factory forgot. Most of us need to keep our SUV's on the road during customization; we'll prefer to do one or two projects at a time, one weekend at a time. If you're planning some radical changes or sending it to a customizing shop, your SUV could have some "down time" that you'll need to plan for – this can sometimes exceed your schedule. Be sure you've got a back-up vehicle available that can handle your usual loads.

Whatever plan you choose, it's best to have one . . . a plan . . . and you're sure to wind up with an SUV that's the envy of the neighborhood!

A blast through the past

Where'd my SUV come from?

Whether you're picking up the kids at school or hauling your boat and family out to the lake for the weekend, the SUV is the one vehicle that can do it all. While the need for these do-anything vehicles is clear to us today, it hasn't always been that way. The SUV's development was more than the bright idea of one manufacturer. The SUV evolved over time, slowly developing its current form. Since it's difficult to trace a direct lineage for the SUV, it's best to think of its development in terms of the characteristics we've come to expect from modern SUV's: 1) The ability to carry multiple passengers in comfort, 2) A cargo area, 3) An off-road capability (improved ground clearance and the availability of four-wheel drive).

Utility vehicles

Almost since the automobile's invention, manufacturers have designed light trucks that could be used to haul the family and its belongings. The early pick-ups and panel-side vans were the first vehicles that offered family utility, but these vehicles were not designed to carry multiple passengers. In these early days, riding in a motor vehicle was considered a privilege, and riding in a pick-up bed or the back of a van was considered perfectly logical. After all, there were no interstate highways, and 30 mph was considered a fast cruising speed.

Chevrolet's Suburban Caryall was the first popular light truck designed to carry both passengers and cargo. Beginning production in 1935, this unique (for its time) vehicle vaguely resembled modern SUV's. Being built on a light-truck chassis meant the Suburban could seat up to eight passengers and also carry a significant cargo load. The fully enclosed steel body had windows all the way around, giving all passengers the opportunity to enjoy the scenery. By 1938, Ford and International Harvester (IHC) responded with their "Commercial Station Wagons." The competition had begun. By the mid-

1950's, all the US truck-makers were producing similar bodies for their light trucks. Although passengers could be carried in greater comfort, these trucks were not luxury vehicles by any measure. Most were used to carry workers and their equipment to worksites, and the interiors were basic and utilitarian.

Off-road vehicles

The first mass-produced off-road vehicles began to appear after World War II. The first of these were four-wheel drive (4WD) military vehicles adapted for civilian use. The Jeep "CJ" (for Civilian Jeep) was introduced in 1945, and the Dodge Power Wagon truck became available in 1947. In 1948, inspired by the military Jeep, Land Rover introduced the first 4WD vehicle specifically for civilian use. These 4WD vehicles were rugged, versatile, and had some limited cargo-carrying capability. However, comfort was not on the design agenda, and you wouldn't want to drive one to a cocktail party. The "open-air" configuration for the passenger compartments were not conducive to comfortable on-road driving.

Putting them together

In 1955, Jeep introduced its 4WD Utility Wagon. While not overwhelmingly popular, this was the first full-size utility-vehicle chassis that had a true off-road capability. By 1957, both Chevrolet and GMC had a 4WD Suburban. Although the market for these vehicles was relatively small at the time, there was a growing interest in these rugged, go-anywhere vehicles that could carry large loads of both people and equipment. These early SUV's were sometimes purchased by large families in remote areas, but more commonly the buyers were businesses, such as telephone and electric companies, that needed to transport people and equipment over unimproved roads.

The modern SUV emerges

The full-size SUV continued to improve through the 1960's. Even with competition from Dodge's Town Wagon, Jeep's Wagoneer and IHC's Travelall, the Suburbans from Chevy and GMC continued to be very popular, with steadily increasing sales. Interiors became more car-like, and comfort options such as air-conditioning and power windows became available. Truck manufacturers began to recognize that these vehicles were being used for family transportation and recreation. Aware of the success of IHC's Scout and Toyota's Landcruiser, Ford made its entry into the arena of recreational SUV's with its Bronco in 1966. Much smaller than the Suburban, the Bronco was a sporty off-road vehicle that had an optional rear seat and removable hardtop. This little SUV found a niche between the larger Suburban and the less-comfortable open-air vehicles. By 1970, there was competition from Chevrolet and GMC who introduced the Blazer and Jimmy. Somewhat larger than the Bronco, these GM SUV's were built on shortened truck chassis and also featured removable hard tops and rear seats. In 1974, Dodge followed the same formula to develop its Ramcharger.

Through the 1980's, SUV's continued to gain more on-road sophistication, emphasizing a smoother ride and passenger comforts. By now, SUV's were typically being equipped like luxury cars, with upgraded seating and power assists. Ford, Chevy and GMC now offered smaller versions of their Bronco and Blazer/Jimmy, based on their mini pick-up chassis. In 1984, Jeep introduced its Cherokee, Toyota its 4Runner and Isuzu its Trooper. Nissan's Pathfinder appeared in 1987. By now, Toyota's Landcruiser had grown into a very large, and very luxurious, SUV.

It's often said that the SUV came into its own in the 1990's. There was certainly an explosion of new models, such as the Ford Explorer and Isuzu Rodeo in 1991, Honda Passport in 1994, Toyota RAV4 in 1996, Honda CRV in 1997, and Dodge Durango in 1998. The CRV and RAV4 were much smaller than the typical SUV and were designed around front-wheel drive chassis (a long

driveshaft joined the front transaxle to a rear differential on 4WD models). These smaller SUV's provided far better fuel economy than a full-size SUV.

By 1995, Chevy and GMC had retired their full-size Blazer and Jimmy in favor of the Tahoe and Yukon. The Trailblazer and Envoy replaced the smaller Blazer and Jimmy in 2002. The big news for Ford fans was the 1997 introduction of the Expedition, finally providing direct competition to the Suburban. The even larger Ford Excursion was available in 2000. The small front/four-wheel drive Ford Escape and the similar Mazda Tribute appeared in 2001.

Also in 2001, the full-size Sequoia and the smaller Highlander rounded out Toyota's line of SUV's. Not to be outdone, Nissan introduced its mid-size Xterra in 2000, its front-wheel/four-wheel drive Murano in 2003 and its full-size Armada in 2004. Beginning with the Lexus "LX" series in 1996, a trend toward ultra-luxurious SUV's had emerged. This has led to the upscale Infiniti QX4 in 1997, the Lincoln Navigator and Mercedes "ML" in 1998, the Cadillac Escalade in 1999, and, in 2003, the Infiniti "FX" and Lincoln Aviator.

While we have mentioned some of the more popular manufacturers, there are many, many more fine SUV's available today. Through its evolution, the SUV has become increasingly comfortable, quiet and luxurious, without sacrificing ruggedness or utility. In fact, today's SUV's haul and tow more than ever before. Fuel economy and power are up, as well, and unique styling gives each its own personality. No wonder SUV's have become so popular. And history has taught us that we can expect even better SUV's in the years to come.

Body
and exterior

There are a lot of options out there when it comes to customizing the exterior of your SUV. There's custom headlights and taillights, body kits with bumper covers and side skirts, running boards, mirrors and custom grilles. You can debadge for a sleek finish, or add aftermarket badges for a unique look. The combination of modifications is endless, and when you're finished, you'll have a completely uncommon vehicle. Of course, it's important to think about exactly what you want to do before you do it. You don't want it to look like you just threw a bunch of mismatched parts at your SUV. Shop around to find parts you really like and look at other modified SUVs for inspiration. You may have to fiddle with some of your prefabricated pieces to get them to fit just right, but pretty soon your vision will really start to come together, and you'll be cruising the sweetest SUV in town.

Detailing

Detailing is much more than simply washing your SUV. A good detail should be done once or twice a year to really clean your SUV. Here are some tips and tricks from the pros to help.

Cleaning trim

A small paint brush with soft bristles will remove the dirt and debris that collects around door handles and at the edges of trim

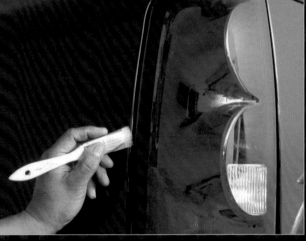

If car wax gets into a gap and dries out it can be difficult to dislodge. One way to remove it safely is with a two-inch-wide paintbrush. Take a clean (preferably new) paintbrush and cut the bristles down to about 1/2 to 3/4-inch in length. Wrap duct tape around the metal band to protect the paint from scratches. This special tool will make short work of wax, dirt and anything else that's hard to remove

The weatherstripping at the bottom edge of your windows can collect all sorts of debris. And if you have tinted windows, this will mean scratches. The best way to loosen up this crud is to scrub it off with an all-purpose cleaner and a toothbrush

Cleaning wheels

To loosen up junk that sticks to the wheel in tight spaces, use a bristle brush like this, or even a paintbrush

Removing decals

To remove a decal from glass, warm up the adhesive with a heat gun, then carefully remove the decal with a razor blade

Here's a trick that's so obvious you'll ask yourself "Why didn't I think of that myself?" Buy a pair of cheap cotton work gloves and use them to loosen up brake dust and grime in really tight corners. (The gloves will also protect your fingers from scratches should you drag them across a small section of "casting flash" or rough edges)

If you need to remove a wheel, put a piece of plastic (or a plastic bag) over the lug nuts to protect them from scratches when you break them loose with a lug nut wrench

Interiors

To clear away dust and dirt from a/c louvers or other hard-to-get-at nooks and crannies, use compressed air. These small cans are for computer keyboards and can be found at office supply stores.

Cotton swabs are great for cleaning those small interior spots that just seem to attract dirt and grime

Super-cleaning paint

A small brush is also handy for dusting off small levers and knobs

Before applying your wax, the paint needs to be as clean and free from oxidation and contaminants as possible. There are dozens of pre-wax cleaners and polishes available at your local auto parts store, but a lot of professional detailers now use detailing clay that will make the surface smooth as silk.

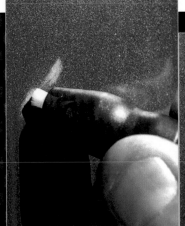

01 Clean the chip thoroughly with a special fiberglass-bristled brush

02 Use a standard touch-up applicator or a paper match to deposit the touch-up color into the cleaned-out chip, or . . .

03 . . . if a better match for your paint is available only in a spray can, aim the spray into the cup from the top of the can and then use that liquid paint for touch-ups with a paper match or toothpick for an applicator

Touch-up

Many minor scrapes and shallow scratches can be eliminated or reduced with nothing more than wax and polishes. Try this first before doing anything more drastic. If that doesn't work, then color it with a touch-up paint.

Most touch-up paint bottles have an applicator inside, or you can use the end of a paper match or a toothpick to apply it. The latter works best in applying only a tiny amount if necessary. The factory brush in the jar puts on way too much paint so that it usually makes a small chip end up looking a lot bigger. If you can't find the color you need for your SUV in a touch-up bottle, check your auto parts store in the spray-paint racks. There is a much wider selection of "original" touch-up paint colors in spray cans than in little bottles.

We illustrate here a method of repair using a "Chip Kit" which has all the supplies you need for a quality touch-up except the actual color to match your vehicle.

 Tip
Basic touch-up paint available from auto parts stores should be a close match to your SUV's paint, but due to the myriad colors and shades that come out each year, it can sometimes be difficult to find touch-up paint for more than a few years back. It is suggested that you buy a bottle or two when you buy your SUV and keep them in the glove box for future use.

Clear lacquer is applied in several coats after the original color paint has **04** thoroughly dried, which usually takes several days

When the repair is built up to slightly above the surrounding paint, the area is sanded flat with several grades of ultra-fine **05** sandpaper wrapped around a soft rubber sanding block

Very fine polishing compound is then used to blend the repair and sanded **06** area into the rest of the paint

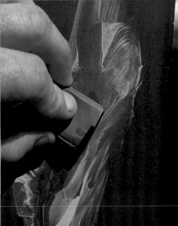

De-badging

You know that old saying about beauty being in the eye of the beholder? Well, you might not see things the same way as The General. Just because Chevrolet put a set of funky badges on your SUV doesn't mean that you're stuck with these eyesores. They're pretty easy to remove, and your ride will look a whole lot cleaner without them.

There's more than one way to remove glued-on badges. One common method is to use a scraper and heat gun on raised plastic letters such as the "CHEVROLET" on your liftgate. Some plastic badges will come off in one piece. But they're just as likely to break as you bend them to lift them off the paint. So if it's important to keep the badge in one piece . . .

01

. . . try using fishing line instead of a scraper. Because the adhesive that attaches the badge to the paint is fairly soft even before it's heated up by a heat gun, a good strong piece of fishing line will cut through it like a knife through butter

02

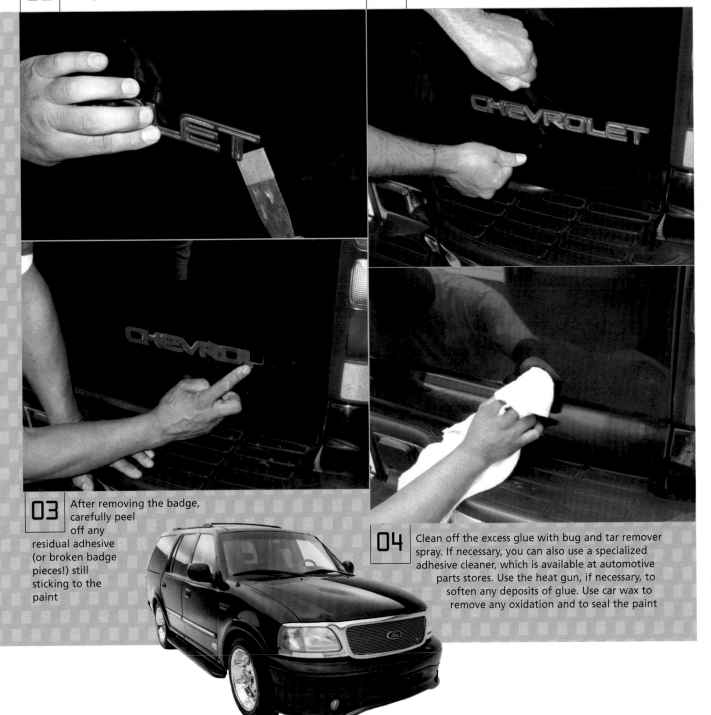

03 After removing the badge, carefully peel off any residual adhesive (or broken badge pieces!) still sticking to the paint

04 Clean off the excess glue with bug and tar remover spray. If necessary, you can also use a specialized adhesive cleaner, which is available at automotive parts stores. Use the heat gun, if necessary, to soften any deposits of glue. Use car wax to remove any oxidation and to seal the paint

Aftermarket mirrors

Installing custom mirrors

01 Carefully pry off the triangular trim panel

There are plenty of aftermarket mirrors out there that can add an interesting touch to your exterior. If you pull a trailer, there are extended mirrors to help you see around that monster you're pulling. Some even have built-in turn signals integrated into the mirror surface. Whether you choose a carbon fiber finish or clip-on accents, they'll certainly be much more exciting than your stock mirrors. You'll see the installation is fairly easy as we dress up a late-model Tahoe with a set of sport mirrors from APC.

Mirror covers that simply snap into place over your stock mirrors are also available from Applied Products Group (APG)

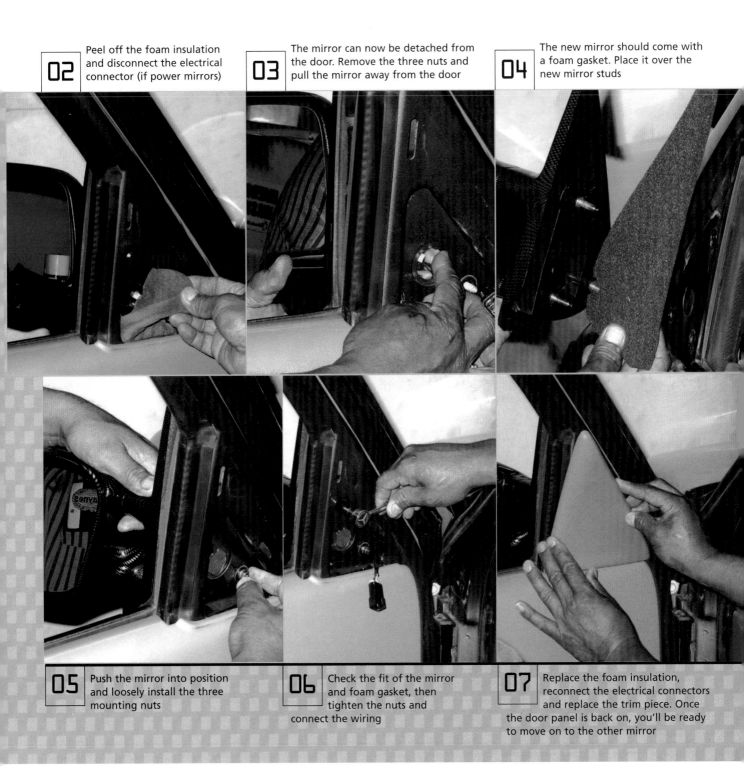

02 Peel off the foam insulation and disconnect the electrical connector (if power mirrors)

03 The mirror can now be detached from the door. Remove the three nuts and pull the mirror away from the door

04 The new mirror should come with a foam gasket. Place it over the new mirror studs

05 Push the mirror into position and loosely install the three mounting nuts

06 Check the fit of the mirror and foam gasket, then tighten the nuts and connect the wiring

07 Replace the foam insulation, reconnect the electrical connectors and replace the trim piece. Once the door panel is back on, you'll be ready to move on to the other mirror

Custom headlights

The front end of your SUV is already pretty nice, but if you want it to stand out from the crowd, you need to make it unique. Start by replacing those stock headlight housings with some aftermarket units. They'll really set it off.

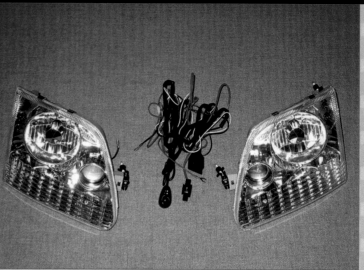

Installing custom headlights

Here's our headlight kit from APC. This particular kit includes a set of fog lights (within the headlight housing) and a relay, an inline fuse, a switch that allows you to turn the fog lights on and off independently of the regular headlights and a wiring harness to connect all of these new components.

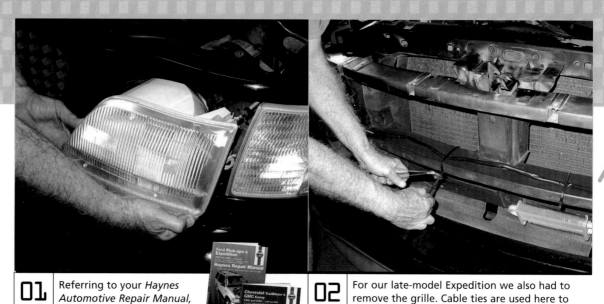

01 Referring to your *Haynes Automotive Repair Manual,* remove the stock headlight assemblies

02 For our late-model Expedition we also had to remove the grille. Cable ties are used here to secure the wiring harness for the new lights

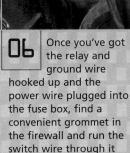

03 Install the new headlight housings in exactly the same manner as the stock units. The headlights use the stock connectors, but the fog lights must still be wired, which is what we'll do next

04 Route the power, ground and switch wiring along the left side of the engine compartment to the fuse box. Secure it with a cable tie or two. Drill a hole in the left inner fender panel and mount the relay and the ground wire with a self-tapping screw

05 Open the fuse box and find an unused spade terminal that's hot all the time and hook up the power wire to it. If there are no vacant 12-volt spade terminals in the fuse box, use a fuse tap to connect the power wire to a 12-volt fused circuit

06 Once you've got the relay and ground wire hooked up and the power wire plugged into the fuse box, find a convenient grommet in the firewall and run the switch wire through it

Remove the adhesive backing from the switch and firmly push the switch onto the dash surface

07

Grab your flashlight and test light, get under the dash and find a switched 12-volt wire (12 volts only when the ignition key is turned to ON) for the switch circuit wire

08

Using a quick-splice type connector, or some other suitable connector, splice into the switched 12-volt wire to complete the installation

09

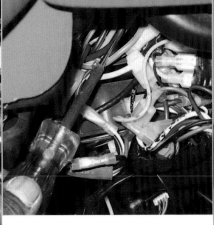
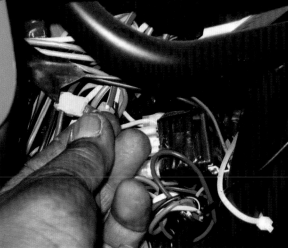

Aftermarket taillight assemblies

One of the hottest styling trends is installing clear, smoked or colored aftermarket taillight assemblies. Basically, all you have to do is remove the stock taillight assemblies and replace them with the aftermarket units of your choice. Don't forget that your running lights and brake lights must be red, your back-up lights clear and your turn signal lights either amber or red. Your stock taillight lenses are already the proper colors for these lights, but you'll have to install the correct color bulbs if your aftermarket housings are clear.

Installing custom taillights

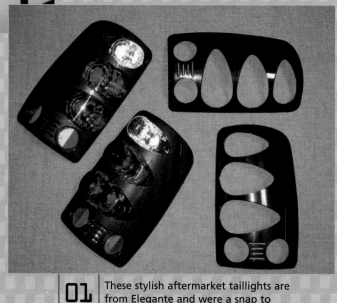

01 These stylish aftermarket taillights are from Elegante and were a snap to install on our late-model Chevy Tahoe

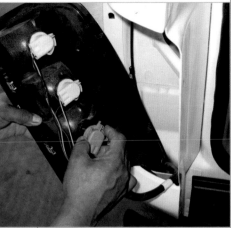

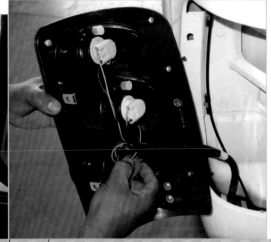

02 Remove your stock taillight housings (refer to your *Haynes Automotive Repair Manual* for the procedure)

03 Give the bulb holders a counterclockwise twist and remove them from the old taillight housing . . .

04 . . . then transfer them to the new unit, giving them a clockwise turn to lock them in place

05 Carefully place the new taillight assembly in position . . .

06 . . . and install the taillight mounting bolts. That's it! Now go and do the other one!

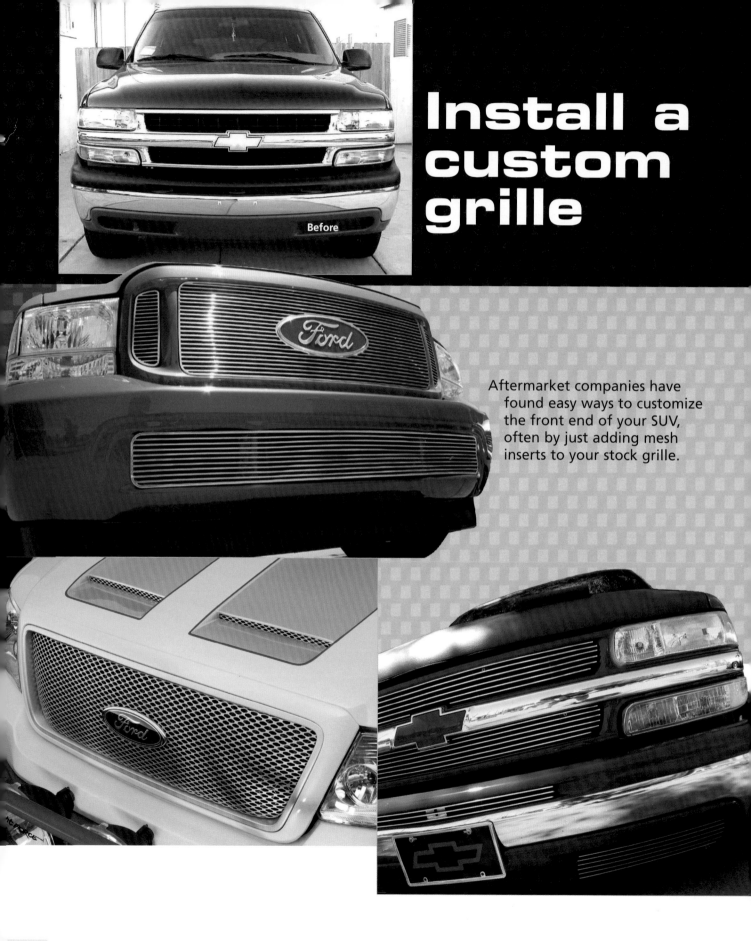

Before

Install a custom grille

Aftermarket companies have found easy ways to customize the front end of your SUV, often by just adding mesh inserts to your stock grille.

01 The front end on our project SUV could use a little something, so we decided to install a GrillCraft sport grille. If you need help removing your grille, refer to your *Haynes Automotive Repair Manual*

02 Install the sport grille over the existing grille and hold it firmly in place

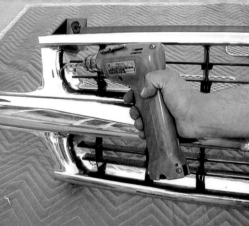

03 Mark the mounting tab holes

04 Using the proper size drill bit, drill the mounting screw holes

05 Attach the mesh grille using the mounting hardware supplied in the kit. That's it! Now go put the grille back on!

Here's a custom grille installation on an Expedition. It's a little more work because the grille stretches across the entire front of the SUV, surrounding the headlights. The end result, though, is a really clean looking front end.

01 First, remove the left and right turn signal/sidemarker housings, then remove the stock grille (refer to your *Haynes Automotive Repair Manual*, if necessary)

02 The stock grille - and this custom unit from ATS Designs - use a couple of spring clips to lock the two lower mounting tabs into their corresponding slots in the lower radiator crossmember. So don't forget to install the two new spring clips on the two lower mounting tabs of the new grille

03 When installing the new custom grille make sure that the lower mounting tabs, with the spring clips installed, are aligned with their respective slots in the lower radiator crossmember . . .

04 . . . then swing the grille assembly up and push the clips into their respective slots until they snap into place

05 The new grille assembly uses the same mounting points as the stock grille: two screws at the left end (shown) and two more at the right end, and five screws across the top to secure the upper edge of the grille bezel to the upper radiator crossmember. That's all there is to it! Now install the two front turn signal/sidemarker housings and you're done!

Body styling

Aside from a set of trick wheels or a custom paint job, a body kit is the biggest visual change you can make to your SUV.

Custom body pieces are not nearly as expensive or tough to install as you might think. The newest styles already fit well, so little if any trimming is necessary.

These pieces can be either fiberglass or high-quality molded polyurethane. Some manufacturers will paint the parts for you based on your truck's color code, otherwise you will need to find a paint shop to spray the parts for you.

Installing running boards

01 The running board is held solidly in place with strong L-brackets

Running boards are one of those modifications that can not only be a useful add-on, but also improve the looks of your SUV. The running boards installed here are from ATS Designs and have built-in lights.

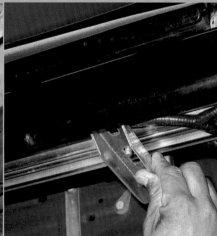

02 Here you can see the various L-brackets in place, awaiting the attachment of the running board

03 The running boards and brackets are adjustable in order to get a perfect fit down the side of your SUV

04 If your running boards are equipped with running lights, you can splice into the parking light circuit to have them on whenever the headlights are on, or with the door courtesy light circuit to come on when one of the doors is opened

Add function and flash to your wheel wells with
Fender flares

If you're adding bigger wheels and tires, and your SUV didn't come equipped with fender flares, consider adding a set. On the practical side, they will keep rocks and mud from wrecking your paint and also give your SUV an aggressive new look.

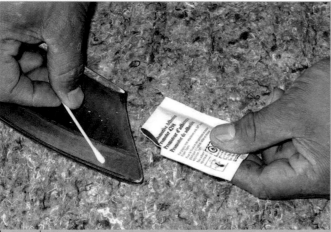

01 The fender flares shown here are from ATS Designs. They are held tightly to the body with a special double-face tape that requires an adhesion promoter, being applied in this photo

02 With the special tape on the fender flare and the fender thoroughly cleaned, peel OFF just a few inches of the tape paper at each end. Do NOT peel off all of the red tape at this time! If you mess up and plant your new flare at the wrong angle, you'll break it before you can unpeel the tape from the fender. This stuff is STICKY!

03 Remove the screws from the inner fender splash shield. Move the flare into position with the ends of the tape sticking out and loosely reinstall the screws

04 Firmly grab the two exposed ends of the red tape and carefully peel off the rest of the red tape. Push the fender flare firmly against the fender, then tighten the screws

Front valances

The stock valances (that plastic piece that sits under your front bumper) on most SUV's aren't bad looking. It's just that they all look alike. Wouldn't it be nice to put something a little different on there? Well, now you can. The aftermarket offers a wide variety of valance styles and colors. We selected this ATS Designs valance because it's different (but not too wild), uses the factory mounting points, and ATS painted it to match the factory color.

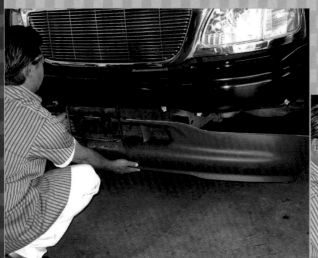

01 First, remove your old valance

02 Test fit the new valance to make sure it's a good fit and all the mounting holes in the valance are aligned with the factory mounting holes. If a factory hole is too far off, use a grease pencil to mark the correct location for the hole and drill a new hole

03 Apply the double-sided tape to the area next to the center tunnel in the new valance. Do NOT remove the red tape yet!

04 Peel back just an inch or two of the red tape now, then insert the mounting bolts from underneath (threaded end facing up) . . .

05 . . . and secure each mounting bolt hex head with a piece of masking tape so that it won't fall out during installation

07 Grasp both ends of the red tape and carefully and slowly pull it off and out through the gap between the bumper and the new valance. Firmly push the valance up against the underside of the bumper. Now go back and tighten all the nuts and bolts securely

06 Using the center tunnel and the two driving light holes to guide the mounting bolts through their corresponding holes in the bumper, install the new valance and secure it with a flanged nut at each mounting bolt. Snug all of the bolts and nuts but don't tighten them yet

Painting and Graphics

Custom painting

Get some ideas of what you like – go to shows, look at books and magazines – and then find yourself a painter who can make it happen.

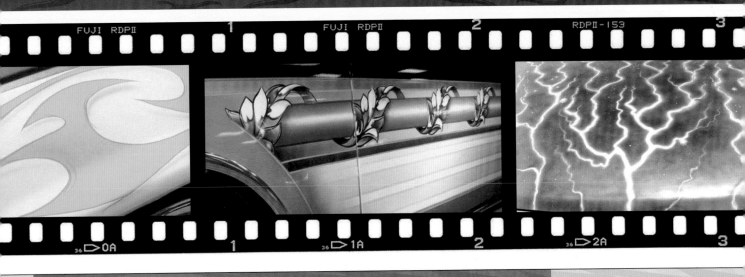

Metallic paints - have microscopic particles of metal in the paint that reflect the light and give off a high luster effect.

"Metal flake" paint - is really just metallic paint with bigger chunks of reflective metal in it.

Candy apple paint - consists of a reflective base coat of silver or gold metallic, with a translucent color coat on top of it and clear coat on top of that.

Pearlescent (or simply pearl) finishes - created by applying multiple layers of paint: first a matte color base, then a colored lacquer coat and finally a clear lacquer coat.

"Flip-flop" pearl or chameleon paint - uses high-tech liquid crystal and interference pigments to produce a finish that looks like one color when viewed from some angles but looks like a different color when viewed from other angles.

How to choose a good paint and body shop

The old adage "you get what you pay for" is especially true of professional bodywork and paint jobs: the best work is very, very expensive. The reason is the labor-intensive nature of the work. It takes a lot of time to do a good job, and time is money.

So, if you decide to take your truck to a shop for body repairs or painting, be prepared to pay plenty for a first-class job. And shop around before deciding where to have the work done. A little time spent checking out body shops in advance will pay off in the long run.

Don't let a shop's location scare you off. Most shops are located in industrial areas that can't be considered good neighborhoods. However, any good shop, regardless of its location, will have safe, secure storage areas - either indoors, outdoors or both - for customer's cars. If a shop doesn't have well-secured parking, keep looking.

As you drive up to a shop, note its general condition, how the surrounding area is maintained and the types of cars that are waiting for attention. If they all seem to be desirable collectors or luxury cars, you might have stumbled onto a top-notch shop. (You might also need to call your banker for a big loan!) Are completed vehicles stored indoors or outside? Are they covered or not? It might not be obvious at first glance, but details like these can make a difference between a great paint job and a good one, so ask the manager when you get a chance.

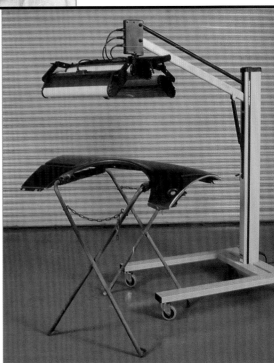

Ask the owner or manager to give you a little tour of the shop. Is it relatively neat and clean, or are there body parts and tools scattered all over the place? Is it well lit and roomy, or dark, dingy and cramped? Are the body repairmen and painters wearing neat new work clothes, or grungy old paint-smeared jeans and T-shirts? Is there plenty of room between the cars that are being worked on, or are they jammed together? Has any effort been made to protect the interiors of vehicles and the exterior parts that don't require work? What about new replacement parts and the old parts that have been removed from vehicles during repairs? Are they shoved into the interiors of the cars, or are they labeled and stored neatly in a separate area?

Look for a frame-straightening fixture, MIG, TIG and oxyacetylene welding equipment, and separate masking and painting booths.

Try to get a close look at some recently completed paint jobs. Note whether any dirt or lint is trapped in the paint. Look for runs and sags and see if the coverage is uniform and complete. Was everything carefully masked off? Or is there paint all over trim pieces? If it looks good, chances are that everything was done right.

If everything so far checks out, there's one more thing you should do: Ask the owner or manager if he would be willing to allow you to contact some recent customers so that you can ask them whether they're satisfied with the work done on their vehicles. If there's any hesitation at all, thank the person you're dealing with and leave. If the owner or manager is willing to put you in touch with recent customers, and if they're happy with the work done on their cars, you need look no farther.

Vinyl graphics

That custom paint job may not be paint at all. Custom vinyl graphics - don't call them decals - have come a long, long, way.

But vinyl isn't perfect. For one thing, it's not that easy to install. Vinyl sorta goes on like a decal, but some vinyl graphics (like the kit shown on the following pages) are often much larger, and far more difficult to install, than a mere decal. And unlike paint, which can be quickly removed with reducer if you screw up, vinyl is pretty much toast if you commit a Major Mistake while applying it. Our graphics kit from Universal Products made our SUV look sharp and installed in only a couple of hours.

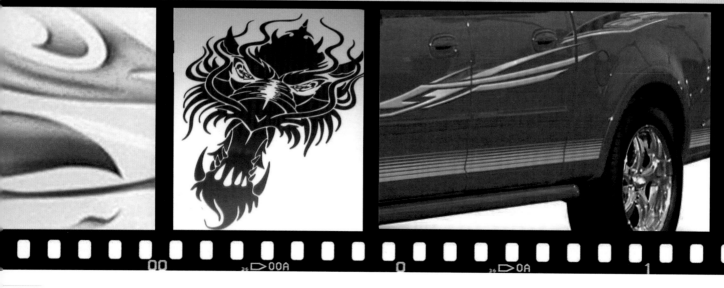

Installing custom vinyl graphics

01 First, round up the stuff you'll need for applying your vinyl graphics kit. We used a special stripping cleaner, isopropyl rubbing alcohol, a spray bottle with a slightly soapy water solution (mix a gallon of water with a single DROP of dishwasher soap), a heat gun, scissors, a gasket scraper (taped to protect the paint), masking tape, lint free shop towels and a squeegee

02 After using the special stripping cleaner, we used a few little pieces of masking tape to "hang" the graphic, to figure out exactly where to put it. Once you've determined the location and the orientation of the graphic, tape it to the truck along the entire upper edge. This long piece of tape will serve as the "hinge" so that you can flip the graphic up and out of the way as necessary during the installation process

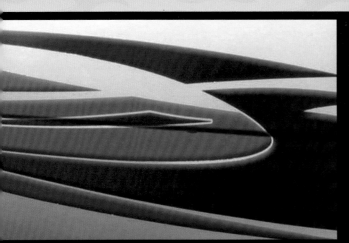

03 Okay, flip up the graphic and secure it to the window with a piece or two of tape, wipe off the area to be covered with alcohol, then spray the surface liberally with your slightly soapy water solution

04 Starting at one end, peel off the liner (the white backing sheet) from the graphic, working your way down in sections

05 As you peel off each section of the liner, spray the exposed back side of the vinyl graphic itself with liberal amounts of the semi-soapy water and apply the vinyl graphic to the truck, spraying and peeling off the liner as you go

06 Once the liner is completely removed and the graphic is applied to the vehicle surface, work out the air and water bubbles with your hand first, keeping the graphic flat and preventing it from moving around. Start at the upper middle part of the graphic and work your way down and out toward the ends to prevent the graphic from bunching up

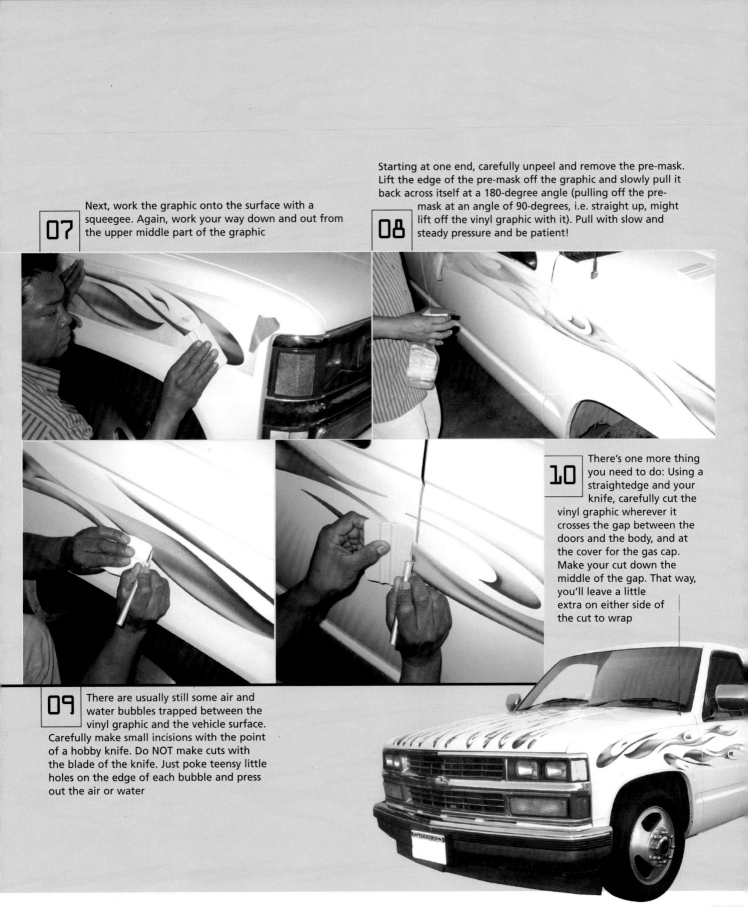

07 Next, work the graphic onto the surface with a squeegee. Again, work your way down and out from the upper middle part of the graphic

08 Starting at one end, carefully unpeel and remove the pre-mask. Lift the edge of the pre-mask off the graphic and slowly pull it back across itself at a 180-degree angle (pulling off the pre-mask at an angle of 90-degrees, i.e. straight up, might lift off the vinyl graphic with it). Pull with slow and steady pressure and be patient!

10 There's one more thing you need to do: Using a straightedge and your knife, carefully cut the vinyl graphic wherever it crosses the gap between the doors and the body, and at the cover for the gas cap. Make your cut down the middle of the gap. That way, you'll leave a little extra on either side of the cut to wrap

09 There are usually still some air and water bubbles trapped between the vinyl graphic and the vehicle surface. Carefully make small incisions with the point of a hobby knife. Do NOT make cuts with the blade of the knife. Just poke teensy little holes on the edge of each bubble and press out the air or water

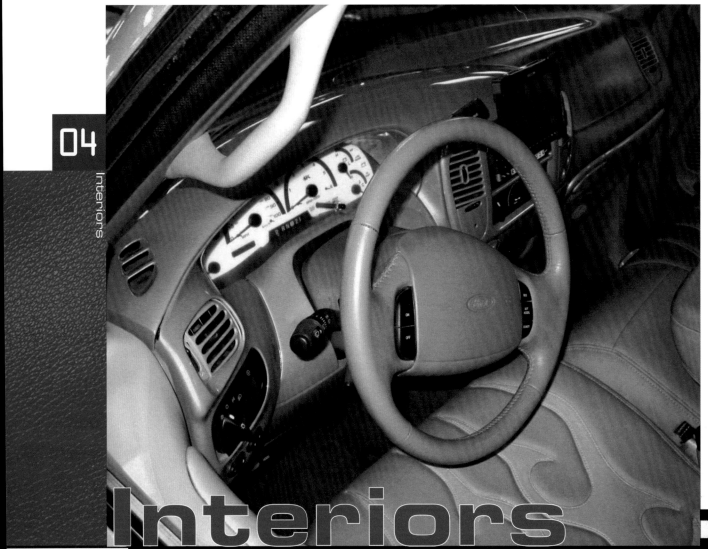

Interiors

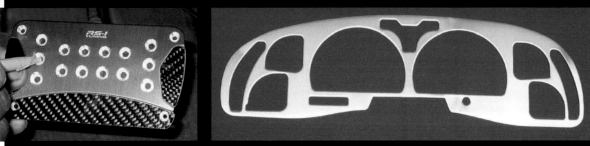

If you're sick and tired of staring at your boring stock interior, there are plenty of ways to trick it out. From aftermarket seat covers to custom trim panels, there are countless options for your SUV. Many are quick and relatively inexpensive to install and they add life to your drab interior. Something as simple as a steering wheel trim ring or a set of custom pedals can make your SUV look a million times better without hours of labor. Or, if you want something that'll really impress your passengers, you can install luminescent gauges with multi-colored lights. There's really no limit as to how far you can go with your interior modifications.

Custom pedals

A custom interior is all about getting the details right. Replacing your stock, worn-out rubber pedal covers with stylish new replacements can be a great upgrade.

Selecting a new set of pedal covers

When selecting a set of pedal covers for your SUV, pay close attention to a couple of things. First, the new pedal covers will have two or more mounting bolt holes in them. When installing the new pedal covers, you'll be using these mounting holes to attach the new covers to the old steel pedal footplates. But you'll also have to drill mounting holes in the old footplates, and those holes must be aligned with the mounting holes in the new covers. So it's a good idea to either take the dimensions of your old steel pedal footplates with you when you go to buy new pedal covers, or to be able to take the new covers out to the parking lot, place them in position on your pedals and eyeball the dimensions. If the new pedal covers have mounting holes sitting over nothing but thin air when you position them over the old rubber pedal covers, think seriously about a different set of aftermarket pedal covers! The stock pedal footplates must be large enough so that you'll be able to drill mounting holes in them without having to relocate any of the new pedal covers. Relocating the pedal covers could cause clearance problems between the pedals. And, more importantly, it could be dangerous to offset the pedals because you might accidentally depress the wrong pedal at the wrong time.

Inexpensive, easy-to-install pedal covers, which slip over the pedal pads and clamp into place, are widely available. Just be aware that, even when installed properly, they have the potential of slipping and interfering with another pedal, which could cause an accident. Securely bolting the pedal cover in place is the safer option.

Installing a set of custom pedal covers

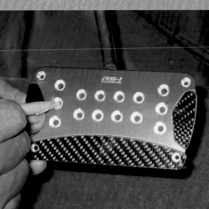

01 Remove the old rubber cover from the pedal

02 When you've got your custom pedal correctly positioned, mark the pedals where the mounting holes will be drilled

03 Use a center punch to make some indentations for the drill bit . . .

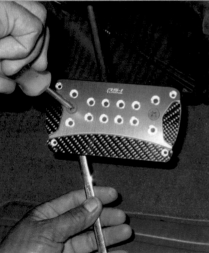

04 . . . then drill the mounting holes in the pedal

05 When you're satisfied that the pedal covers are correctly positioned, tighten the mounting bolts securely. We can't overstress the importance of making sure the pedal cover mounting bolts are tight. It's a good idea to check the tightness of the bolts a few weeks after installing them and periodically thereafter

06 And that's it! One customized set of pedals!

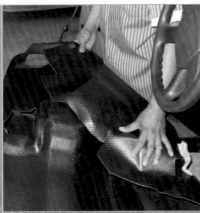

01 The first step to new carpet is to get the old carpet or vinyl floor covering out of the vehicle. But, before you can do that, you have to remove the sill panels, kick panels and seats. If your SUV is equipped with a center console, remove that as well. Refer to the *Haynes Automotive Repair Manual* for your specific vehicle to get more details on these procedures

02 When all the seats are out you can pull out the old floor covering. Vacuum or sweep the interior and check for rust. If you find some, make sure to remove it and treat the area with a rust-inhibiting paint

03 Use the old flooring as a stencil, trace all the edges and holes onto the new carpet with chalk or a grease pencil

Let's face it, even if you've got floor mats, chances are the carpet in your SUV is pretty dirty. And, if it's equipped with vinyl floor covering instead of carpet, it's easy to clean, but nothing special to look at. So, what you need is brand new carpet to match all your other interior modifications. It's going to take a little bit of work - including removing the seats - but it'll all be worth it when you see how much new carpet can perk up your interior. Carpet kits that are pre-formed for specific makes and models are commonly available and make this job a lot easier. The one shown here is from J.C. Whitney.

Installing carpet

04 After the new carpet is marked-up, position it onto the floor of your SUV, smoothing out any wrinkles or lumps

05 Using a sharp knife, trim off any excess carpet and cut out the holes. It may be easier to make a small slit instead of a hole and trim around the object after it's pushed through the slit

06 Now, just reinstall your seats, kick panels and sill panels, and you're done!

Custom styling rings for airbag-equipped steering wheels

Even though you can't legally replace an airbag-equipped steering wheel with a custom aftermarket steering wheel, you can upgrade the appearance of your stock wheel with a custom styling ring. Each ring is custom molded to fit over the stock steering wheel. Styling rings are available in decorator colors like blue, red, silver, white, and yellow; in carbon fiber; and in simulated woodgrain such as burlwood or rosewood. Ours, from Grant Products, was easy to install and turned an ordinary airbag-equipped steering wheel into a stylish, elegant "new" steering wheel.

Carefully position the styling ring over the steering wheel. Before pressing it onto the steering wheel, make sure that the spoke covers on the ring are perfectly aligned with the spokes on the steering wheel. Then press the styling ring onto the steering wheel. Work your way around the circumference of the wheel, pressing down firmly all the way around to make sure that the styling ring is firmly attached. Easy, huh?

01 Clean off the steering wheel with a mild degreaser. Remove all dust, oil and silicone protectant

02 Peel off the protective strip covering the adhesive

03

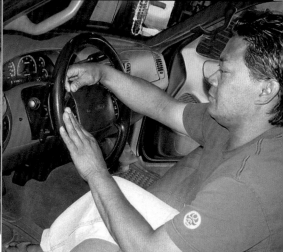

Interior trim

Add a little color to your interior

Automotive exteriors come in lots of nice colors, but most stock interiors are still mainly black, gray, or beige. Boring!

But it doesn't have to be that way. There are three ways to add a little (or a lot of) color to your interior: paint it, film it or re-cover it with new trim pieces. Interior trim film is a new high-tech product that you can buy in sheets and cut to fit various trim pieces on the dash, the center console and the doors. Film is UV and heat resistant and it's available in a variety of finishes - simulated woodgrain, carbon fiber, etc. - and colors. Trim covers are also available in a similarly wide range of finishes and colors.

Painting trim

01 First, remove the trim panels you want to paint. We decided to start with the inside trim panels for the outside mirrors (refer to your *Haynes manual* if you're unfamiliar with how to remove these pieces)

02 Give each piece a really good scrubbing with a Scotch-Brite pad to rough it up (paint adheres better to a rougher surface). When you're done, give it another soap and water bath, then dry it off

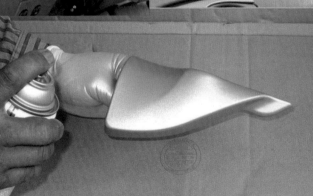

03 Apply a mist coat of primer. This step is essential to help the paint stick to the plastic. Allow the primer plenty of time to dry

04 Apply the first topcoat very dusty, which means you must spray from a little further away than normal, letting the paint fall onto the job, rather than blasting it on using the full force of the aerosol spray propellant. Some colors need several coats before they look right. Allow time for each one to dry (several minutes) before applying the next coat

05 When you're done with both sides, re-install the mirror trim pieces and *voilà!*

Applying film

01 First, remove the trim panel(s) you want to film. (refer to your *Haynes manual* for help). Using a suitable degreaser, clean up the surface you want to film. If you're hoping to film a heavily grained finish, be aware that the grain will show through thin film, and the film won't fully stick to a heavily grained surface either

02 Cut the film to the approximate size and carefully warm up the film and the panel itself with a heat gun. Peel off the backing sheet, and make SURE that the film stays as flat as possible. Also make sure that, when you pick up the film, you don't allow it to stick to itself!

03 Carefully apply the film. If you're installing a patterned film (like the carbon-fiber-look film shown here), make very sure that you apply the film with the pattern aligned horizontally and vertically. Starting at one edge, work across to minimize air bubbles and creases. If you get a bad crease, unpeel the film a bit and try again. Don't try to shift the position of the film once you've begun to apply it; the adhesive is far too sticky

Before trimming your filmed panel, work out the air bubbles with a soft cloth. Then make sure the film is sticking well by going over it firmly **04** with the edge of a plastic credit card

Trimming the panel can be tricky. It's easier to trim the more complicated edges after heating up the film with a hairdryer or heat gun. But don't overdo it! Also, make sure that the hobby knife you're using is SHARP. A blunt **05** knife will ripple the film, and might even tear it

To get the film to wrap neatly around a curved edge, make several slits almost up to the edge, then heat up the area you're working on, wrap each sliver of film over the edge and stick it on firmly. If you heat the film sufficiently, it wraps around and keeps its shape. Without the heat, the film **06** might spring back, ruining all your hard work

Electro-luminescent gauge faces are one way to add a little light to your instrument cluster. Custom-made cluster trim panels are another. They're less expensive and easier to install than custom gauge faces and are available in a wide array of colors and finishes. We obtained the trim panel you see here from APC. The procedure shown here for installing the trim panel is typical. However, the actual dashboard trim panels on your vehicle might be slightly different than the ones on our project vehicle, so refer to your *Haynes Automotive Repair Manual* for help if necessary.

Instrument cluster trim panels

01 Unpack your new instrument cluster trim panel and read through the instructions carefully

02 Remove the trim panel that covers up the steering column opening (refer to your *Haynes Automotive Repair Manual*)

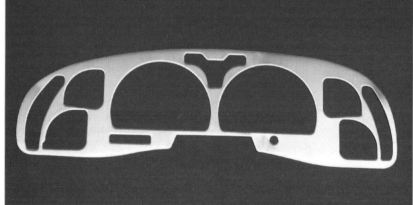

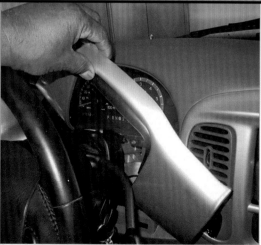

03 Remove the instrument cluster bezel (refer to your *Haynes Automotive Repair Manual*)

04 Remove the screws that secure the lens to the instrument cluster

05 Remove the lens

06 Place the new cluster trim panel in position to make sure that it's a good fit

07 Peel off the backing protecting the adhesive on the backside of the cluster trim panel. The front side has a clear protective film that will be peeled off once the panel is in place

08 Okay, here it comes! Take a deep breath and CAREFULLY place the cluster trim in position, then push it onto the instrument cluster. Make SURE that the trim panel is perfectly horizontal and that the gauge face cutouts in the trim panel are aligned with the gauge faces before you press the trim onto the cluster. There is zero margin for error here. If you stick this thing onto the cluster crooked, you'll never get it off without bending or kinking the trim panel and possibly damaging the cluster assembly, so take your time and do it right!

09 Whew! That wasn't so bad (was it?). Once you've thoroughly tamped down the entire surface of the new trim panel onto the cluster assembly, peel off the protective sheet from the front of the cluster trim, then install the lens immediately before dust has a chance to settle onto it. Then install the instrument cluster bezel and the steering column trim

Installing a custom trim panel kit

Interior trim kits come in a variety of styles and colors, custom-fit for nearly all SUVs. Ours, from Woodview, was a snap to install and really dressed-up the dash and door panels. These pieces fit right over the stock ones so there's no need to take apart your dash or doors.

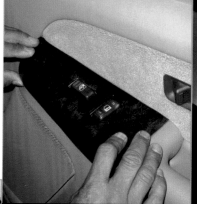

01 Before removing the adhesive backing paper, test-fit the armrest panel

02 Wipe off all oil, dirt, silicone protectant, etc. with rubbing alcohol

03 Now apply the adhesion promoter to the surface of the trim piece. Some kits include a pen-type promoter like this one, which is convenient, neat and precise. Other kits give you some promoter in a small container, which you apply with a cotton swab

04 Peel off the adhesive backing from the new trim panel . . .

05 . . . and press the panel into place

06 Once you've installed the two armrest trim pieces, use the same procedure to install the big single piece for the dashboard

Billet Accessories

If you've ever spent time at a car show, you've seen that the little custom details are what sets those vehicles apart from the stock models on the street. Adding a few billet accessories may give you just the look you're after.

A few of the more popular interior billet pieces, some shown here from Empire Motor Sports:
- Shift handle
- A/C vents
- Speaker grille covers
- Door panel inserts
- Window cranks
- Door sill plates

Billet accessories from Lokar Performance Products were a snap to install and really dressed up the interior.

With the steering wheel removed (see your *Haynes Manual*, especially for airbag info), a single screw secures the turn signal lever.

Above - Billet pedals are also a nice interior touch

Left - Turn signal and tilt steering wheel levers

Gauge face upgrade

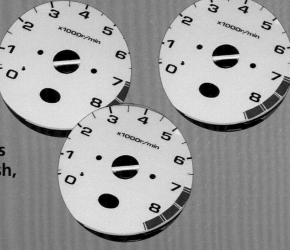

White, colored, even glow-in-the-dark . . . changing out your stock black gauge faces will really add a custom touch to your dash, like this set from APC.

01 First thing we removed was the instrument cluster

02 On this particular model we separated the cluster bezel from the cluster assembly . . .

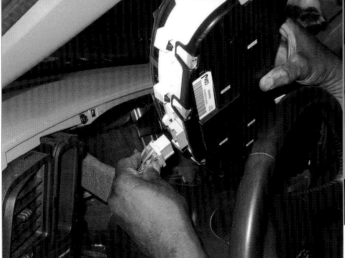

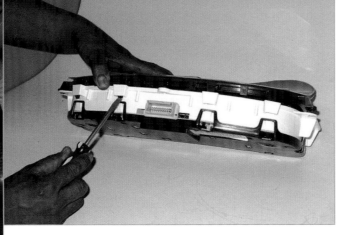

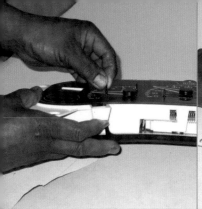

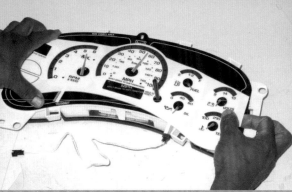

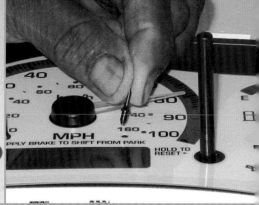

03 . . . then carefully pulled off the little black plastic needle "stop" posts

04 We installed the new gauge face onto the cluster by very carefully working each of the gauge needles through their respective holes

05 Once the new gauge face was in position, we reinstalled the needle stop posts

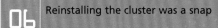

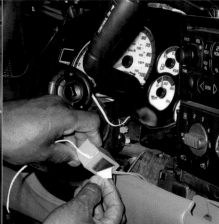

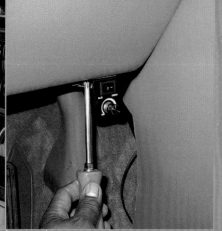

06 Reinstalling the cluster was a snap

07 We picked a convenient spot for the converter box and affixed it using the adhesive backing

08 Same goes for the switch housing. A couple of self-tapping screws and in no time it was attached to the underside of the dash

Just make sure you get the right kit for your truck, and don't start stripping anything until you're sure it's the right one. Look carefully at every detail. Applications for replacement faces should be very specific for model and model year. This is one mod that is not ONE SIZE FITS ALL.

09 Finally, we connected all the wiring, made a final test to find a circuit that's hot only when the parking lights are turned on, then connected the power. That's it. We're done!

Upgrading your basic stock seats with soft leather, custom-fit for your SUV is an easy and relatively inexpensive project you can do at home. Our leather covers from Katzkin Leather fit like a glove and installed in only a couple of hours. They can even do custom embroidery like the "Katzkin" stitching shown here.

Custom Seat Covers

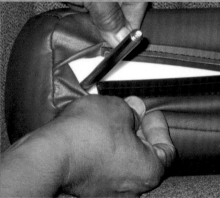

01 The first thing you need to do is remove the seats

02 Before you get started on re-covering the seats, start by removing the headrests. Simply push on the mounts and pull the headrest from the seatback

03 Unsnap the plastic fastener on the underside of the headrest and remove the old cover

04 Install the new cover and fasten, then tuck in the ends

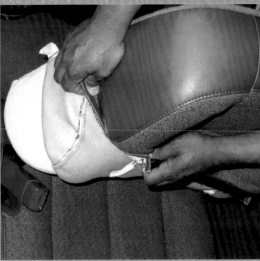

05 For the seat back, follow the supplied directions and remove the old upholstery

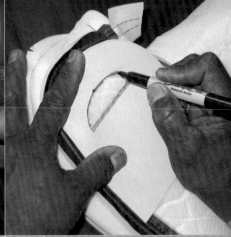

06 Our seats had built-in seat belts which required some careful marking and cutting of the new cover

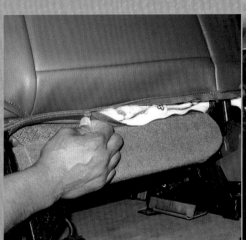

07 Pull the new cover all the way down the seat back, tuck the material in at the bottom and zip it up

08 The bottom of the seat may have electrical connectors that will need to be disconnected before unbolting the seat frame and removing the stock upholstery

09 Turn your new seat bottom cover inside out and install it onto the seat, folding it over the sides. Just secure the new cover to the seat, bolt up the frame and you're ready to reinstall your seats

Window tinting

First, pick your day, and your working area, pretty carefully - on a windy day, there'll be more dust in the air, and it'll be a nightmare trying to stop the film flapping and folding onto itself while you're working. Applying window tint is best done on a warm day (or in a warm garage), because the adhesive will begin to dry sooner. Don't try tinting when it's starting to get dark!

01 Step one is to get the window that will be tinted extra clean inside and out. Do not use glass cleaners or any other product containing ammonia or vinegar, since both of these ingredients will react with the film tint or its adhesive and create a mess. It is also worth cleaning the working area around the windows because it is too easy for stray dirt to attach itself to the film tint. On door windows, be sure to lower them down partially to clean all of the top edge

02 Spray the outside of the window with a weak, soapy water solution. Some film tint kits will provide a cleaning solution for your vehicle, but if not, use a little bit of dish soap in a spray bottle and apply the solution sparingly to the windows

The downside to tinting is that it will severely try your patience. If you're not a patient sort of person, this is one job which may well wind you up - you have been warned. Saying that, if you're calm and careful, and you follow the instructions to the letter, you could surprise yourself.

In brief, the process for tinting is to lay the film on the outside of the glass first, and cut it exactly to size. The protective layer is peeled off to expose the adhesive side, the film is transferred to the inside of the vehicle (tricky) and then squeegeed into place (also tricky). All this must be done with scrupulous cleanliness, as any muck will ruin the effect (difficult if you're working outside). The other problem which won't surprise you is that getting rid of air bubbles and creases can take time. A long time. This is another test of patience, because if, as the instructions say, you've used plenty of spray, it will take a while to dry out and stick.

03 Before you even unroll the film tint, beware - handle it carefully! If you crease it, you won't get the creases out. Unroll the film tint and cut it roughly to the size of the window. Lay the sheet of tint onto the glass, with the protective film (liner) facing you. Check this by applying a small piece of sticky tape to the backside and front side of the corners of the tint and film and carefully separate them. It will then become obvious which side is the sticky side of the tint and which side is the protective film. Once the film is in place, spray it with more of the soapy water solution

04 Use a squeegee to get rid of the air bubbles. Remember, the protective film will be facing out. Use a sharp knife and be sure not to damage your paint or window rubber. Trim the perimeter of the tint to the outside of the window. On door windows, leave a little extra material along the bottom of the window (it can be trimmed later, after the film has been applied and the window has been rolled up). On some rear glass, there are wide black bands on the edges of the glass. Cut your tint to the inside of these bands or the tint will not fit when it is transferred inside

05 Once you've got it cut to size, roll the tint off the window, with the protective layer on the inside

06 Now go inside the vehicle and prepare the glass for receiving the tint. Tape some plastic sheet below the window to prevent water damage when the tint is applied. When applying tint to door windows, it is a good idea to remove the door trim panel first, before going ahead with the job. Spray the inside of the glass with a soapy solution. Remember, no ammonia products such as glass cleaner or vinegar

07 To really get that glass clean, lubricate the window with the soapy solution and scrape the entire surface with a razor blade

08 Lightly spray the window with the soapy solution after the glass is completely clean. Partially unroll the tint, peeling the protective film from the first few inches of tint

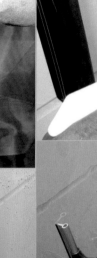

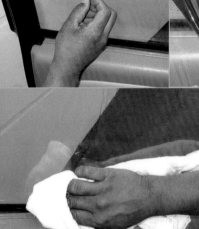

11 When you've finished, and the tint is dry, clean the window one more time and wipe it down with a soft cloth

09 Press the adhesive side of the tint onto the edge of the window. While an assistant holds the tint to the glass at one end, pull the protective film in the opposite direction, gradually unrolling the tint into place. If things start to get sticky, spray a little more soapy water onto the tint

10 Once you've got it on, spray the tint with soapy water and carefully squeegee it into place, working from the top to the bottom. It is easier to use the squeegee blade separated from the handle to access the corner spots. If necessary, soak up any excess water at the base of the tint with paper towels. If the edges of the tint refuse to stick, use a hair dryer to gently warm the tint at the base to assist with the adhesion. Be very careful when using a squeegee on a dry surface. Do not lift the tint off the glass. Be patient, the tint will stick. Persistence will pay off

12 The end result is a nice, dark window that's worth the effort

Wheels & tires

If there is one crucial first customizing step in the process of getting your SUV noticed, it's the tires and wheels, and of those two it's 90% the wheels. The right wheels can set your SUV apart in a way that makes it stand out from two blocks away, even if the rest of the vehicle remains unimpressively stock.

Going with big wheels on your SUV may mean upgrading the disc brakes as well. Standard discs will look (and perform) too small

Big aluminum discs like these (sandwiched between the brake hub and the wheel) can conceal drums/discs, prevent black brake dust on your wheels, and really set your wheel design off, especially when the discs are painted like these - they may decrease brake cooling though, so they might not be suitable for performance driving or towing

Choosing wheels

Choosing the right wheels for your SUV is an important decision - besides how they look, do your research on quality, fitment, durability and offset before making the investment

Custom wheels are mostly purchased to attract attention, but they do have practical considerations. A wider wheel allows you to install wider tires for better handling. A set of custom aluminum wheels may be lighter than your stock steel wheels and thus reduce the amount of unsprung weight in the chassis, which leads to improved handling. However, the weight savings of the aluminum may be negated if you go much bigger than stock in the new wheels. A 20-inch-diameter or larger aluminum "show" wheel might actually weigh more than your stock steel wheels!

Have in mind the style of wheel you like long before you enter the tire/wheel store. Once you're in the store, the vast display of wheel choices can make the final selection more headache than fun. Observe the other SUVs you see at shows and on the street and look at the wheels/tires closely. If you can find the owner, ask him if he had any problems with the tires/rims he chose. Once you spend the money to get new rolling stock, you'll want to be happy with them for a long time to come.

Also look at SUVs like yours in magazines and see which wheels appeal to you, as well as scoping out the wheel advertisements. When you see wheels you like on an SUV like yours, read further and see what other modifications may have been made to accommodate those tires/wheels. Was the vehicle lowered, and did it have custom wheelwells or an aftermarket body kit? Those custom body alterations may have given the clearance needed for those tires/wheels, in which case the same combination of rolling stock may not fit your SUV unless you do the same body modifications. Getting a picture of how complicated the simple act of choosing wheels and tires can get?

Two-piece wheels have the center section joined to the aluminum rim, either by fasteners or by welding (arrow indicates machine-welded seam on the backside of the wheel)

RIM WIDTH

Rim width on custom wheels is measured at the inside of the wheel lips, not the outside as you might have thought

Plan ahead

If you're the type who is mostly interested in extracting total performance from the engine, while leaving your SUV pretty much stock as far as suspension and the body are concerned, you can just add tires and wheels that fit your vehicle just the way it is. However, if you think that later on you'll lower your vehicle with some aftermarket springs, spindles or even airbags, you must consider the clearance between the tires and the fenderwell lip. It's cool to have a tire/wheel combo that fills the wheelwell, but not so cool to drive around with the outside edges of your tires worn away from rubbing the body.

A tire/wheel package that fits your vehicle now may create interference when the vehicle is lowered an inch or two. You can tell the guys whose tire-to-body fit is less than optimal. They're the ones who enter the driveway of your favorite hangout really slow, and at an extreme angle to the driveway to keep from having rubber meet paint. That's what has made the airbag suspension so popular today; you can stay high enough to get wherever you need to go, but when you're there or just cruising, you can really get down!

If you are thinking of adding flared fenders or a custom body kit at some point, this will have a major impact on your wheel/tire choice. If you want really wide tires and big rims, you may have to run something aftermarket in terms of bodywear just to clear the tires. On the other hand, you may have a good amount invested in the custom wheels/tires currently and they may look too small if you add a body kit. Figure the cost of new rims and rubber into your budget if you are going to utilize a custom body kit on your SUV.

A big tire/wheel certainly makes a statement, but try to keep rolling radius close to stock - here we have a stock Chevy 16-inch wheel (center) with 75-series tire and 29-inch RR - the wheel at rear is a 22-inch Boyd's but using a short 40-series tire keeps the RR to 31.5 inches, while the front tire shown is a 20-incher with a really low 35-series tire and comes out actually shorter than the stock wheel/tire

This wheel sticker's information includes: wheel offset, 40mm; bolt pattern, 4 bolts on a 100 mm circle; hub bore; and date of manufacture

Rolling radius

Rolling radius is the distance from the center of the wheel to the edge of the tire's tread. Most of us simply look at the tire/wheel diameter, rather than the radius. Without having to find the exact center of the wheel, you can measure the diameter with a tape measure simply by going from the ground to the top of the tire. Since tires vary in height as well as width, just knowing that a vehicle has 20-inch wheels doesn't tell you how tall the rolling radius is, but a handy pocket tape measure will.

The existing final drive ratio in your rear axle is affected by the rolling radius of the tire/wheel size you choose. For performance purposes, the gear ratio in some SUVs is barely adequate with the stock tires and wheels. With a taller rolling radius at the tire/wheel, the effect is to make the final drive even more of a "cruising" ratio, which is not what you and I want for acceleration.

If you don't want to increase the rolling radius but still make the upgrade to taller wheels, you'll have to choose a tire that is shorter in section height. If your stock tire was a 75-series or 60-series, for instance, changing to a wider 55 or 50-series tire on your one-inch bigger new wheels may give you the same rolling radius as your stock tires and wheels, without taking away any gearing effect on performance. If you go up one rim size, decrease profile one size.

Confused? Well, a 205/55x15 tire (that's a 15-inch wheel, obviously) has a rolling radius of 607mm. Upgrading to a 17-inch wheel means fitting a 215/40x17 rubber with a nearly-identical rolling radius of 606mm. Stay within ten percent of your original height and you should be okay. If you are adding more power with engine mods, you can get away with a higher-than-stock

Some wheels are marked only with decals rather than cast-in numbers - this sticker indicates the wheel load rating and the maximum recommended tire diameter (rolling radius)

rolling radius, otherwise expect some reduction in acceleration with big wheels, and lower cruising rpm on the highway. The taller rolling radius is going to reduce your cruising rpm to a point far off the torque band the engine was designed for. If you have a stock engine whose torque peak is 3500 rpm and you now cruise at 70 mph at 1800 rpm, you may have a dog on the highway, so select the tire profile that will keep your rolling radius close to original.

Another reason to stay close to your stock rolling radius is braking. When you run really tall wheels/tires, your braking performance is going to suffer because the wheel and tire have more "leverage" against the stock rotor/caliper. By putting more torque or twist against your stock brakes, you'll find hard-stop performance will suffer, even if you don't notice much difference in easy stops. This is one of the two reasons customizers install larger-diameter brake upgrades on their vehicles; to make up for the big wheels and of course, it also looks better proportionately when observers don't see a little brake behind a huge wheel.

If you're really serious, use a common bathroom scale to weigh the wheels - the lighter the better for handling

Wheel weight

If there were no other considerations when buying wheels, we'd always go with the lightest available. Lighter wheels are easier to accelerate or slow down and they are easier on your suspension. Unsprung weight is that weight that has to bounce up and down over the road with your tires. If you have a big set of tires they can improve traction, but the heavy unsprung weight is like asking the suspension to work harder. Unfortunately, really light wheels are expensive! Most of us are more concerned with the outward appearance of the wheels than their performance benefit, so we pick the wheels that have the best compromise between the factors of weight, looks, and price.

Weight is not really an issue with off-road or rock-crawling applications, where the important factors are the offset that is best to fit the chosen tires to the vehicle, and the strength to take serious punishment. Special steel wheels are used on rock-crawler vehicles for strength. If a steel rim gets bent in action, it can be hammered back enough to re-air the tire and get home, while an aluminum wheel may just have a chunk broken off and can't be repaired in the field. In this respect, a two-piece aluminum wheel may be better than a cast one for reparability.

Gearing selection

Adding lower gears for your rear end is the answer for the overdrive/big wheel blues. To find out what your "cruising" rpm will be on the open highway, the formula is: MPH x gear ratio x 336 divided by D (diameter of the tire/wheel, or rolling radius). If you are running an overdrive trans as many do today, multiply the result by the top-gear overdrive ratio. If your overdrive is called a "30%", that means your final ratio is 0.70. Thus, if you have 3.00 rear end gears, 27-inch tall rear tires, 30% OD and want to find out the projected engine speed at 70 mph (where permitted, of course), it would go like this: 70 x 3.00 x 0.70 x 336, divided by 27 = 1829 rpm.

Now, trying that formula for an off-road SUV with big 33's, you learn that you would need at least a 4.00 gear to sustain 70 on the highway. If that same vehicle did not have overdrive, then the cruising rpm would be 2850, which offers plenty of passing punch. Gearing is always a compromise. A target of 2200-2800 rpm will be a good compromise for most SUVs with unmodified engines. Rely on wheel/tire combos that you know have worked successfully on other SUVs like yours, plus listen to the advice of a good tire and wheel shop. They've probably seen all the right and wrong combos! If you are going after tall off-road tires, then you may be in the market for new rear-end gears.

On the subject of gearing and tire/wheel changes, any of these modifications can alter the speedometer accuracy in your vehicle. You can easily get an expensive ticket if you don't know what your real speed is! You can change the little plastic speedometer gear in trucks so equipped. These gears are usually color-coded and your dealer parts man should be able to tell you which one is right for your change of gears or tire/wheel size. Many late-model vehicles have an electronic speed sensor in the transmission - there are no speedometer gears. Your dealership may be able to alter the electronic speedometer's programming with their factory scan tool, although there may only be a program for tire/wheel sizes that could be stock or optional to your specific vehicle. The other alternative is to purchase an aftermarket "performance reprogrammer" (see Engine Performance Chapter). Besides their primary function to give your truck more power by optimizing fuel/spark curves, many of these programmers can also correct your speedometer readings to compensate for gear or tire changes.

Wheel offset has perhaps the most influence on tire/wheel fit - this truck wheel has a great, deep shape for style, but note how much offset to the outside there is (you have to make sure ahead of time that such a tire/wheel combo fits your vehicle)

Wheel offset

There's much more to the measurement of a wheel than its diameter. The amount of wheel offset is critical to fitment problems with the body and even the brakes. That flat, machined section on the back of a wheel that fits directly against your brake drum or hub is the area we're concerned with. If that section is in the exact center of the wheel (in a side or end plane), the wheel is considered to have no offset. If the mounting plane is closer to the back of the wheel than the front of the wheel, that wheel will stick further out than a "centered" wheel.

A wheel with a certain offset or wheel-center design may not clear the brake calipers or some other suspension parts on your SUV, but most vehicles running wheels two inches or more taller than the stock rims usually won't have problems with this kind of interference.

There are no universal standards for marking wheels with their offset dimensions. Some have the offset cast into the back of the wheel, some have a sticker on the rim, and some are unmarked. However, the offset of a wheel is easily measured with a ruler and straightedge. Lay the wheel down on a flat surface and measure the width of the rim. If the measurement is 8 inches, then the

To measure a wheel's offset, lay a straightedge across the back of the rim, then measure from there down to the wheel's mounting surface - this measurement compared to the wheel's theoretical center gives you offset

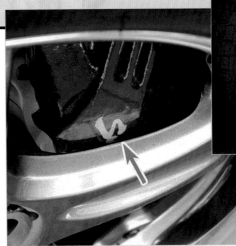

If you have upgraded your brakes, you need to check for caliper clearance if you haven't also gone to larger-diameter wheels

On this vehicle, note how the owner matched the upgrade in his brake size to the upgrade in wheel diameter - the combo looks great and there's plenty of braking power for towing or performance driving

center of the wheel is at 4 inches. Place a straightedge across the wheel on the backside and measure from that edge down to the flat mounting surface of the wheel where the bolt pattern is. Let's say that measurement is 5 inches. This measurement is also called the backspacing, and it means the wheel has the mounting surface one inch further to the outside of the wheel than the theoretical center. The offset is one inch.

For purposes of checking a wheel's offset, measuring the width of rim as described works fine, since we're just looking for the centerline measurement. However, when wheel sizes are described, the width measurement that is used is only the space between the tire-mounting beads, not the lip-to-lip measurement. A wheel that is nominally 17x8 would be eight inches between the two tire beads. Measuring between the outside edges would be too confusing, since wheel designs vary greatly in the amount of lip width.

Used wheels

If you tend to swap parts around between your vehicle and your circle of buddies, or you contemplate buying a set of wheels at a swap meet, there are a number of things to check. Bring a tape measure that has both inch and metric measurements. We've just outlined above the simple measurements that determine rim width and offset.

Another thing to worry about when selecting wheels is the bolt pattern. Most SUVs have five or six nuts holding each wheel to its hub. Different manufacturers use different bolt patterns for their wheels, so, just because two wheels have the same number of lug nuts doesn't mean they will interchange.

Take one of your existing wheels off and make a paper or cardboard template of the bolt pattern. Place the paper over the machined mounting surface at the back of the wheel and rub a lead pencil over the paper until the location and dimensions of the bolt holes are clearly outlined. Keep this paper with you when you are wheel shopping and you won't get stuck with a set of wheels that won't fit. Hold the paper behind the wheel you're examining and all the holes should line up with the bolt holes in the wheels.

Many wheels have plastic or metal rings inserted on the backside to make an exact hub-fit on a particular application; always make sure the ring is in place before mounting a wheel

Stay centered

How a wheel is located on a particular vehicle's hub can vary. A "hub-centric" wheel is one that is located on the hub by a closely-machined opening in the center of the wheel that is matched to that hub's diameter. Some wheel are "lug-centric", which means that the center of the wheel doesn't locate perfectly over the hub, but the lug nuts and lug nut holes are tapered to locate the wheel that way.

Your original wheels are machined at the center to locate properly on your hubs. Most good aftermarket wheels are also machined to fit a specific application. There are some companies, however, that make most of their wheels in a basic, one-size-fits-all dimension, and rely on inserts that go behind the wheel to achieve the correct fit to center the wheel on various makes of vehicle.

"Get the size right the first time"

Going away from your stock tire and wheel sizes can really bring on some headaches. Most people will simply find a good tire and wheel dealer and trust his judgement about what will look good and fit right.

The tool shown here is one way to help take the guesswork out of tire/wheel sizing. From Wheel Concepts, this gauge is bolted onto the wheel hub and then the two slide gauges are moved in or out to approximate various tire and wheel widths, offsets, diameters, etc. In just a few minutes the tool will show exactly what wheel/tire combination will fit – and, perhaps more importantly, which ones won't.

Wheel lug nuts/studs

The relationship between the wheel studs in your hubs and the lug nuts used to secure the wheels on those studs is a critical safety consideration. Where most enthusiasts get themselves in trouble in this area is by using wheel spacers to achieve a look or fit by increasing the offset of a wheel. Spacers go between the wheel and the hub to move the wheel outboard a little.

If you use the same lug nuts that you had originally before the spacers were added, the amount of wheel stud that is threaded into the lug nuts is reduced by the thickness of the spacer.

Most wheel experts dislike wheel spacers, preferring their customers buy the right wheel for the job in the first place. There is no hard-and-fast rule about how many threads need to be engaged between the stud and the lug nut, but you should never reduce this dimension beyond the amount engineered by your vehicle's manufacturer. If necessary, install longer studs.

To protect the finish on your wheels during removal/installation, use special plastic liners over your lug socket or wrap the socket with electrical tape

To protect your investment in cool tires and wheels, you'll want to use a set of locking lug nuts - use one per wheel, and don't lose the special "key" adapter required to remove them

Lug nuts are important! The two types are tapered (left) and straight (right) - the tapered ones (like stock lugs) center the wheel over the hub, while the straight ones don't exactly, so the wheel must have an exact center at the hub

Lug nuts may look alike, but pay attention to their markings or you could strip your wheel studs - this one is marked "12x1.5", which means it's for a 12 mm stud with 1.5 thread pitch

Some wheels have a thicker mounting flange than your stock wheels - using a thicker wheel or wheel spacers means you should have longer studs pressed into your hubs for full thread engagement

Lug nuts also come either open at the ends or closed

When monster mudders or snow chains just won't do the job . . .

Turn your SUV into a tank! MATTRACKS rubber track conversion systems bolt right up to your wheel hubs and give you the ability to venture into areas a wheeled vehicle wouldn't dare go. They can handle rocks, mud, silt, swamps and snow with ease, and can also be used on smooth surfaces if necessary.

Choosing tires

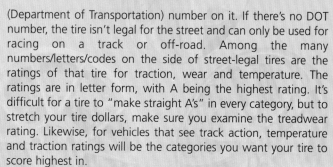

Along with the custom wheels, tires are an important part of both the looks and performance of your SUV. If you want the ultimate look for a lowered vehicle, you'll get the tires and wheels that are as close as possible to looking like a rubber band has been wrapped around a 22-inch wheel. Not only is this nice to look at, it's race-inspired. In hard cornering, stock tires do not stay centered on the wheel. They "roll under," so that the tread area actually moves away from the center of the wheel. When this happens, the tread distorts, the tire "breaks away" and starts sliding. On low-profile tires, roll-under is almost non-existent, so the tire can keep a consistent tread "patch" on the road. Additionally, the treads of low-profile tires are often designed for maximum adhesion, so they stick to the road better. Tires designed for long tread life are usually made from a very hard rubber compound and therefore will last a very long time. But hard-compound tires don't stick to the road as well. So most high-performance low-profile tires are made from softer, stickier rubber compounds that will allow better traction for cornering and acceleration - but the tires will tend to wear out faster.

On the other hand, if you're going for the "adventure" type driving with your SUV, the tire issue presents a new set of compromises. Off-road tires have plenty of cush for absorbing impacts, and they're built to do just that. But the tread selection is your biggest buying decision, and it should be based on exactly what kind of driving you plan to do. There are treads for dirt driving, sandy washes, rocky terrain, and even tires designed specifically for mud. The tougher the expected conditions the more gnarly the tread design, but the downside is that those terrain-grabbing treads make a lot of noise when travelling on the highway. You have to make a compromise, or if your off-roading is confined to occasional weekend trips, then keep the off-road tires/wheels in the garage and only put them on when you go adventure-seeking.

If you do most of your driving on the street in normal traffic and on the highway, take a closer look at the sidewall markings while you're out tire shopping. First of all, the tire must have a DOT (Department of Transportation) number on it. If there's no DOT number, the tire isn't legal for the street and can only be used for racing on a track or off-road. Among the many numbers/letters/codes on the side of street-legal tires are the ratings of that tire for traction, wear and temperature. The ratings are in letter form, with A being the highest rating. It's difficult for a tire to "make straight A's" in every category, but to stretch your tire dollars, make sure you examine the treadwear rating. Likewise, for vehicles that see track action, temperature and traction ratings will be the categories you want your tire to score highest in.

So don't just go into a showroom and point to the wheels and tires that look the best - with that level of research, you're almost sure to be disappointed. Talk to the salespeople and technicians at the tire store and find out about the ride quality and treadlife of each tire, as well as its cost. Tire technicians who install a lot of tires can help you figure out how big a tire/wheel combination you can run. And if you're planning on lowering the vehicle, tell them about that, too, since it will have an effect on maximum tire size. When in doubt about maximum tire size, contact the tire manufacturer for their recommendations.

Many people try to measure their own wheelwells with a tape-rule to determine how much clearance they have for larger tires and wheels. Even if you take these measurements with the front wheels in their extreme turn positions, there are many other variables that are very hard to calculate. For example, the new wheels will likely have more offset than your existing wheels.

If you are planning on lowering your SUV with airbags, make sure the wheels/tires you purchase aren't going to be too tall or too wide for the body in the extreme-lowered (on the ground) stance - the last thing you need is a fenderwell to cut your tire

Deal with an experienced tire shop with a good reputation to sort through the many choices in tire sizes, aspect ratios and tread design

For all-weather traction on the street and light off-road use, choose the "M&S" designated tires (mud&snow) - for more serious off-road driving on rocks, gravel, sand and mud, look for the "MT" mark that indicates a maximum traction design, but expect more noise on the highway

Some high-performance tires are "directional" in their design - the arrow marking means it must roll in this direction, so you can't rotate these tires side-for-side

Even off-road tires must have the DOT (Department of Transportation) code on the side if you ever run them on public roads

The most important markings on a tire are these for the tire size, profile and speed rating - this is a short-and-sporty 255/40 ZR17 94W on a customized street SUV

Tire size markings

All tires carry standard tire size markings on their sidewalls, such as "195/60 R 15 85H".

195 indicates the width of the tire in mm.

60 indicates the ratio of the tire section height to width, expressed as a percentage. If no number is present at this point, the ratio is considered to be 82%. This section ratio is also called the aspect ratio or the "profile." A low number here means a low-profile tire that won't be as tall as a higher-ratio tire. Some tires for tall wheels have an aspect ratio as low as 30.

R indicates the tire is of radial ply construction.

15 indicates the wheel diameter for the tire is 15 inches.

85 is an index number which indicates the maximum load that the tire can carry at maximum speed. Ratings on cars and light trucks range from 70-110, with our subject tire above having a load rating of 1,135 pounds (per tire). A rating of 95 here would mean a load of 1,521 pounds.

H represents the maximum speed for the tire, which should be equal to or greater than the vehicle's maximum speed.

Note that some tires have the speed rating symbol located between the tire width and the wheel diameter, attached to the "R" radial tire reference, for example, "195/60 HR 15".

You may also see tires with an "LT" designation in their tire sidewall description. Although it stands for "light truck", it is generally applied to tires for 3/4-ton and one-ton trucks. Additionally, when you see a tire with a "half size" rim dimension, such as 8.00R-16.5 (with or without the LT designation), this is also a tire designed for heavy-duty light trucks.

Overall tire-and-wheel height and width will be different than the wheel measurements themselves. And don't forget about suspension movement - you don't want to have the tires rub every time you go over a bump! No, it's best to let the experts determine your maximum tire and wheel size, and they are usually happy to help. And if the combination doesn't work, you'll have someone to blame beside yourself!

Enthusiasts who do their own research generally make better buying decisions, and on wheel/tires you need to look at all the examples of modified SUVs you can. Check out their tires and wheels and see not only how they look, but also how evenly they are wearing in the application. Look at the backside of the front tires, if possible, and see if the tire or wheel has been rubbing on any suspension or body parts. If the outside edge of the tire's tread is chewed or worn excessively, it could indicate this wheel/tire combo is too wide for the vehicle. Always compare "apples to apples." If the SUV you really like has a body kit or flares on the fenders, don't assume that the wide tires he's sporting are going to fit your stock vehicle.

Speed rating symbols for radial tires

Symbol	mph
P	93
Q	99
R	106
S	112
T	118
U	124
V (after size markings)	Up to 150
H (within size markings)	Up to 130
V (within size markings)	Over 130
Z (within size markings)	Over 150

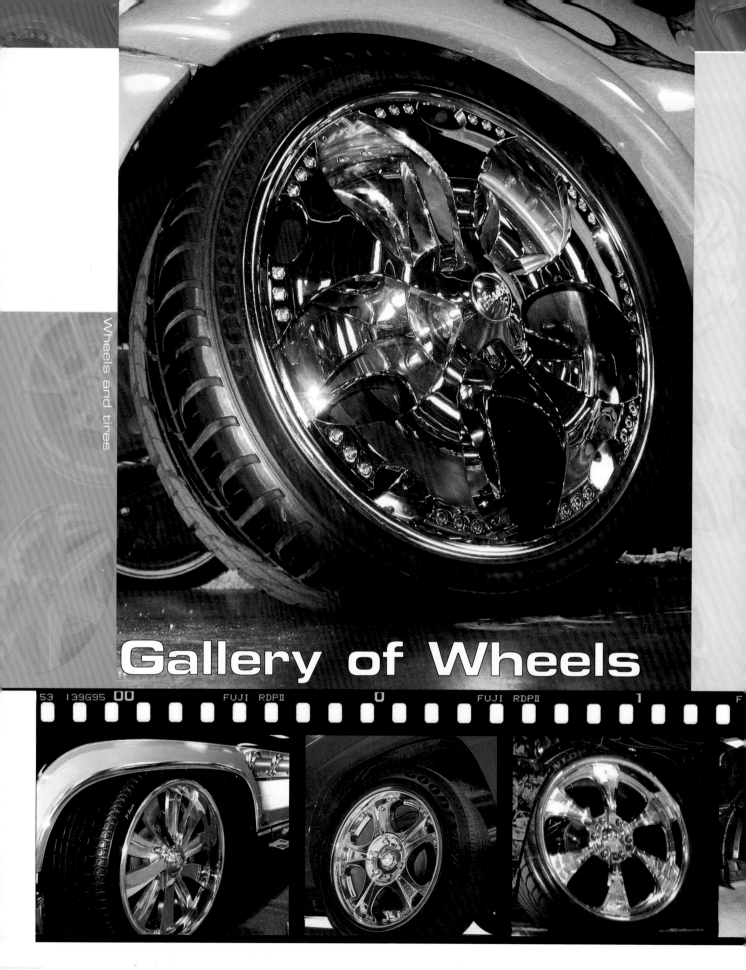

Gallery of Wheels

53 139G95 00   FUJI RDPII   0   FUJI RDPII   1   F

06 Suspension

Suspension - it's generally considered one of the first mods to be made to a custom SUV, along with custom wheels. And raising or lowering your rig just screams out "Not stock anymore!"

Raising or lowering your SUV? You've probably already decided which look you're after, but how do you get there? Can you really do it yourself?

Or maybe the stance of your vehicle is just fine, but you'd sure like to improve the handling and ride a little bit. Perhaps you really use your SUV and are tired of seeing the rear end dragging every time you load the back and hitch up the boat.

All of these relate to your SUV's suspension system – a group of components that work together to prevent your head from going through the roof at every dip in the road. That's usually easy for a car. But an SUV often needs to transform to the needs of the owner, whether that's routinely carrying heavy loads, traveling off-road or cruising the twisty back roads.

What we're going to show in this Chapter are some common ways to raise or lower your SUV. For the actual component replacement procedures on your particular vehicle, we suggest you refer to your *Haynes Automotive Repair Manual*. We'll also cover a couple of issues to help you keep the red light of Mr. John Law out of your mirrors. So before you throw down any green or even think about touching a wrench, read on . . .

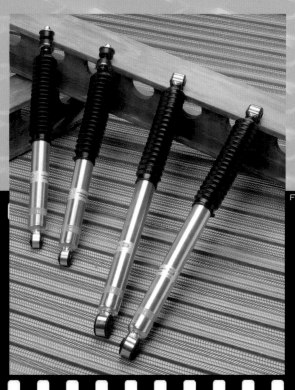

Is the sky

the limit?

While there's no doubt that a lifted SUV is a cool sight, there are several factors other than appearance to consider before you go out and buy a lift kit and big tires. First of all, are you willing to deal with the hassle of getting in and out of a taller vehicle, the potentially less-comfortable ride quality, diminished handling, parts wearing out more frequently, etc.? More importantly, though, is staying within legal limits and not building an SUV that is so high that it becomes dangerous to drive. Yes, there are *laws* governing how high you can go. They vary from state to state, but you'll want to check into this before you go shopping (your local Department of Motor Vehicles should be able to help you). For example, the California Vehicle Code states that the lowest portion of the frame on a passenger vehicle (excluding motorhomes) cannot be more than 23-inches from the ground. Additionally, the lowest portion of the body floor can't be more than five inches from the top of the frame. Some states also have bumper height regulations. Keep in mind that even if you do stay within the legal constraints, the vehicle is not going to handle like it did when it was in stock form.

As far as how high is too high, most experts feel that anything more than a six-inch suspension lift is excessive. An eight or ten-inch lift, combined with larger diameter tires, raises the center of gravity so high that a rollover is almost imminent if an abrupt defensive maneuver must be taken. Front-to-rear brake bias is also seriously affected. If an SUV is going to be lifted to an extreme height, the vehicle's track should also be widened to compensate for the relocated center of gravity.

Lifted vehicles are prone to wearing out U-joints more rapidly than those of stock height. The same is true for driveaxle CV joints on the front end of 4WD vehicles with Independent Front Suspension (IFS). Bushings, balljoints, wheel bearings and brake linings are other components that may suffer as increased loads are imposed upon them.

If the vehicle is going to see off-road action, it's not a good idea to go any higher than necessary. Necessary, in most cases, means just high enough to run the size tire you want.

When you finally settle on a scenario that's right for you and your SUV, purchase all of your lift components from the same manufacturer. Mixing components from different brand kits can be frustrating, since the parts haven't been engineered to work with each other. It can also be dangerous.

How low can you go?

Plenty low, really. In most states, no part of the vehicle (except for the tires) can be closer to the road surface than the lowest spot on the wheel rim. Any lower than that would be impractical anyway, except for when the vehicle is parked.

Apart from the good looks that are gained, you lose two things when you lower a vehicle: suspension travel and, in most cases, ride quality. Lowering springs are shorter but stiffer and will yield a pretty jarring ride. Airbag systems can give the most amount of drop and are adjustable, but if a bag or line springs a leak you'll be calling the

flatbed. Repositioned leaf spring mounts and axle flip kits can give you lots of drop out back, but your SUV's load carrying capacity will be reduced. With any significant drop, speed bumps, potholes and driveways will become annoyances. All of this may or may not matter to you, just be prepared for a compromise in the comfort department.

On the bright side, a lowering job done right will make your SUV handle like a slot car.

Coil spring front suspension

Suspension 101

So what type of suspension do I have now?

Coil springs

These springs are constructed from a length of spring steel rod, heated and formed into a coil. Some springs are made with a progressive rate; the coils at one end are wound a little tighter than the ones at the other end. This will give the vehicle a smooth ride but, as the suspension compresses to a certain point, the spring becomes stiffer. On most applications rubber or polyurethane insulators are used on each end of the spring to reduce noise and road vibration.

Working with coil springs can be very dangerous, as there is a tremendous amount of energy stored in a compressed spring. Whenever working with a coil spring a special compressor tool must be used to harness the spring (the exception to this would be when removing a spring from a solid axle suspension, where the axle could be lowered slowly to safely extend the spring). These tools are available at most auto parts stores.

Leaf springs

Made from long, flat plates of spring steel, these springs consist of one or more leaves, usually shaped into an arc. The ends of the top leaf are formed into round "eyes" and serve as the mounting points. Bushings are inserted into these eyes. At the front end the mounting point is stationary and is called the spring hanger. The spring is fastened at the rear by a shackle attached to the frame. This shackle allows the spring to extend as it is compressed. On multi-leaf springs the individual leaves are held together in the center by a bolt, and along their length by clips. The rear axle housing is mounted either above or below the spring, and attached to the spring with U-bolts and a mounting plate.

Leaf spring rear suspension

Shock absorber/coil spring assembly

· Some later model vehicles utilize a coil-over shock absorber assembly. These units are sometimes erroneously referred to as struts, but they play no role in keeping the wheel upright.

Aftermarket shock bodies are available that are equipped with threaded adjuster rings; this type of shock body will allow ride height adjustment.

Although removal and installation of the shock absorber/coil spring unit doesn't require any special tools, changing the shock absorber or the coil spring requires a special spring compressor, which can be obtained at most auto parts stores. The job can't even be attempted without it. Even with the tool it's a potentially dangerous procedure.

Torsion bars

This type of spring is fabricated from a long spring steel bar, with either splined or, more commonly, hex-shaped ends. The front ends of the bars are attached to the control arms (usually the lower control arms). The rear ends of the bars are attached to levers; the ends of these levers bear against adjustment bolts which are threaded into nuts cradled in the crossmember. The positions of these bolts in their nuts determine the ride height of the front end.

Just as with any spring, there is a great deal of energy stored in the torsion bar. Before performing any work to any part relating to the torsion bar, make sure you know how to relieve the tension on the bar. Refer to your *Haynes Automotive Repair Manual* for your specific vehicle for the procedure.

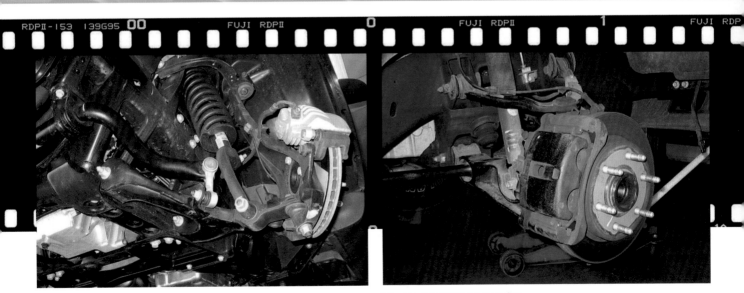

Coil-over front end

Torsion bar front suspension

Going UP

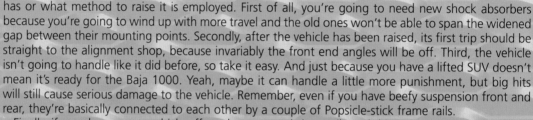

Courtesy of Full Force Suspension, Inc.

Suspension

There are lots of ways an SUV can be lifted, but a couple of things hold true no matter what kind of suspension the vehicle has or what method to raise it is employed. First of all, you're going to need new shock absorbers because you're going to wind up with more travel and the old ones won't be able to span the widened gap between their mounting points. Secondly, after the vehicle has been raised, its first trip should be straight to the alignment shop, because invariably the front end angles will be off. Third, the vehicle isn't going to handle like it did before, so take it easy. And just because you have a lifted SUV doesn't mean it's ready for the Baja 1000. Yeah, maybe it can handle a little more punishment, but big hits will still cause serious damage to the vehicle. Remember, even if you have beefy suspension front and rear, they're basically connected to each other by a couple of Popsicle-stick frame rails.

Finally, if you do use your vehicle off-road, stay on existing trails and drive responsibly.

Solid axle

Front or rear, this is the most straightforward type of suspension design to lift. Up front, the required components include new leaf springs with a greater arc (or, on coil spring models, longer springs), longer shock absorbers, a bracket to lower the track bar mounting point, and a dropped Pitman arm, which is necessary to maintain proper steering linkage geometry. At the rear, new leaf springs can be combined with lift blocks, installed between the axle and springs, for additional height. Some kits also include replacement shackles. On models with coil spring rear suspension, longer springs can be installed.

Leaf spring packs that utilize thinner leaves, but more of them, give a better, more compliant ride than spring packs that are made up of fewer but thicker leaves.

Whenever thicker leaf spring packs or lift blocks are used, new, longer U-bolts are required.

One important thing to remember: It is dangerous, and illegal, to install lift blocks between the front axle and leaf springs. This is because if a lift block breaks, the spring will drop down to the axle and could cause a loss of steering control.

A common side effect of raising a vehicle with leaf spring suspension is an improper differential pinion angle. This can occur at the rear of a raised two-wheel drive vehicle and at both ends of a vehicle with four-wheel drive. On the front end of a raised solid axle vehicle this not only changes the pinion angle, it also messes up the caster angle and can cause serious handling issues. To correct this problem, wedge-shaped shims are available that are installed between the axle and leaf spring. When the wedges are installed, the differential pinion will be tilted up towards the transmission or transfer case and will reduce the angle at which the driveshaft U-joints have to operate (and up front, will bring the caster back to where it's supposed to be). Most lifting blocks have this angle built into them. Failure to use these wedges will cause premature U-joint wear, and you'll also notice an annoying surge at low speeds as the U-joints rotate through a severe angle.

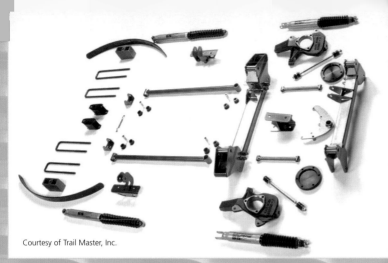

Courtesy of Trail Master, Inc.

Independent Front Suspension (IFS)

Independent front suspension is found on all modern 2WD models, and non-heavy duty full-size 4WD models. Employing upper and lower control arms, coil springs or torsion bars, the front end will track more precisely over bumps and rough terrain, with less change in camber, than a solid axle front end.

Front suspension lift kits for these SUV's include (depending on spring type, kit design and amount of lift) longer coil springs or heavy duty torsion bars, upper control arms, spindles, crossmember, differential mounts, and support struts between the transmission crossmember and replacement front crossmember. Some manufacturers make "economy" lift kits for the front end that consist of nothing more than thicker coil spring insulators. Certain states don't allow coil spring spacers, though, so be sure to check with your Department of Motor Vehicles before installing one of these kits.

On models with torsion bar front ends you can obtain up to about 1-1/2 inches of lift by simply tightening the torsion bar adjuster bolts, equally, a few turns. This places a greater preload on the torsion bar (that's why it raises the front end) and, as a side effect, will most likely result in a harsher ride.

Body lift kits

If you need more clearance to run big tires or just want that off-road-ready look, a body lift kit is an option that will enable you to do that without losing your stock ride quality. Some SUV owners combine body lifts with suspension lift kits to really gain some altitude, but some body lift kit manufacturers state that their kits are NOT to be used with suspension lift kits.

Body lift kits consist of spacers that fit between the body and frame mounts to raise the body off the frame, and a good kit will contain everything else necessary to complete the job. Items that may need modification or replacement include the steering shaft, shift linkage, clutch linkage, brake and clutch lines, wiring harnesses, fuel hoses and filler tube, fan shroud and radiator mounting, radiator hose, air intake duct, power steering hoses, air conditioning lines, bumper mounts, and maybe more, depending on the vehicle. So, while economical when compared to a suspension lift kit, a body lift kit could involve a considerable amount of work. Most kit manufacturers also state that a body lift kit should not be installed on a vehicle with a Supplemental Inflatable Restraint (airbag) system.

If you decide to go this route, obtain a kit from a reputable manufacturer - don't try to fabricate your own.

Extended brake lines

Whenever a lift kit is installed, make sure your brake lines are still long enough to accommodate the full distance the suspension is capable of travelling - not just when the vehicle is standing at ride height. They may reach the calipers just fine with the truck sitting there, but when the suspension rebounds what's going to happen?

Anything more than a minor lift will require longer brake lines. So, as long as you have to change them, you might as well go with a set of braided stainless-steel lines. They're tough and will give you better brake response (less prone to "ballooning"). These examples here are from Full Force Suspension.

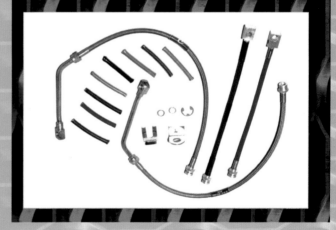

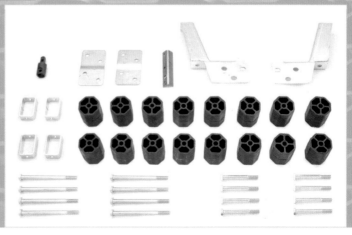

Gettin' down

So you've decided to go low. Nice. The following text explains how different types of suspensions can be lowered, but there are a couple of things you need to know. Number one is shock absorbers; when you lower your SUV using any method that reduces the amount of total suspension travel, the existing shock absorbers might still fit but they'll be in a more compressed state. This means the piston rods are near the end of their travel and might bottom out when a bump is hit, limiting your suspension travel and knocking the fillings out of your teeth. Replacing your shocks with a set designed for lowered suspension will be necessary.

The other bit of info you should store in the back of your mind is how the vehicle's handling characteristics will be changed. With its new lower center of gravity (and stiffer springs, if you've gone that route), low profile tires and maybe a set of stabilizer bars, it's probably going to be able to corner harder than it did before, and without all of the tire-bending/squealing/understeering nonsense. Hard-cornering vehicles are fun to drive. But beware - they are also less forgiving. When you start pushing it through the twisties and reach the tires' limit of adhesion on a turn, it's gonna let go and you're probably not going to be able to save it. So mellow out and drive like a civilized person so you don't wad-up your machine, or worse!

Oh, don't forget: Whenever a vehicle is lowered the front-end geometry changes. That means a front end alignment will be necessary right after the kit has been installed.

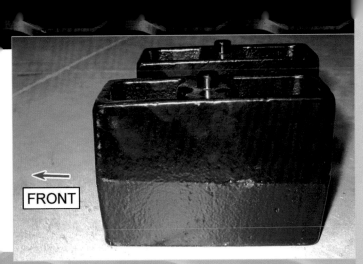

Solid axle

With a solid rear axle, lowering can be accomplished a couple of different ways. If the rear axle is mounted above the leaf springs, lowering blocks can be placed between the axle and the leaf springs. If the axle is mounted under the leaf springs, a "flip kit" can be installed which relocates the axle above the springs. Lowering shackles can be installed at the rear ends of the springs, which will take a little height out of the back end. Replacement spring hanger mounts can be installed which relocate the front ends of the springs a little higher; these mounts combined with lowering shackles will give you some drop, and when used in conjunction with lowering blocks or a flip kit, can produce just about any amount of lowering you desire. On models with coil spring rear suspension, shorter springs can be installed. Some of these setups will require notching and reinforcing the frame rails to provide clearance for the axle to travel.

A more radical approach would be to scrap the springs altogether and install a subframe, four-link setup and an airbag system.

Independent Front Suspension (IFS)

The typical independent suspension front end uses upper and lower control arms and coil springs; lowering can be achieved by the use of shorter coil springs or lower control arms with recessed spring pockets, or dropped spindles. If you decide to go with drop spindles, you can use your original coil springs - this means your ride quality won't suffer.

Other SUVs with IFS use torsion bars instead of coil springs. On these models, loosening the torsion bar adjuster bolts equally a few turns will give you a couple inches of drop.

Ford models with Twin-I Beam front ends can be lowered by installing shorter coil springs, but doing this will leave you with way too much negative camber. Not only will this look rank, it'll wear out your tires on the inside edges. So, the proper way to lower a Twin I-Beam front end is to install beams with more drop built into them.

Of course, if you really want to scrape the pavement, there's always the airbag option.

Installing a rear stabilizer bar

Even with stock suspension, most SUVs handle pretty well. But if you've lowered your vehicle, or like to cruise a little harder than normal through the canyons, handling limitations will quickly become apparent. Most often this will come in the form of a "push," also known as understeer.

Stabilizer bars reduce the tendency of the vehicle's body to "roll" (or tilt towards the outside of a turn) when cornering. Your SUV probably already has a stabilizer bar at the front, and maybe even one at the rear. But even if you have stabilizer bars front and rear from the factory, a good set of aftermarket performance bars will do you a world of good - you won't believe how flat your SUV will corner!

Here we're going to show the installation of a rear stabilizer bar. The vehicle has already been lowered, so psychologically it's going to be more difficult for its driver to hold back. But this stabilizer bar will get rid of the understeer problem and make it handle as if it were on rails!

Replacing the existing front stabilizer bar bushings with aftermarket polyurethane ones will help that bar function more efficiently.

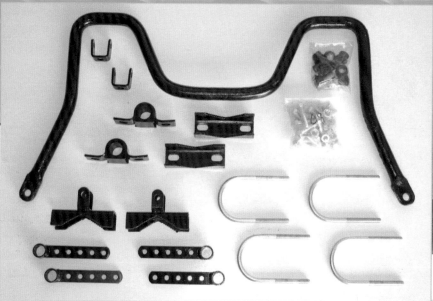

This kit from Hellwig includes a pair of polyurethane bar clamp bushings and brackets, U-bolts and saddle brackets (for the axle and the crossmember), links and bushings, clevis brackets and all the necessary hardware to complete the installation. Read and follow the instructions that will come with the kit you purchase

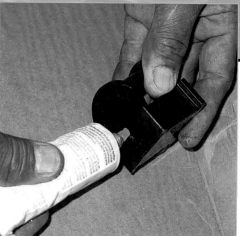

01 Prep the new bar bushings by lubing them up with a good waterproof grease and then slide them over each end of the bar

02 Place the U-bolts on top of the axle tubes, then guide the saddle brackets, stabilizer bar and bushing brackets up into place, installing the washers and nuts (be sure to use the right size U-bolts). Make sure the U-bolts pass between the brake lines and the axle tubes (you might have to bend the brake lines a little, but be careful not to kink them)

03 Place the U-bolts for the link saddle brackets over the crossmember then install the link saddle brackets, washers and nuts

04 Insert the polyurethane bushings into the upper links and attach them to the saddle brackets

05 Attach the link clevis brackets to the ends of the stabilizer bar

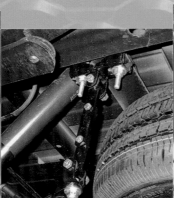

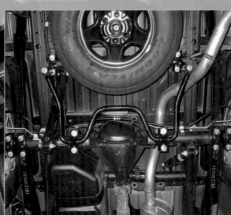

06 Insert the polyurethane bushings into the lower links and attach the links to the clevis brackets on the stabilizer bar

07 Swing the lower links up and connect them to the upper links, using two bolts and nuts per side. Adjust the position of the stabilizer bar and link brackets so that the ends of the bar are as close to horizontal as possible when the vehicle is at normal ride height, and the links are as close to vertical as possible

08 With stabilizer bar centered on the axle and everything adjusted in the proper relation to each other, tighten all of the fasteners to the torque values listed in the kit manufacturer's instructions. Our kit came with extra nuts to be used as "jam" nuts on the ends of all of the U-bolts to really lock them in place

09 And there you have it! A nice, clean stabilizer bar installation (too bad nobody's going to see it, but *you'll* know it's there!)

Shock absorbers

The shock absorber's job is to dampen the action of the suspension, preventing the body and wheels from bouncing uncontrollably as they travel over surfaces that aren't perfectly smooth.

A typical shock absorber is constructed of a sealed tube with a rod and piston protruding down inside. The tube contains oil and the piston has valving and orifices through which the oil is forced as the suspension travels through its range of motion. This converts the oscillations of the springs into heat, reducing unwanted compression and rebound cycles of the suspension. Shock absorbers play no part in supporting the weight of the vehicle.

Shock hoops like this enable you to easily install a dual-shock setup on each front wheel

Courtesy of Full Force Suspension, Inc.

Conventional oil-filled shock absorbers can suffer from foaming of the oil when they have to work too hard. The result is a lag in damping. To combat this, gas-filled shock absorbers are available. These shocks are similar to non-gas-filled units in construction, but contain an additional piston, behind which is a nitrogen-filled chamber. The force exerted on the shock absorber's oil chamber by the nitrogen-charged piston prevents the shock oil from aerating.

Most vehicles are equipped with one shock absorber per wheel, and this is usually adequate. Vehicles used off road sometimes need more than one shock per wheel. This is because a single shock just isn't capable of converting all of the violent suspension action into heat. Multiple shock setups also look really cool! Kits are available that allow you to convert your single-shock setup into a multiple shock-per-wheel rig. The most common type is a front dual-shock kit that uses an aftermarket upper shock mount, or hoop, that bolts to the frame and the existing upper mount.

Whenever lowering or raising your vehicle, be sure to match the shock absorbers to the travel of the new suspension. Even though the standard length shock absorber can be compressed and will fit between its mounts, it will be very close to being bottomed-out and will limit the travel of the suspension. Solution? Shorter shock absorbers. Obviously, on a raised vehicle longer shocks will be needed.

Vehicles that need occasional extra load-carrying capacity can benefit from a set of air shocks installed at the rear. These shock absorbers are like a cross between a regular hydraulic shock absorber and an air spring. When it's time to pull a trailer or carry a lot of weight in, the shocks can be charged with compressed air, which counteracts the sag caused by the heavy load. When the hauling job is done, the shocks can be deflated to return the vehicle to its normal ride height.

Steering stabilizers

When you're running big off road tires and the terrain turns ugly, a steering stabilizer will help keep the steering wheel in your hands and greatly reduce driver fatigue. These stabilizers are similar to shock absorbers, but mount between the frame or axle and the steering linkage to dampen harsh feedback through the steering system.

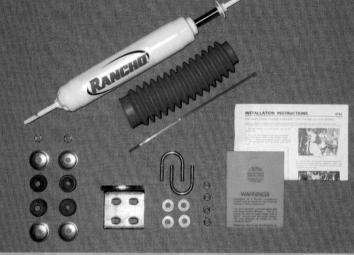

Bushings

Every point where a suspension component contacts the chassis is insulated by a bushing. Most original equipment bushings are rubber and work just fine for stock applications. When modifications are made, or when the stock bushings wear out, these rubber bushings can be swapped out for a set of polyurethane or graphite-impregnated polyurethane bushings. These bushings are less compliant and will transfer more road noise and shock to the chassis, but they will also reduce the "slop" that is inherent to rubber bushings. The result is a suspension system that more closely retains its design tolerances during operation, and transmits better "road feel" to the driver.

Urethane bushing kits usually include a special grease that is to be applied to the friction surfaces of the bushing to reduce noise. Graphite-impregnated bushings don't require this special grease, but some experts maintain that the properties of the urethane are compromised with the addition of graphite (meaning they might not last as long). Regardless, aftermarket bushings are the way to go to "tighten-up" the suspension.

For actual bushing replacement procedures, refer to the *Haynes Automotive Repair Manual* for your particular vehicle.

Courtesy of Trail Master, Inc.

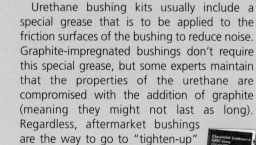

Air suspension

Air suspension systems provide the ability to raise or lower the vehicle instantly, from the driver's seat, or even from a distance on systems equipped with a remote control. Many consider this the ultimate suspension system, since you can lower your rig as low as you want for shows and cruises, but still be able to easily raise it to a reasonable ride height for your daily commute. The main components are air "springs" (which are airbag-like assemblies with no coil springs) filled with compressed air. Pumping air into the air springs increases the air pressure and raises the vehicle, while releasing air from the springs lowers the vehicle. The system also has an electric air compressor, valves and air lines to deliver and release the compressed air. Air suspension systems also have a high-tech look: the compressors are often highly polished and sometimes chrome or gold plated - they can really dress up your engine compartment!

The primary disadvantage of an air suspension system, as you might have guessed, is cost: generally, they run more than twice the price of a traditional lowering kit. And the ride quality will likely be worse than with the stock suspension system. Another disadvantage is that the systems can cause damage to your vehicle's suspension and chassis if they are not set up and used carefully. The systems should be set up so that there will be no fender rub or metal-to-metal suspension bottoming when the air is released. Sometimes systems can leak down when the vehicle is left sitting for an extended period.

There are a variety of air suspension systems available, and installation procedures vary. The air compressor is generally installed under the hood. Many owners choose to install a large separate storage tank for compressed air that allows rapid, repeated cycling of the system ("bouncing" the vehicle up and down). Some owners use compressed nitrogen rather than compressed air. When installing any air suspension equipment, refer to the manufacturer's instructions and recommendations.

Air Assist

There are other forms of air suspension that aren't intended to transform your ride into a slammed sled. These come in the form of helper springs (airbags) that are installed between the leaf spring and the frame, and an air compressor mounted under the hood. These systems are great for vehicles used for towing or carrying heavy loads, since the airbags can be inflated when they're needed for extra load carrying capacity and deflated when not, so the ride quality can be preserved.

Air cylinder installation

Air cylinders are a great way to increase your load or towing capacity. They're a good choice because they can be inflated when necessary and will reduce the amount of sag in the rear of the vehicle, but when the towing or hauling job is done they can be deflated, returning the vehicle to stock curb height and ride quality. Here we're going to show a typical installation on a 1500 Suburban, which occasionally pulls a trailer.

01 Raise the rear of the vehicle and support it securely on jackstands placed under the frame rails (this will allow the axle to hang down with the coil springs extended). On this vehicle the rubber insulator at the top of the coil spring had to have the center of it trimmed to make a larger opening for the stem on the air cylinder. A hobby knife did the trick

02 On our vehicle the exhaust pipe is fairly close to the right rear coil spring, so we had to install the supplied heat shield. First we bent the mounting tabs into the proper angles . . .

03 . . . then mounted the heat shields on the pipe and secured them with the hose clamps

04 Push a length of air line up through the hole in the upper insulator (don't cut it yet because you don't know how long it needs to be)

05 Remove the cap from the stem on the air cylinder, roll the cylinder up from the bottom to push out as much air as possible, then reinstall the cap to keep the cylinder deflated

06 Work the cylinder through the coils then remove the cap; the cylinder will begin to suck air in but you might have to help it get back into shape. Be sure to follow the directions with the kit; on some vehicles the cylinder must be installed with the stem pointing up, but on others it must be pointing down

07 Install the protector over the stem end of the cylinder . . .

08 . . . then attach the end of the hose to the stem, securing it with the hose clamp. Once you've done this, set the protector down around the stem

09 Find a good place to route the air lines, keeping them away from moving suspension components and hot exhaust pipes. Use the supplied T-fitting and clamps to join the two lines from the air cylinders, then secure it to the underside of the vehicle with the mounting strap and screw. The third line from the T-fitting gets routed to the Schrader valve, used for inflating the cylinders

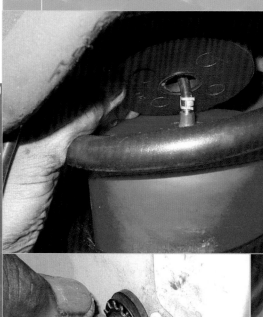

12 . . . then the valve was passed through the hole and fastened into place with the insulator, washer, locknut and nut

13 Our kit came with a sticker listing the minimum and maximum pressures for the system. Even when the bags aren't being used to give the back end a boost, the minimum pressure must be maintained to keep the bags inflated enough to prevent them from becoming chafed

10 We decided a good out-of-the-way spot for the Schrader valve would be just inside the right side rear door - easy to get to, but not in an area where it could get damaged easily. So, the hole was drilled . . .

11 . . . the Schrader valve was secured to the hose and the nut, washer and insulator were placed on the valve . . .

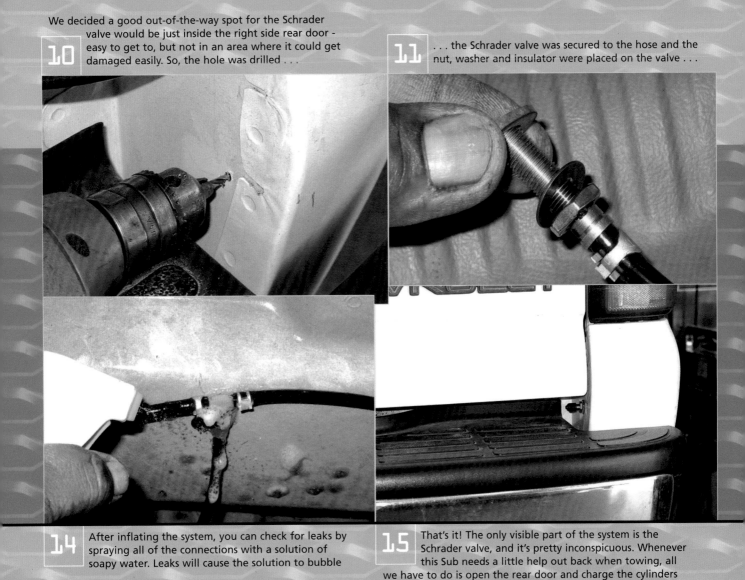

14 After inflating the system, you can check for leaks by spraying all of the connections with a solution of soapy water. Leaks will cause the solution to bubble

15 That's it! The only visible part of the system is the Schrader valve, and it's pretty inconspicuous. Whenever this Sub needs a little help out back when towing, all we have to do is open the rear door and charge the cylinders with air (keeping an eye on the maximum allowable pressure, of course)

07 Brakes

Brakes. Always there when you need them - or are they? Modern brakes are pretty bulletproof and require a minimum amount of attention. But add a lift kit and/or large diameter wheels and tires and you might realize that a bit more effort is required to bring your SUV to a stop. Those big tires act as large levers trying to overcome the resistance of your brakes, and on lifted vehicles the higher center of gravity means your front brakes are going to take more of the punishment than normal. This can only lead to one thing: increased wear in the brake system. Solution? Upgrade your brake system's "horsepower!" But first, here's a little refresher course to bring you up to speed on the most important system on your vehicle.

Brake pedal

Where it all starts, from your point of view. The pedal itself is a mechanical lever, and has to provide enough leverage to work the brakes if the power booster fails. Manufacturers use "brake pedal ratios" to express this - a low-ratio pedal, for instance, will give quick-acting but hard-to-work brakes.

Booster

The power brake booster is either vacuum or hydraulically operated, and it produces extra force on the pistons inside the master cylinder when the brakes are applied, reducing brake pedal effort. Modern vehicles are equipped with boosters because they are also equipped with disc brakes (at least up front), and disc brakes require more force than drum brakes do (they aren't self-energizing).

Master cylinder

Below the brake fluid reservoir is the master cylinder, which is where the brake pedal effort (force) is converted to hydraulic effort (pressure), and transmitted to each brake through the hydraulic lines and hoses.

Brake fluid

Pressing the brake pedal moves the brake fluid through the lines to each brake, where the hydraulic pressure is converted back to mechanical force once more, as the pads and shoes move into contact with the discs and drums. Fluid does not compress readily, but if air (which is compressible) gets in the system, there'll be less effort at the brakes and you'll get a fright. This is why 'bleeding' the brakes of air bubbles whenever the system has been opened is vital.

Brake hoses

For most of the way from the master cylinder to the wheels, the fluid goes through rigid metal brake pipes. At the suspension, where movement is needed, the pipes connect to flexible hoses. The standard rubber hoses are fine when they're new, but replacing old ones with great-looking braided hoses is a good move - in theory, it improves braking, as braided hoses expand less than rubber ones, and transmit more fluid pressure.

Calipers

These act like a clamp to force the brake pads against the discs - fluid pressure forces a piston outwards, which presses the brake pads onto the disc. Generally, the more pistons your calipers have, the more surface area the brake fluid has on which to push, providing greater clamping power. Most vehicles have only one or two per caliper, while exotic calipers may contain three, four or even more!

Discs

Clamped to your wheel hubs, the discs spin around as fast as your wheels. Over 90% of braking is done by the front brakes, which is why all modern vehicles have front discs - they work much better than drums, because they dissipate heat better. The bigger the disc diameter, the greater pad area available, with greater stopping power (think of a long lever as compared to a short one).

Drum brakes

Up until recent years, all of the vehicles covered by this manual were equipped with drum brakes on the rear wheels (and on really old models, the front wheels too). In this type of brake a pair of shoes are expanded outward, by means of a hydraulic wheel cylinder, onto a spinning drum attached to the wheel hub. This causes friction and heat, which slows down the drum and, in turn, the vehicle.

Drum brakes are very efficient until they get wet or too hot; they don't shed water or heat nearly as well as a disc brake does. They're also harder to work on or upgrade.

Pads and shoes

Both have a metal backing plate, with friction lining attached. Brake linings used to be made of an asbestos compound, which had excellent heat-resisting qualities but could cause cancer or asbestosis in people who breathed in the dust. Now they come in non-asbestos organic (stock), or for higher-performance applications, semi-metallic or carbon metallic.

Anti-lock Brakes (ABS)

Bottom line: Two cars are cruising down the road and a hay truck pulls out from a side road. Both drivers stand on the brake pedal. The car without ABS "locks up" the wheels and starts skidding, ending up sideways in a ditch. The car with ABS is able to slow down and safely maneuver around the truck. Great stuff, and here's how it works.

ABS works by detecting when a particular wheel is about to lock. It then reduces the hydraulic pressure applied to that wheel's brake, releasing it just before the wheel locks, and then re-applies it.

The system consists of a hydraulic unit, which contains various solenoid valves and an electric fluid return pump, wheel speed sensors, and an electronic control unit (ECU). The solenoids in the hydraulic unit are controlled by the ECU, which receives signals from the four wheel sensors.

If the ECU senses that a wheel is about to lock, it operates the relevant solenoid valve in the hydraulic unit, which isolates that brake from the master cylinder. If the wheel sensor detects that the wheel is still about to lock, the ECU switches on the fluid return pump in the hydraulic unit and pumps the fluid back from the brake to the master cylinder, releasing the brake. Once the speed of the wheel returns to normal, the return pump stops and the solenoid valve opens, allowing fluid pressure back to the brake,

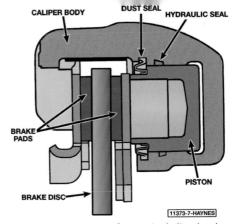

Cutaway of a typical disc brake

and so the brake is re-applied. Pretty impressive, especially when you consider all this is happening in a fraction of a second! You may feel your ABS system working in a hard braking situation. The brake pedal will "pulse" as the pressure varies. But don't let up or "pump" the pedal yourself - let the ABS do its job.

If you have any problems with an anti-lock brake system, always consult an authorized dealer service department or other qualified repair shop.

Why upgrade?

Stock brakes are just fine on a stock SUV; the manufacturer has made sure that they'll be up to any task the vehicle was designed to perform. Obviously, if you carry heavy loads or tow a trailer on a routine basis, you're going to wear out your brake pads faster, and eventually the brake discs too. Wear is an inherent feature of the brake system.

Brake wear can easily be monitored by following a good preventive maintenance program, and problems can be taken care of before any damage occurs. But what about overtaxing your brakes? Is this possible? Absolutely, and the symptoms of an inadequate brake system can reveal themselves suddenly, with "unpleasant" results.

How could this happen? There are two common ways: 1) the installation of large diameter wheels and/or oversized tires, and 2) the installation of a lift kit, especially when combined with big wheels and tires. Why is this? Because the stock brakes were designed to work with a wheel/tire combination of a certain rolling radius. When the rolling radius is increased it's as if a much larger lever is trying to rotate through the clamping action of the brakes, which is going to generate more heat. The brake can become so hot that the pads can no longer maintain friction against the disc, which will cause the brakes to "fade," or even fail completely. In the case of a raised vehicle, more weight is transferred to the front brakes *every* time the brake pedal is applied, meaning they have to work harder than normal. This can also lead to brake fade.

One common, relatively inexpensive way to upgrade your brakes is with the installation of aftermarket high-performance brake pads that can operate at higher temperatures. Another way is to swap out your stock brake discs with ones that are grooved, which will help them dissipate heat. If you really need to increase your stopping power, you can install larger diameter brake discs; these will directly counter the forces generated by the bigger wheels. They are also available in grooved or cross-drilled versions which help them cast off heat more quickly.

There's an added benefit to large-diameter, grooved/drilled discs: they look way better behind large diameter wheels than those puny stock units!

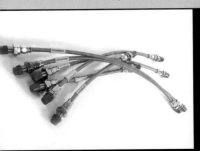

Grooved and drilled discs

Besides the various brands of performance brake pads that go with them, the main brake upgrade is to install performance front brake discs and pads. Discs are available in two main types - grooved and cross-drilled (and combinations of both).

Grooved discs (which can be had with varying numbers of grooves) serve a dual purpose - the grooves provide a 'channel' to help the heat escape, and they also help to de-glaze the pad surface, cleaning up the pads every time they're used. Some of the discs are made from higher-friction metal than normal discs, too, and the fact that they seriously improve braking performance is well-documented.

Drilled discs offer another route to heat dissipation, but one which can present some problems. Owners report that drilled discs really eat brake pads, more so than the grooved types, but more serious is the fact that some of these discs can crack around the drilled holes after serious use. The trouble is that the heat 'migrates' to the drilled holes (as was intended), but the heat build-up can be extreme, and the constant heating/cooling cycle can stress the metal to the point where it will crack. Discs which have been damaged in this way are extremely dangerous to drive on, as they could break up completely at any time. Only install discs of this type from established manufacturers offering a useful guarantee of quality, and check the discs regularly.

Performance discs also have a reputation for warping (nasty vibrations felt through the pedal). Justified, or not? Well, the harder you use your brakes, the greater the heat you'll generate. Okay, so these wicked discs are meant to be able to cope with this heat, but you can't expect miracles. Cheap discs, or ones which have been abused over thousands of miles, will warp.

Performance pads can be mated to any brake discs, including the stock ones, but are of course designed to work best with heat-dissipating discs. Unless you plan on regularly pre-running off-road race courses, or hit the autocross circuit frequently, don't be tempted to go much further than 'fast road' pads - anything more competition-orientated may take too long to come up to temperature on the road. Remember what the brakes on your old ten-speed bike were like in the rain? Cold competition pads feel the same, and at regular street speeds may never get up to their proper operating temperature.

Lastly, installing all the performance brake parts in the world is no use if your calipers have seized up. If, when you remove your old pads, you find that one pad's worn more than the other, or that both pads have worn more on the left wheel than the right, your caliper pistons are sticking. Sometimes you can free them up by pushing them back into the caliper, but this is a sign that you really need new calipers. If you drive around with sticking calipers, you'll eat pads and discs. You choose.

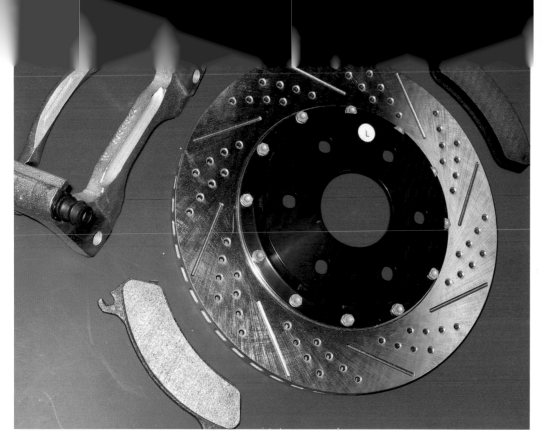

Installing upgraded discs and pads is a simple modification that takes a couple of hours max, and can make a huge difference. Since they do wear down over time, and are also prone to warpage, there's a chance you'll have to change your discs anyway, so why not upgrade them at the same time?

Upgraded
discs and pads

Warning: *The dust created by the brake system is harmful to your health. Never blow it out with compressed air and don't inhale any of it. An approved filtering mask should be worn when working on the brakes. Do not, under any circumstances, use petroleum-based solvents to clean brake parts. Use brake system cleaner only!*

01 Loosen the wheel lug nuts, raise the front of the vehicle and support it securely on jackstands. Now unscrew the caliper mounting bolts, lift the caliper off and hang it with a piece of wire or rope (DON'T let it hang by the hose!)

02 Pull the brake pads from the caliper mounting bracket . . .

03 . . . then unscrew the bolts and detach the caliper mounting bracket from the steering knuckle

04 At this point the brake disc should slip right off the hub, but if it's stuck, a little persuasion with a universal speed wrench (hammer) will usually do the trick

The following procedure is typical for a late-model Chevrolet. Purchase a Haynes Automotive Repair Manual for your vehicle to get specific instructions for this job.

Some good things to know about working on brakes

- Brakes create a lot of dust from the friction linings. Although usually not made from asbestos (very bad stuff) anymore, the dust is still something you'll want to avoid. Spray everything with brake cleaner and don't blow it into the air where you'll breathe it.

- Brake fluid is nasty stuff - poisonous, highly flammable and an effective paint stripper. Mop up spills promptly and wash any splashes off paintwork with lots of water.

- Do not use petroleum-based cleaners and solvents on or around brake parts. It will eat away all the rubber parts and hoses. Use only brake cleaner.

- Most brake jobs you can do without loosening or removing the fluid hoses and lines. If you mess with these you'll let air into the system and then have to "bleed" the brakes, which can be tricky. If you finish your job and then step on the pedal and it goes all the way to the floor, or feels soft or "spongy," you've let air into the lines.

- Which brings up a good point. After working on your brakes, start the engine and pump the pedal a few times to bring the pads into contact with the discs, and to make sure all is well before charging down the street.

05 There's the old disc on the right and the new one on the left. The bigger disc will generate more braking torque, and the slots and holes will allow the disc to dissipate heat faster; two important traits, especially if you're increasing the rolling mass the discs have to contend with (by installing larger diameter rims or big tires)

06 After cleaning the hub surface with a wire brush, it's time to install the new disc over the wheel studs. Beautiful, isn't it?

10 . . . and the outer pad

⚠ **Caution:** *New pads of any sort need careful bedding-in (over 100 miles of normal use) before they'll work properly - when first installed, the pad surface won't exactly match the contours of the disc (even if the disc is new) so it won't actually be touching it over its full area. This will most likely result in a set of very underwhelming brakes for the first few trips, so take it easy for awhile.*

11 Install the brake caliper and mounting bolts. You'll probably have to push the piston(s) back into the caliper to make room for the new pads; this can be done with a C-clamp and an old brake pad placed over the piston(s). Keep an eye on the brake fluid level in the master cylinder as this is done. Don't let it overflow. If necessary, remove some of the fluid with a suction gun

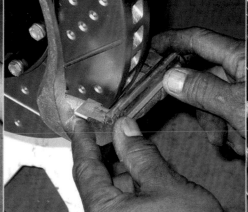

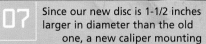

07 Since our new disc is 1-1/2 inches larger in diameter than the old one, a new caliper mounting bracket was required (it mounts just like the stock one, though). Tighten the bolts to the torque listed in your *Haynes Automotive Repair Manual*

08 Install the pad support plates on the upper and lower surfaces of the mounting bracket where the pads ride . . .

09 . . . then install the new inner pad . . .

12 Finally, tighten the caliper mounting bolts to the torque listed in your *Haynes Automotive Repair Manual*. When your brake job is complete, be sure to pump the brake pedal a few times to bring the pads into contact with the disc

13 Big improvement! Emphasis on *big*; so big that the stock wheel won't fit over it! With this kit the smallest wheel that can be run is an 18-inch. But we're going with 20's, and these drilled and slotted discs will look great filling up the space that those rims will create

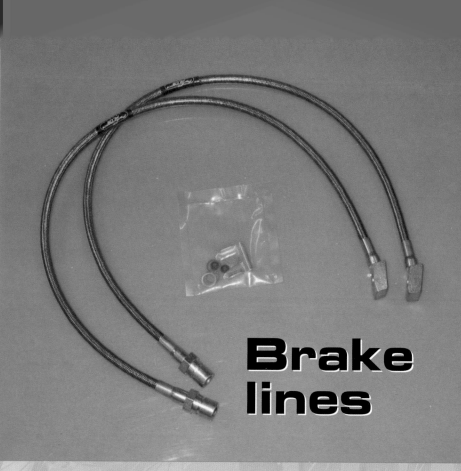

Brake lines

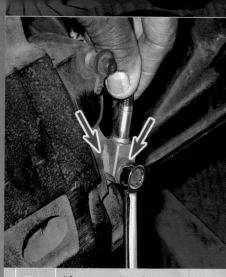

01 After removing the old brake hose, attach the new line to the brake caliper. Be sure to use new sealing washers on each side of the fitting, and tighten the fitting bolt to the torque listed in the *Haynes Automotive Repair Manual* for your vehicle

With any substantial lift you're going to run the risk of winding up with brake lines that are too short. You can solve this problem one of two ways: brake line extensions or longer brake lines. While there's nothing wrong with installing brake line extensions, longer replacement lines are preferable. Braided steel-covered lines. They look great and they're also less prone to swelling under pressure, so in theory more brake pedal force is transferred hydraulically to the calipers and (if equipped with drum brakes) wheel cylinders.

This upgrade isn't just for raised SUV's; the same benefits apply to lowered vehicles, as well.

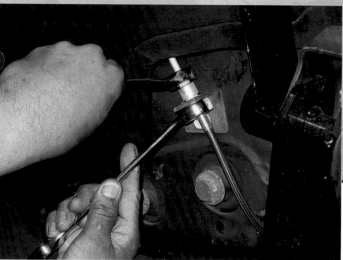

04 Pass the other end of the line through the frame bracket and thread it by hand to the hydraulic fitting, then tighten the fitting nut with a flare-nut wrench while holding the hose fitting with another wrench (a flare-nut wrench will prevent damaging the corners of the nut)

02 Route the line into place, avoiding sharp bends. Attach it to any existing brackets to keep it from contacting other components. In many cases, brackets or clips will have to be fabricated or modified to work with the new line. This one here bolts to the underside of the upper control arm

03 Here the line has been secured with a clip fastened to the upper control arm mount

05 To complete the installation, slide the spring clip into the groove on the hose fitting. Repeat on the other side

06 Now that the line is in place, turn the steering wheel from side-to-side and actuate the suspension through its range of motion, making absolutely sure the line doesn't bind, kink, stretch or chafe on anything. When you're satisfied everything is good to go, bleed the brakes as described in your *Haynes Automotive Repair Manual*

Bigger power-adders like this Eaton supercharger will give you plenty of horsepower and torque, but you need a systems approach so other aspects of your engine, like exhaust, intake and programming, are compatible

The performance needs of most SUV enthusiasts can be quite different from passenger cars. We all love performance, but SUVs need power to do work, like towing, hauling loads or off-roading. High-rpm starts and low ET's at the dragstrip are lower on our priority list.

Engine performance

An engine built to make 600 horsepower at the racetrack is not going to idle smoothly, get good gas mileage or go 200,000 miles between overhauls. Performance modifications are frequently called upgrades, but we need to keep in mind that the performance end of the operational spectrum is what's being upgraded, and often you'll have to give up some of the smooth, reliable and economical operation you've come to expect from your SUV.

So it's best to have a plan for your project, even if you don't have all the money to do everything right away. Most of us will want to build an SUV that is a compromise: one that has power to do what we need it to do while also being fun to drive. It should have some sauce to it when we hit the throttle, but still be practical to drive to work every day. Many upgrades, such as an exhaust header, cat-back system, and air-intake tube give free horsepower, with the only compromise being more noise (which is not necessarily a bad thing). These upgrades are also relatively

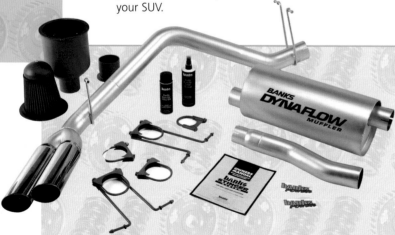

Among the "basic" modifications performed on most sport SUVs are improvements in intake flow and the exhaust system – you can include these items on your SUV one at a time or get a kit like this BanksPower "Stinger" kit for the Ford Expedition, which includes everything you need for the exhaust system and a free-flowing air intake

Mistake number one

Ya gotta have a plan! The most common mistake when enthusiasts start to modify their SUVs is getting dazzled by those seen at shows or in magazines. This leaves the temptation to just start throwing parts at your SUV in an effort to be as cool as those show vehicles. Every level of performance for your SUV should be a coordinated effort. Have a performance goal in mind that is a realistic compromise for your driving needs and budget.

Many enthusiasts start out buying parts

Torque vs. horsepower

These two terms are perhaps the most used and misunderstood measures of an engine's power. Torque is the twisting force exerted on the crankshaft, while horsepower introduces a time factor that indicates how quickly the engine makes power. Most enthusiasts read about how much horsepower a racing engine makes and they want the same for their vehicle, but power in a useable range is what we need for SUVs. Torque is what pushes you back in your seat when launching across an intersection. You could say that horsepower rules the track, while torque rules the street! Making engine modifications that increase low-end torque will give you the power you want for all your street needs: fun driving, tire-smoking or towing. Off-road driving, hill-climbing, or rock-crawling also require lots of low-end torque, and we'll be telling you some of the proven methods of gaining torque. One route that we don't cover here in detail is increasing your engine's displacement, i.e. making your engine internally bigger. This is the time-honored path to increased torque, but this is not a bolt-on operation by any means. Boring the cylinders and/or installing a stroker crankshaft that has a longer-than-stock stroke both require removing and rebuilding your engine. However, there are a number of factory and aftermarket sources for crate engines. If your engine has seen better days and you're contemplating a new one, why not invest in one that's the same physical size as yours but already has a stroker crank?

inexpensive and are no-brainers for any SUV project, since they come with no harmful side-effects.

When you get into nitrous, turbos and superchargers, you'll be spending more money and, unless you make changes to your engine management system, also getting into more risk of engine damage. High-rpm camshafts and big-port/valve cylinder head work will reduce your low-speed driveability and frequently decrease your gas mileage. Often, when these modifications are designed to increase high-rpm horsepower, you'll actually lose some low-rpm power, and for most of us, that's where we need power the most.

Torque is the commodity we're most interested in for our SUVs – this isn't an inexpensive bolt-on, but swapping in a performance crate motor could be what you want for brute torque in a stroked small block or big block – Smeding Performance has new engines for Ford and Chevrolet – these stroker Ford "small blocks" are available from 347 all the way to 427 cubic inches

that really don't help their engine at the performance level they're seeking. For instance, an aftermarket ignition system will add nothing to your relatively-stock engine except looks. The stock ignition works fine for most purposes, so unless you're building to a high level, you don't absolutely need the hot coil and amplifier. However, when you get to the bigger modifications like a supercharger or turbocharger, that performance ignition system will be required in order to fire the engine with the increased cylinder pressures.

Planning ahead means you won't have a garage full of expensive parts you bought and then later took off after you switched to higher or lower-phase parts when things didn't perform the way you expected.

On the more basic and affordable level, a chip upgrade or reprogramming for your SUV's computer is simple to perform, and can help with economy as well as performance

You're going to need some fuel economy to help defray the cost of those oversize tires and the flamed paint job – a cold air intake is one of the first mechanical mods for improved efficiency on the road

Fuel economy

There was a time when *fuel economy* and *SUVs* did not appear in the same sentence, but today's SUVs can achieve quite decent economy, with some simple modifications to both the vehicle and your driving style!

Vehicle modifications

The advent of computer-managed, electronic-fuel-injected engines, coupled with federally-mandated CAFE (Corporate Average Fuel Economy) ratings has given us the best-performing, most efficient SUVs of all time. Once we got past the Eighties, auto makers began producing better and better SUVs in every way. The computer advances, improved oxygen sensors and the now-standard multi-port, sequential fuel injection have done wonders for driveability, economy and cleaner air, plus put some perfor-mance back into our favorite work/play vehicles.

When it comes to modifications done most typically to sport SUVs, some of the same mods that we install for performance gains will also help us save some precious petrol.

It's old advice but still valid – check your tire pressure regularly, because low air in the skins means increased rolling resistance and a nick in your gas mileage

An improved air intake system is a common bolt-on modification for performance that can add power, but which may also help economy. By allowing the engine to breathe air in easier, there's a little gain in efficiency, but this gain is from giving the engine's induction system a straighter, smoother path for incoming air. The "cold" part of a cold-air package is really for performance rather than fuel economy. In fact, the warmer the air coming in (up to a point) the better most engines work in terms of mileage and emissions. There is some increase in noise from the incoming air in a typical cold-air intake package compared to the torturous passages in a stock intake system (designed to reduce the engine noise as much as possible), but overall, the long-term benefit in performance and a small help in economy will definitely pay off for you in the long run.

Perhaps the best modification for help with fuel economy as well as performance is the exhaust system. Your engine is basically an air pump, after all. Any restrictions in the path of air getting into the engine will choke it to a degree, and likewise anything that restricts the hot exhaust gasses from getting out of the engine will also restrict the engine. The bigger the engine, the bigger the engine's need to get increased airflow in and out. While a two-inch diameter intake pipe and the same size exhaust pipes may work for a small engine, this won't be sufficient for a larger one. The usage of the engine or vehicle is also a factor. For high-performance purposes where the upper rpm range is utilized, there is greater need for efficient airflow because the time allotted in each cycle for the air to get in and out is much shorter. An engine that spends most of its life at lower rpm will likewise not need so much airflow.

Modifying exhaust systems to gain more power and economy is practically as old as the automobile, and it's one of the few engine mods that doesn't have some undesirable side effect, unless you're bothered by the higher sound level of a performance exhaust. Right, we didn't think so! Enthusiasts love the performance sound, so that's not much of a drawback.

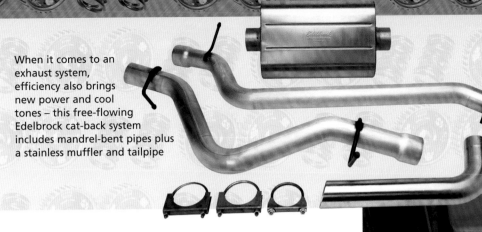

When it comes to an exhaust system, efficiency also brings new power and cool tones – this free-flowing Edelbrock cat-back system includes mandrel-bent pipes plus a stainless muffler and tailpipe

Below: Even if you retain a stock system, check underneath yours occasionally, especially if you have a lowered SUV or do any off-roading – a big dent in the head pipe like this can restrict the exhaust and also dent your fuel economy

If you refer to the section in this book on exhaust systems, you'll see that gaining performance from the exhaust system isn't that difficult.

A computer upgrade is a common performance modification, and, combined with a new air intake and a good exhaust system, will definitely give you a performance enhancement you can feel. Don't expect improvements in fuel economy, though. Most chip programs increase ignition timing and alter the fuel curve, which usually requires you to upgrade to premium fuel. The extra expense of the higher-grade gas can bring your dollars-per-mile rating down some.

It's how you drive

You know how the advertisements of new vehicless always include the caveat "your mileage may vary?" The reason it will vary is partly the terrain where you live but mostly it's your driving patterns. The device most critical to good fuel economy isn't a radical new throttle body or gas tank additive, it's your right foot!

Here are some driving tips for economy:

A) Keep your engine properly tuned (filters, plugs, clean injectors, etc)
B) Tires should be properly inflated (under-inflated tires cause vehicle drag)
C) Don't install items that increase your SUV's wind resistance (cargo carriers on the roof, etc)
D) Buy your gas in the early morning (gas is colder and denser then)
E) Air conditioning costs fuel economy, so run it only if you need it (roll down the window?)
F) Automatic transmissions use more fuel (but they're worse if you're low on fluid or have a slipping converter)
G) There are no "miracle inventions" to radically improve your economy (don't get suckered)

Here's one final tip, and a good one: buy a vacuum gauge for your SUV. They're inexpensive, easy to install and really tell you a lot about your engine. The gauge becomes the silent monitor of your driving style. The more time you spend with the vacuum high, the better your economy; it's as simple as that. When you've driven for a month or so with a vacuum gauge where it's easy to see, you'll know instinctively what to do or not do to keep the gauge reading higher vacuum. That driver training can gain you more economy that many expensive aftermarket components!

Perhaps the most effective "miracle economy" device is an ordinary vacuum gauge – it'll teach you how to drive for economy and it's a great engine diagnostic tool as well

A good cold air intake package (BBK here) on your 4.6L Ford SUV is one that works for both economy and power

The stock engine compartment is not really something you'd want to show off

Engine compartment dress-up

Open the hood on an SUV and what do you see? Black plastic air filter housing, black air intake duct, black battery, black radiator and heater hoses, black vacuum hoses, black fuse box, black electrical harnesses, black accelerator and cruise control cables, black valve cover (with, of course, a black oil filler cap), black . . . well, black everything. Black, black,

black everywhere! A sea of black! It's as if the engine compartment was dressed for a funeral or some other somber occasion.

We took this engine compartment from stock-and-filthy to attention-getting with inexpensive, easy-to-install parts from our local auto parts store. This Chapter shows you how we did it.

Here's how it looks after you're done

Silicone spark plug wires

Want better looking spark plug wires? Silicone spark plug wires and plug wire boots look better than those boring black plug wire sets, because they're available in a wide variety of colors. You say you want functionality too? Silicone plug wires and boots have better electrical insulating capabilities than conventional rubber plug wires and boots! And they can withstand heat, cold, vibration and fuel and oil vapors better than rubber insulated wires.

Disconnect the first spark plug wire and boot from its corresponding spark plug. The boots on some vehicles are rather long, and sometimes difficult to disconnect. Do not pull on the wire itself; pull only on the boot. Auto parts stores sell special plier-like tools with plastic coated tips that wrap around and grip the spark plug boot, making it easier to remove

01 The most important advice for this job is to replace one plug wire at a time! Each new wire must go back to its original location or your engine won't run.

02

03 Disengage the first spark plug wire from any cable guides on the valve cover or anywhere between the distributor and the spark plugs

04 Carefully disconnect the spark plug wire from its tower on the distributor cap

05 Each spark plug wire, whether original equipment or aftermarket, is a specific length because each spark plug is closer to or farther from the distributor. Before installing each new spark plug wire, make sure that the cable lengths are similar and that the boots at both ends are identical

06 Plug in the new silicone spark plug wire to the same high tension tower from which you just disconnected the old spark plug wire

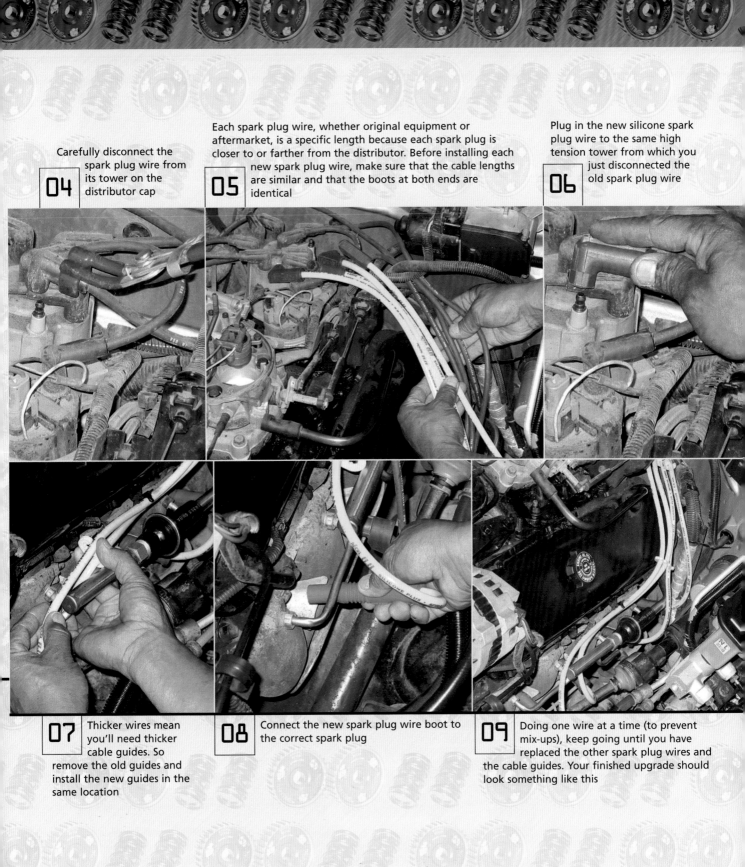

07 Thicker wires mean you'll need thicker cable guides. So remove the old guides and install the new guides in the same location

08 Connect the new spark plug wire boot to the correct spark plug

09 Doing one wire at a time (to prevent mix-ups), keep going until you have replaced the other spark plug wires and the cable guides. Your finished upgrade should look something like this

Braided metal hose covers

Braided covers are available from automotive retailers in a variety of lengths and diameters. Typical cover kits include six feet of material for vacuum lines, fuel hoses or heater hoses. Radiator hose covers are available in three or six foot lengths, each of which is available in 1-1/2 inch or 1-3/4 inch diameters.

Most aftermarket manufacturers of stainless-look braided cover kits also include anodized aluminum "clamps" which look just like the more expensive fittings used on race car plumbing. Except that they're just aluminum rings, machined to look like big nuts, which fit over a standard hose clamp (which you can easily hide by putting it on the side of the hose that nobody will ever see).

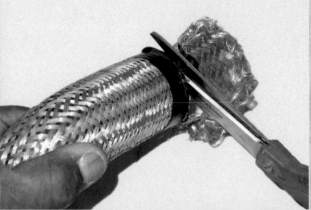

01 To cover a radiator hose, first wait until the engine cools off completely. Drain the engine coolant (refer to your Haynes manual if necessary), then loosen the hose clamps, slide them back and disconnect the hose

02 Insert a short section of PVC pipe (usually included in your kit) into one end of the braided cover to hold the cover in a rigid tubular shape, then wrap the end of the cover with electrical tape, remove the PVC pipe and cut off the frayed ends of the cover

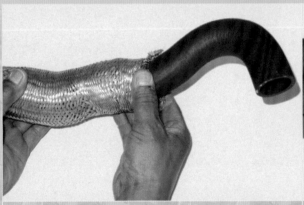

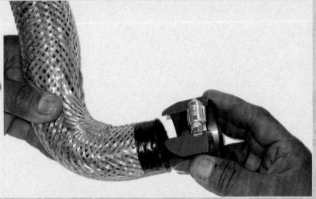

03 Now run the upper radiator hose through the braided cover

04 Install a hose clamp and clamp cover on each end of the radiator hose

05 Install the hose, then tighten the hose clamps at both ends

01 The first thing you need to do is remove the spark plug wires and the breather hose so you can unscrew the valve cover bolts

02 Lift off the valve cover, pulling it away from the cylinder head. If the cover's stuck, tap it loose with a rubber mallet. Do not pry it off with a sharp object, or you may damage the mating surface

Chrome valve covers

A quick way to spruce up the look of your engine compartment is to replace those boring old valve covers with something a little more flashy. If you want your SUV to look really sharp under the hood, get yourself a set of chrome valve covers. They're easy to install, and the results will be more than satisfying.

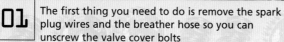

03 Install your new gasket on a clean surface, or you won't get a tight seal

04 With the valve cover in place, tighten all the bolts by hand. Then, working from the center, cinch the bolts down. Be careful not to overtighten the bolts, or you'll warp your brand new valve cover

05 Buff off any fingerprints and smudges so your valve cover is nice and shiny. Repeat on the other cylinder bank, then step back and give yourself a pat on the back for all your hard work. It looks great, doesn't it?

Air cleaner cover

If you thought replacing your valve cover was easy, try trading your stock air cleaner cover for chrome. It's the simplest thing you can do to make your engine compartment shine.

01 Unscrew the fastener and lift the cover off the air cleaner

02 Put your new chrome cover on, and replace the fastener

03 Polish off those fingerprints so you can admire your handiwork. Too easy, right?

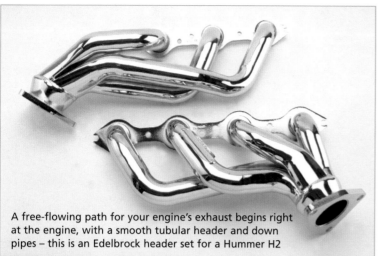

A free-flowing path for your engine's exhaust begins right at the engine, with a smooth tubular header and down pipes – this is an Edelbrock header set for a Hummer H2

After wheels and tires, perhaps the most noticeable aspect of an SUV is its exhaust; the right look and the right sound can make points plus score you power and fuel economy too!

Modifying exhaust

Of all the bolt-on modifications you can make, improving the exhaust system is one that pays benefits in several areas, regardless of the level of performance you're after. Once you have a free-flowing system, it'll work with all future mods.

When you assemble the right package of exhaust components that allow your engine to really breathe, the vehicle is going to sound as good as it performs. It bears repeating here that the exhaust system is one of the few aspects of modifying that gives you the performance you want without any of the drawbacks or compromises that usually come with engine mods. On the contrary, the exhaust work should have no effect on your idling or smooth driveability, and your fuel economy will actually go up, not down! The cool sound is a bonus, too.

The goal of performance header design is to have the right size and length pipes and arrange them so each pipe complements the others in terms of timing the pulses, and having smooth bends that reduce backpressure better than factory cast-iron manifolds

The exhaust from your catalytic converter on back is as important as a good header. Here are three examples of exhaust pipe bends: at bottom, a crinkle bend often found on stock pipes that detracts from good flow; middle, a better bend made with a hydraulic bender at a muffler shop; at top is a smooth mandrel-bent pipe that provides the smoothest exhaust flow

The classic performance muffler is a straight-through design, in which there is a perforated core surrounded by fiberglass sound-dampening material – they used to be called simply glasspacks and have always been noted for their performance sound – also popular today are chambered performance mufflers that do not utilize fiberglass

If you have lowered your Chevy SUV, this special Y-pipe from Edelbrock replaces your stock Y-pipe but gives you 1-5/8 inch more ground clearance – pipes that get squashed on driveways will cost you performance!

Backpressure and flow

Even a stock engine that operates mostly at lower speeds has to get rid of the byproducts of combustion. If it takes fuel and air in, it has to expel those gasses after the reciprocating components have turned the cylinder pressures into work. The exhaust system needs to allow swift exit of those gasses, and any delay or obstruction to that flow can cause engine efficiency to suffer. If there is an exhaust flow problem somewhere in the system, the pressure waves coming out with the gasses can back up, which can cause the cylinders to work harder to complete their four-stroke cycle. In exhaust terms, this is called backpressure, and getting rid of it is the chief aim of performance exhaust system designers.

We know that the right-sized length of straight pipe, with no catalytic converter and no muffler, would probably offer the least backpressure to the engine, but it's not very practical (or legal) for a street-driven machine. For our purposes, we have two main components between the exhaust valves and the tip of the tailpipe: the headers, and everything from the catalytic converter back (which includes the converter, exhaust pipe, silencer, muffler and tailpipe. If we can improve flow both ahead of and behind the converter (which we must keep to be legal), we'll have the best street exhaust system possible.

Custom exhaust systems are as popular on diesels as on their gas-powered brethren, but they go big – this is a Banks "Monster" Exhaust package of four-inch pipes with five-inch tip for Ford Powerstroke diesels

Headers

The first major components of your performance exhaust system are the headers, tubular replacements for your stock cast-iron exhaust manifolds. In some OEM SUV applications the stock exhaust manifolds aren't too bad, at least for the needs of your stock engine. The exhaust flow needs of an engine go up exponentially with the state of performance tune. The flow and backpressure needs of a stock engine aren't excessive, especially when the engine spends the bulk of its driving life under 4000 rpm. But what happens when you modify the engine and then take advantage of those modifications by using the high end of the rpm scale, or start towing a boat, horse trailer or some other heavy load? The exhaust system that was once adequate is now restrictive to a great degree.

How much power you make with just the headers depends on several factors. On an SUV with a really restrictive stock exhaust system, particularly exhaust manifolds full of tight bends and twists, headers will make a bigger improvement than on an SUV with a decent stock system to start with. What's behind the headers can make a big difference as well. If the stock exhaust system includes restrictive converter and muffler designs, small-diameter exhaust pipes and lots of wrinkle bends, the headers aren't going to have much chance of making a big improvement in performance. Good headers on a typical SUV engine with few other modifications can be expected to make only 5-10 horsepower, depending on how good or bad the stock manifold had been. That's with a stock exhaust system from the headers back.

That sounds disappointing, but if we take a case where the engine has numerous modifications yet still has a stock exhaust manifold, the same aftermarket headers could release much more than 10 horsepower. Any of the big power-adder modifications, including nitrous oxide and supercharging virtually require headers and a free-flowing exhaust system to take advantage of their power potential.

Installation of performance headers is quite easy. Most aftermarket headers are made to use all the factory mounting points. Make sure before buying headers that you give the shop your exact year, model, engine, 2WD or 4WD and other pertinent data. The location of the oxygen sensor varies among models. Most headers we've seen do not have provisions for bolting on a factory tin heat shield (if your SUV had one) over the headers, but we're pretty sure you want to show off your new pipes anyway.

If you can, buy your headers with a high-temperature ceramic-type coating. It looks almost as good as chrome, but will not turn color or burn off and it has a scientific plus also. The coatings will retain heat inside your headers, and that helps performance in two ways. The coating allows less exhaust heat into the engine compartment, and keeping exhaust heat inside the headers means the hotter gasses will move out of the system.

01 Here's the stock exhaust on a 2000 Chevy – it's serviceable, but the giant (too quiet) muffler and single exhaust pipe just don't cut it for our purposes of performance, sound and appearance – Marco Muffler of Sacramento, CA upgrades these day in and day out for dealers and customers

02 This is important – before any welding is done on a computer-controlled vehicle, you must disconnect the battery to prevent electrical spikes from smoking your computer! At Marco, they use an alternative method: this surge protector device attached to the ground and positive lugs underhood – it's easier and you don't lose your radio presets

03 Most factory exhaust systems are welded together on the assembly line, so the only way to remove it is to cut – here Rich has supported the giant stock muffler and uses a Sawzall to liberate it

04 The stock pipe ahead of the muffler is a 2-1/2 inch – here a hydraulic bender is being used to form a new piece of three-inch aluminized pipe to the same shape as the stock pipe – foot controls operate the bender

Cat-back system

Once the exhaust gasses leave your efficient new headers, they must travel a ways to get out from under your SUV, and our goal is to make it more of a freeway than a mountain road. First off, there is the catalytic converter, usually bolted right there just behind your exhaust manifolds. For most of us, this is not an option because we have to have it to pass emissions tests. That's fine, because the converter does do a great job of cleaning up engine emissions, and the designs of current converters are more free-flowing than older ones, so the converter isn't something to whine about too much.

Most of the aftermarket exhaust systems are called cat-back, because they include everything from the converter back. The system may be in several pieces to simplify packaging, shipping and installation, but it should bolt right up to the back flange of your converter and include whatever silencer(s) and muffler(s) are needed. Many of the

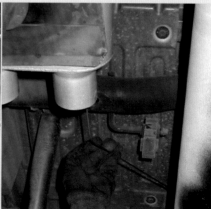

08 The stock hanger and rubber donut isolator support the back of the 3-inch front pipe – the hanger is being welded to the pipe, after which the excess length of hanger will be trimmed off

09 The new Flowmaster performance muffler has a large single inlet for applications like this and two 2-1/2 inch outlets for twin tailpipes – this is a 40-series muffler for aggressive sound, but there are quieter 50 and 60-series models

10 Muffler shops very often use a long length of welding wire to make a pattern for a custom pipe they're going to bend – experience tells them just where to bend the pattern and the new pipe

05 The flange is cut off the stock pipe and bolted to the vehicle's cat-back assembly – then the new 3-inch pipe is aligned and tack-welded to the flange

06 Compare the old pipe and the new (here with the stock flange fully welded to the new pipe) – the increase in pipe diameter will reduce backpressure in the system

07 The single rear tailpipe has been removed, and with the new front pipe bolted back on the vehicle and supported by a stand, the planning for the performance muffler and two new rear pipes can begin

cat-back systems include the muffler(s), which on most SUVs is something designed strictly for noise reduction.

The muffler you choose determines a proportionately large share of both the sound level and backpressure of your total exhaust system. We all like a good growl or purr, but a really free-flowing muffler may be loud to the point of annoying. Maybe what we want is like the sound of a Ferrari: purrs at idle, draws attention when accelerating, and at full song it's like music. Some muffler companies actually have their mufflers divided into classes, with one group having the most aggressive sound, another a little more subdued, and one that's described as mellow. The perfect sound is such a

subjective thing, you may want to just listen around when you're at events with a lot of customized SUVs. When you hear an SUV whose tone suits you, check for a name on the muffler or ask the owner.

When shopping for a pre-made cat-back exhaust system, make sure the system can accommodate your exact vehicle. In SUVs, there is no "one kit fits all." Even the make and type of trailer hitch on your SUV can make a difference. SUV options like towing packages (suspension) and extra or larger-capacity fuel tanks can make routing pipes more difficult, especially when trying to install two pipes on an SUV that only came with one. For these reasons, many enthusiasts like to have a

11 The wire pattern is held next to the hydraulic bender, where the new 2-1/2 inch tailpipes are bent to the same angles

12 Routing pipes requires the installer to check for any possible interference between the proposed pipe and something on the vehicle like shocks, stabilizer bars, etc. – here one of the SUV's cables has been cinched down with three zip ties to keep it away from the left tailpipe area

13 Not all the bends are made at once - after each bend the pipe is tried on the vehicle again. Here, the point where the last bend will be made is being marked – note that pipes are left long because the bends really shorten the pipe beyond your initial guesstimate

14 The entire system is only tack-welded together until every piece is fitted and the hangers are in place - you can see the routing of the two custom tailpipes in their final shapes

15 All stock or custom hangers must be in place; you can't leave any spot unsupported – the front hanger for the left tailpipe is being welded in position

16 Muffler men are never without a measuring device, since they use their fingers. The tailpipes are located evenly by a one-finger distance between them and the bumper, and a three-finger distance to the side from the large flanges on this SUV's trailer hitch assembly

17 The chromed tips can accommodate several sizes of tailpipes – our tips are enlarged on this swaging tool on the hydraulic bending machine, until the tip just fits over a 2-1/2 inch pipe sample, also located on the bending machine for efficiency

custom system built for their SUV. Check around and find a local shop with a good reputation. Most installations take only a few hours to complete, and you get to pick the kinds of mufflers you want, from mild to raucous, and have the tailpipes exit at the location of your choice.

Changing the exhaust of your SUV for a performance system is one of the modifications with more perks than almost any other. You get increased power, improved fuel economy, the sound that will complement your performance profile, and parts that make your ride look better, too. All that, and there's no real downside or sacrifice as with most engine mods.

18 The new tip is slipped over our extra-long tailpipe until it's lined up aesthetically with the rear bumper – a mark indicates where the pipe and tip should be welded, but the pipe is actually cut off a little ahead of this mark

19 The tall stand supports a large bar used to align the tip with the pipe. The tip is tack-welded in four places around the tailpipe

20 The SUV's owner is going to be very happy – a muscle-car sound, improved power and economy, and a great pair of chromed tips!

No, this BanksPower setup isn't emissions-legal, but it is an example of serious turbo power for a gasoline Chevy V8! – with two turbochargers, one for each bank, and all the right parts you can get 700 or more horsepower

Turbochargers

Of the three major "power adders" (nitrous oxide, superchargers, and turbochargers), the turbocharger offers the biggest power potential of all. Its durability and practicality has been proven many times over on production cars and trucks worldwide, whenever extra power was needed without the trouble and expense of fitting the vehicle with a bigger engine.

How it works

There are basically three main elements to a turbocharger: the exhaust turbine, the intake air compressor, and the housing/shaft/bearing assembly that ties the two pressure-related sections together. The turbine is composed of an iron housing in which rotates a wheel covered with curved fans or blades. These blades fit precisely within the turbine housing. When the turbine housing is mounted to an engine's exhaust manifold, the escaping hot exhaust gasses must flow through the housing and over the vanes, causing the shaft to spin rapidly. After the exhaust has passed through the turbine it exits through a large pipe, called a downpipe, to the rest of the vehicle's exhaust system.

Within the compressor housing is another wheel with vanes. Since both wheels are connected to a common shaft, the intake wheel spins at the same speed as the turbine, so the compressor draws intake air in and the rapidly spinning wheels blows the air into the engine's intake side. The more load there is on the engine, the more the turbocharger works to give the engine horsepower. As the engine goes faster, it makes more exhaust, which drives the turbocharger faster, which makes the engine produce more power.

The unit in the center of this turbo sandwich has the important function of reliably passing the power between the two housings.

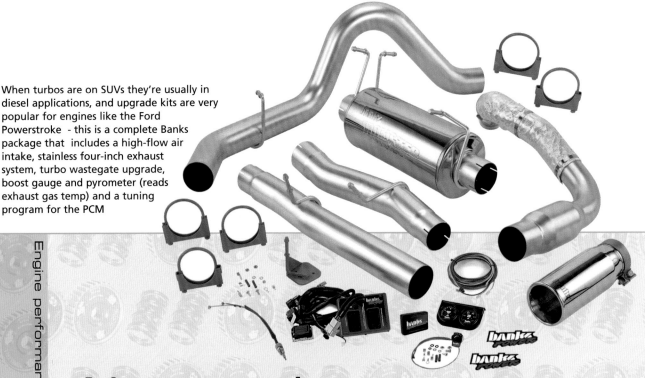

When turbos are on SUVs they're usually in diesel applications, and upgrade kits are very popular for engines like the Ford Powerstroke - this is a complete Banks package that includes a high-flow air intake, stainless four-inch exhaust system, turbo wastegate upgrade, boost gauge and pyrometer (reads exhaust gas temp) and a tuning program for the PCM

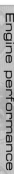
Advantages and disadvantages of the turbocharger

Compared to the supercharger, the turbo is smaller, lighter, quieter, and puts less direct load on the engine. The not-at-all-times boost of the turbocharger is an advantage for fuel economy, operating noise level and driveability, but in some cases may be a drawback when compared to the mechanical supercharger. While a roots-type supercharger adds boost in relation to rpm (i.e. the faster the engine goes, the faster the blower pumps), it runs up against physical limitations eventually and can't pump any more. In order to make any more boost with a supercharger, you have to change the pulleys or gearing that drives it.

The limitation for the blower-equipped vehicle is in top end performance, and this is where the turbocharger has the distinct advantage. The turbocharger is much more customizable, with various wheels and housings available to suit whatever the intended engine or purpose. Boost can be made to come in early, or come in later at a higher boost level.

The same basic turbocharger can be used for street use or modified to make more boost than your engine can live with! Such customizing, called sizing, should be done by an experienced turbo shop that can select the exact components for your engine size and power requirements.

Intercoolers

One of the serious disadvantages of the turbocharger is the heat it will put into the intake air charge, which is why most successful turbo systems utilize an intercooler to combat this. Air coming from the turbocharger tends to be hot because it's compressed and also because of its close proximity to the exhaust.

The most effective and common method of dealing with intake air temperature on a turbocharged vehicle is an intercooler. This is a honeycomb affair much like a radiator, usually mounted out in front of the vehicle's radiator in an opening below the bumper where cooler air is found. The boosted air from the compressor is ducted through pipes and into the intercooler, then to the intake of the engine. Thus, the cooler is between the compressor and the engine, so it's called an inter-cooler. Since cooler air produces more power, intercoolers are very popular.

Turbocharging kits

A complete turbocharging kit from most reputable aftermarket companies will include virtually everything you need for your application, with a cost from $2500 to $4500 for the package. For late-model, gasoline-powered V8 SUVs, there are few turbo kits available, since plumbing the exhaust from two banks of the engine to a single turbo can get complicated, especially if it is to meet emissions standards with catalytic converters.

An intercooler cools the intake charge after it leaves the turbo and before it enters your engine – this is a "Techni-Cooler" kit from Banks with all the hardware to add an intercooler to your Ford Powerstroke diesel for more power

Ironically, for diesels, which usually come turbocharged in stock form, there are numerous kits to upgrade the stock system for more boost and/or add an intercooler.

Durability with a turbo

Problems with turbo installations usually crop up because of detonation caused by too much boost, or not enough fuel under boosted conditions. A turbocharged performance vehicle can be both reliable and pleasurable to drive, even on a daily basis. If you keep in mind the limitations, you'll be fine.

The low octane of today's pump gas will be the biggest limiting factor on street-driven machines. With a reasonable boost level of 5-10 PSI and the proper precautions, you can run pump gas. With an electronic timing controller, you can switch from one timing program to another depending on the octane rating of the gas you have available.

Proper fuel mixture is very important. One lean-out and you'll fry at least one piston or valve! Keep checking your spark plugs and have a good programmable fuel controller. A fuel pressure regulator that can handle boosted conditions, a boost-capable MAP sensor, and a fuel system that can deliver extra pressure under boost should keep things under control.

We can't address every aspect of turbocharging here, but other steps to improving durability include keeping the engine cool, with the use of a good radiator and fan, external engine oil cooler, and of course an intercooler to chill the intake tract temperature. If you consistently run high boosts, internal engine upgrades will have to be made, such as forged, low-compression pistons, forged aftermarket rods, improved-flow oil pump, and a blueprinted rotating assembly.

The Banks "Six-Gun" diesel tuner kit is available separately to tune your SUV's factory software with regards to pulse width, timing and fuel pressure – six levels of tuning can be selected from a dash control

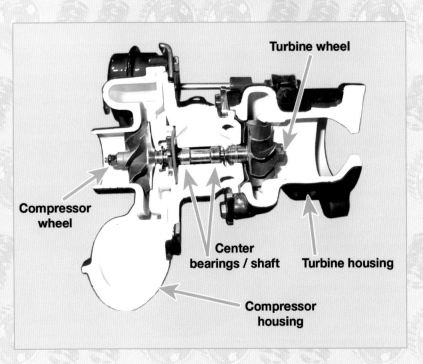

Turbine wheel

Compressor wheel

Center bearings / shaft

Turbine housing

Compressor housing

A good example of the merits of supercharging is this 2004 Chevy with a twin-screw Whipple blower – with 91 octane fuel and only six pounds of boost, the owner has great low-end power and loads of tow capability – the kit comes with computer controls and all the hardware needed for installation

Superchargers

Your engine is in a constant state of combustion when running. It sucks in air and fuel, burns it to make the pistons go, then expels what's left. With a supercharger, instead of having to use its own energy to suck in the mixture, your engine is force-fed, and the difference can be worth 50% and more in horsepower. Boost is good!

Inside a positive-displacement blower (Eaton design from Magnuson Products shown here) you can see the two rotors that, when turned, grasp the fuel/air mix firmly and compress it into the engine – as engine speed goes up, boost does, too

Right - Centrifugal superchargers are sort of like a turbo with a mechanical drive - the Powerdyne unit shown here has a unique internal belt-drive for quieter operation

A turbocharger is similar in function to the supercharger, but differs in that the turbo is driven by exhaust gasses, rather than by mechanical means. A supercharger (also called a blower) is driven by the engine, either with gears, chains or belts, so there is direct correlation between the engine speed and the boost produced by the supercharger.

While the turbo-charger may have the upper hand when you're talking about all-out high-rpm performance on the track, the supercharger shines at improving street performance almost from idle speed on up. Low-rpm power is very helpful for across-the-intersection performance and freeway passing power when towing or when you have a relatively high gearing with overdrive.

Ford's family of 4.6L and 5.4L overhead-cam "modular" engines really rev well, but don't have as much low-end torque as many pushrod V8's. Adding a positive-displacement supercharger is the perfect mod to gain low-end punch, for the best of both ranges. The GM Gen III modular engines also benefit from a supercharger.

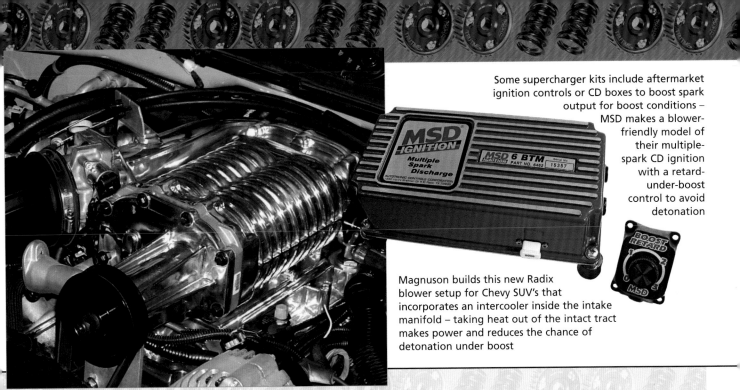

Some supercharger kits include aftermarket ignition controls or CD boxes to boost spark output for boost conditions – MSD makes a blower-friendly model of their multiple-spark CD ignition with a retard-under-boost control to avoid detonation

Magnuson builds this new Radix blower setup for Chevy SUV's that incorporates an intercooler inside the intake manifold – taking heat out of the intact tract makes power and reduces the chance of detonation under boost

Boost

Boost is any pressure beyond normal atmospheric pressure (14.7 psi). If you look at a vacuum/pressure gauge on a boosted engine, as you begin to spin the blower, the vacuum side of the gauge (negative pressure) starts to go towards zero, then you start to show positive pressure or boost. So, if you have a turbo or supercharger that is making 14.7 psi of boost, you have effectively doubled normal atmospheric pressure or added another "atmosphere." Twice that amount of boost and you've added two atmospheres, and you command the bridge of a rocket ship!

However, we must be realistic about boost levels. There is a finite limit to the boost your blower can make, and probably a much lower limit of how much boost your engine can take,

regardless of how the boost was generated. You'll find most street supercharger kits are limited to 5-7 psi, to make some power while working well on a basically stock engine that sips pump gasoline.

Some kits on the market have optional pulleys that will spin the blower faster for more boost, but, as with any power adder, you can only go so far in increasing cylinder pressure before you have to make serious modifications to strengthen the engine (forged pistons, aftermarket connecting rods, etc.).

Your engine's existing compression ratio is a factor in how much boost you can run. To run lots of boost (10 psi or more) your static compression ratio shouldn't be higher than about 9:1, and if you plan on doing any towing, then it shouldn't be much higher than 8.5:1 or 8:1.

Heat and detonation

Knock, ping, pre-ignition and detonation are all terms that describe abnormal combustion in an engine - they also describe big trouble. An increase in boost also increases the combustion chamber temperature and pressure, often leading to these problems that can destroy pistons, valves, rods and crankshafts.

The two main factors in detonation and its control are heat and timing. Ignition timing does offer some ways to deal with detonation. Supercharged engines generally like more timing, especially initial advance, but once you are making full boost and the vehicle is under load, too much ignition advance can bring on the death rattle of detonation that you don't want to hear. How much advance your application can handle is a trial-error-experience thing, but if you are using a production blower kit from a known manufacturer, these tests have already been made and some kind of timing control program should be included.

Anything you can do to control engine temperature and intake air temperature in particular will help stave off

detonation also. Better oil circulation, a better radiator, an intercooler and an engine oil cooler are proven modifications to control excess heat that can contribute to detonation.

If you like SUV performance, you'll love having a supercharger! - this is a Powerdyne installation on a Lincoln Navigator, with the result being comparable to a fast heavyweight boxer . . . in a tuxedo

Allen Engine offers this Eaton-blower kit for '97-'02 F-150's; with an air-to-water intercooler inside the intake manifold it gives a 4.6L 80 more ponies and boosts the bottom-end torque by 100 ft-lbs

Blower kits

There are several types of small superchargers used in kits designed for SUV engines. The two main types of supercharger design you will see are the Roots type or positive displacement, and the centrifugal design.

The Roots-type mechanical blower uses a pair of rotors that turn inside a housing. As the rotors turn, they capture a certain amount of air and propel it to the inner circumference of the case and out to the intake manifold. Each time they turn around, they capture air, hence the "positive" description. The benefit of this type is that it starts making boost at very low rpm.

A variation of this type of blower is the screw-type. These have two rotors with helically-wound vanes that, as the name implies, look like two giant screws. When the two screws mesh together (there is a male and a female rotor), the air is actually compressed between the screws.

The other major type of bolt-on supercharger is the centrifugal design. From a quick examination, the centrifugal blower looks just like the compressor half of a turbocharger, being a multi-vaned wheel within a scroll-type housing. Unlike a turbocharger, this type of blower isn't driven by exhaust but by a mechanical drive from the engine, usually a belt. These types of blowers are not positive-displacement, and thus do not necessarily make their boost down on the low end, but have plenty of air-movement potential when they are spinning rapidly.

Most reputable blower kits have everything you need to install the system and use it reliably. Contents include the blower, intake manifold (if needed), belt, mounting hardware, instructions and some type of electronic gear to control fuel delivery and/or ignition timing. Some kits use a larger-than-stock fuel pump that replaces your in-tank pump, and a special fuel pressure regulator that may be boost-sensitive.

Other included components could be hoses, wire harnesses, air intake, a new MAP sensor that can tolerate pressure as well as vacuum, an intercooler, and parts that relocate items in the engine compartment to provide room for the blower.

Some superchargers use a bypass valve that reduces losses during idle and cruise conditions – the valve is inside on this MagnaCharger blower and is actuated by the external vacuum control

The typical customized SUV engine compartment has had some modifications to the engine – usually to the "in-and-out" sides like a cold air intake for improved sound, looks and breathing power, and a performance exhaust system to do the same for the engine's exit path – a supercharged engine like this one has even more need for a serious intake

More torque in the mid-range for pushrod 5.0L Ford engines is available by stepping up to this Edelbrock "Performer truck 5.0" intake manifold – this and a bigger throttle body could make your modified engine feel like its bigger brother, the 351

Induction systems

Performance air intakes have become so common as to be almost required equipment on even the most mildly modified SUVs. They're universally used because they're legal, cool looking and easy to install, plus, they give the engine a little more intake noise and improved horsepower!

The least expensive and easiest intakes to install are the short ram types. You'll spend longer getting the stock air filter box and inlet tube out than installing the short ram. If you have any doubts about removing the stock components, consult the Haynes repair manual for your model. Short-ram intakes place the new filter relatively close to the engine, and modifications to the engine or body are rarely necessary. Most short-ram installations take only a half-hour to install and may be good for 4 to 8

horsepower, depending on the application. And of course, they look and sound really nice. The more free-flowing they are, the more intake noise you'll hear, but that's OK with us, right? Short-ram intakes usually have a plastic or sheetmetal dam around the filter area to keep hot engine air away from the intake. The dam usually seals to the hood with a weather-stripped edge when the hood is closed.

For purposes of performance, the colder the air the more power you make. Cold-air intake (CAI) systems are

The simplest modification you can make to your stock air induction system is to open the factory airbox, lift out the OEM paper air filter, and replace it with a high-flow aftermarket, pleated-cotton replacement like this K&N - these can be reused over and over by washing, then treating them with a special oil

Typical aftermarket air intake kits like this Airaid will give you some horsepower and a more-impressive sounding engine – such kits are very easy to install and one of the least expensive engine mods you can make

A throttle body spacer like this Airaid unit can easily be installed between the throttle body and the intake plenum, and helps passing power by increasing plenum volume

one of the most-widely-installed bolt-on performance improvements on the SUV scene. They are usually the first modification made and have become so common that people would install one whether it made any more power or not. Most do make some power, for two reasons. The airflow path from the new high-flow filter to the throttle body is usually smoother-than-stock, and the cooler air is denser than hot underhood air around the engine.

Aftermarket cold air intake systems can be worth 8 to 20 horsepower, depending on the design and how modified the engine is. A stock engine doesn't need to gulp huge quantities of air, but a modified engine does. Obviously, a cold air intake is going to need some bends in order to reach the cold air, but if there are too many bends or bends made too sharp, the horsepower gain from the colder air could be offset by a reduction in airflow.

The rest of your induction system will be fine unless you're making bigger engine modifications, such as hotter cam(s), cylinder head work, increased compression and/or power adders like a blower or nitrous oxide. When you're really going for all you can get from your engine, you can add a bigger throttle body and a high-flowing aftermarket intake manifold to really perform at high rpm. Just remember that modifying your engine to run its best at high rpm means it isn't going to be so hot anymore at low, around-town speeds, and throttle response can get seriously doggy unless you're constantly blipping the right foot pedal.

A modification that is very common on today's SUVs is a throttle body spacer. As the name implies, the spacer fits between the stock throttle body and the intake manifold, effectively lengthening the intake tract somewhat without making the diameter bigger, as a larger throttle body would. The spacers are relatively inexpensive and easy to install; just follow the Haynes repair manual for your SUV and, of course, read the manufacturer's instructions. Spacers generally offer little extra power at the bottom end, but can be helpful for mid-range performance, such as towing or highway passing.

Most SUV enthusiasts install both an air intake and an improved exhaust system. To let your engine management adjust to the new, free-breathing parts, it's a good idea to disconnect your SUV's battery for about an hour, then reconnect it. The next time you start the vehicle, the PCM will start adjusting to the new intake and exhaust parameters, and you'll get a bit of additional horsepower from the combo. On some models, the vehicle may not run its best for a period of 20-50 miles, until the relearning process is completed.

A new aftermarket throttle body of increased bore size can add 5-10 horsepower, depending on your application – this CNC-machined aluminum unit from BBK is an 80-mm size for Chevy SUV's

More Power and Fresher Breath for SUVs!

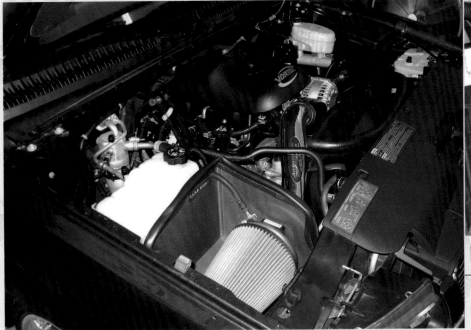

01 Our Airforce One cold air intake utilizes a high-performance cone-type air filter that is kept behind a metal dam to keep the hot engine compartment air from getting to the engine's air intake. This model (installed here by Aftermarket of Carmichael, CA) looks good and has a C.A.R.B. approval sticker

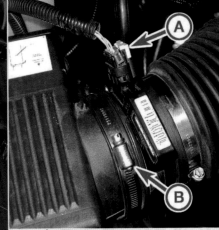

02 Disconnect the battery, then disconnect the electrical connector (A) from the MAF sensor. Fully loosen the clamps (B) securing the MAF sensor in the stock air tubing

03 Pull the air hose and MAF sensor out of the factory air filter box, then twist the MAF sensor out of the tubing and set it aside in a safe place

04 Fully loosen the clamp screw at the throttle body so the stock elbow and air tube can be removed from the vehicle

05 You can remove the Chevrolet filter-box by rocking it a little, then pulling it straight up – it's retained only by pins on the bottom that fit into rubber grommets

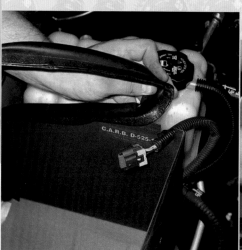

09 A weatherstrip seals the box against the hood to keep hot air out. Press the strip in place around the top edges, but slip the MAF sensor connector and wires into this notch first

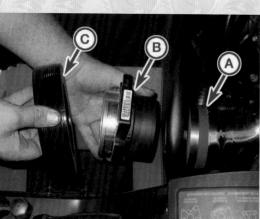

10 The MAF sensor (B) is the center part of a sandwich between the air tube (A) and the rubber adapter (C) that accepts the new cone-type filter

11 Push the MAF sensor through the cold-air box and into the blue silicone hose on the air tube, then install the four long mounting screws from the engine side of the airbox. Now install the two hose clamps and tighten them

06 With the filter-box removed, it is easy to remove the four bolts and this metal plate. Once the plate is out, the new cold-air box can be bolted down with the same four bolts where the plate was located

07 The new Airforce One elbow can be slipped onto the throttle body at this time, then the new polished-stainless air tube can be slipped into the elbow and the tube roughly lined-up with the cold-air box

08 Tighten the clamps at the throttle body and air tube, but allow enough slack for minor tube alignment at the cold-air box

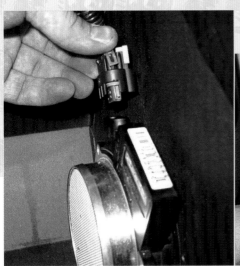

12 Inside the airbox, connect the electrical connector to the MAF sensor

13 The new, pleated-element air filter can now be slipped over the filter adapter and the clamp secured

14 Now's the time to go back and make sure all hose clamps are secured – so you'll be ready for the road and your engine can breathe more freely

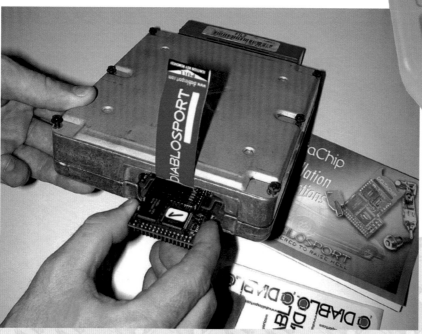

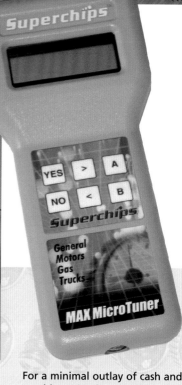

Computers
and chips

For a minimal outlay of cash and trouble, a simple upgrade for your PCM can improve engine response with increased timing. This is a typical hand-held programmer that works on most late-model SUVs when hooked to the diagnostic port at the dash

The engine controls in our modern vehicles were developed to make them more fuel-efficient and emissions cleaner, using computer-controlled electronic fuel injection. The side benefit for performance enthusiasts is that engine control modifications to the fuel and ignition systems are relatively easy.

This is a plug-in Power Programmer for a Chevy from Jet Performance – for some models, computer upgrade work can be done by mail and Jet will ship it back to you in 24 hours, all with special packaging they will supply

Engine management basics

Automotive computer systems consist of an onboard computer, referred to by manufacturers as the Powertrain Control Module (PCM), and information sensors, which monitor various functions of the engine and send data to the PCM. Based on the data and the information programmed into the computer's memory, the PCM generates output signals to control various engine functions via control relays, solenoids and other output actuators.

The PCM is the brain of the electronically controlled fuel and emissions system, and is specifically calibrated to optimize the performance, emissions, fuel economy and driveability of one specific vehicle/engine/transaxle/accessories package in one make/model/year of vehicle.

Non-serviceable chips must be carefully unsoldered from the board, which is why this is usually done by a specialized company or tuning shop with the proper tools and reprogramming equipment

Computer codes keep track

You may have heard of the term OBD or OBD-II. This means On-Board Diagnostics and refers to the ability to retrieve information from the PCM about the performance characteristics and running condition of all the sensors and actuators in the engine management system. This is invaluable information in diagnosing engine problems. The PCM will illuminate the CHECK ENGINE light (also called the Malfunction Indicator Light) on the dash if it recognizes a component fault.

So, if your dashboard warning light comes on you know the computer has spotted something it doesn't like. To then figure out what it has found, you (or your mechanic) need to access the diagnostic code that the computer has stored in its memory for that fault. On some vehicles, getting these codes is an easy in-the-driveway job. On others, it takes an expensive scan tool. Your Haynes repair manual will give specific information for your make and model.

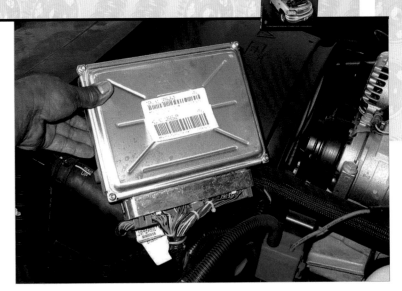

Add-on chips and computers

For improved performance, many enthusiasts upgrade their engine management systems with aftermarket equipment. The advantages are increased fuel flow, an improved ignition advance curve and higher revving capability. While replacing or tuning computer components can provide substantial performance gains when combined with other engine upgrades, they also have their downside. Perhaps most importantly, replacing any original-equipment computer components can void your warranty or cause you to fail an emissions inspection. Nevertheless, if you are into modifying your engine, at some point you will have to consider dealing with the computer.

The factory programming in your SUV's PCM is a highly developed, extensively-tested system that works perfectly for your engine in stock condition. Remember that the goal of the factory engineers is maximum fuel economy, driveability, longevity and efficiency. Our goals as enthusiasts are more in the high-performance sphere and our programming needs are slightly different. The average SUV owner will never see 5000 rpm in the vehicle's lifetime, but the average *enthusiast* wants to see the upper power band now and again and also experience more power down low as well.

Where the factory PCM programming needs some help for performance use is in the ignition timing and fuel curves. Most new SUVs are designed to run on the lowest grade of unleaded pump gas, with an 87-octane rating. To get more performance, the ignition curve can be given more timing and the fuel curve adjusted for more fuel at higher rpm, but the octane rating of the gas now becomes a problem. When more timing is added, the engine may have more tendency to exhibit detonation or ping, signs of improper burning in the combustion chamber and potentially dangerous to the lifespan of the engine. Thus, if you want more timing in your computer for more power, you'll probably have to up the grade of gasoline you buy. In fact, the more serious engine modifications you make, the more you will probably have to reprogram your PCM.

Before you order a custom chip for your SUV, you must copy all the information from the label on your PCM, so the techs know exactly what program and spark/fuel parameters they're working with

While most simple bolt-on engine modifications will work well with increased timing, the serious power adders like nitrous oxide, superchargers, turbochargers and even just high-compression pistons will require less ignition advance. The big gains in horsepower come from modifications that increase the cylinder pressure in the engine, the force pushing the pistons down. Increases in cylinder pressure really raise the octane requirement in a hurry. The best you can get at most gas stations won't be enough to stave off detonation, unless you're lucky enough to live near one of the few stations that sells 100-octane unleaded racing gas, and that gets pricey.

So, over the process of modifying your SUV's engine, your programming needs may change. As you make more and different changes, different tweaks need to be applied to the brain. Hopefully, you have located a trustworthy customizing shop near you. They'll be able to help you with computer upgrades.

On all modern fuel-injected vehicles, the programming that affects the areas we want to modify is part of a chip on the motherboard of the PCM. The chip is a very small piece of silicon semiconductor material carrying many integrated circuits. These are usually called PROM chips, for Programmable Read Only Memory. In some cases, the chip is a plug-in which can be easily removed from the PCM and replaced with a custom chip, while other chips are factory-soldered to the board. Vehicles with plug-in chips are the easiest to modify, but many PCMs do not have replaceable chips.

It isn't recommended to remove a soldered chip from the motherboard at home. Your factory PCM is very expensive to replace and just a tiny mistake with the

solder or the heat source could ruin it. Aftermarket companies offer reprogramming services for these kinds of PCMs, and some tuning shops also have equipment to do this. In most cases you remove your PCM and send it to the company by overnight mail, they modify it and overnight-mail it back to you.

The performance chip will not void your warranty, but you might want to remove it if you bring your vehicle in to a dealer for diagnostic work, in case the dealership downloads an updated factory program as part of your service.

Based on the information you have given them about your vehicle, driving needs, and modifications you have made to the engine, they will custom-program the timing, fuel and even the transmission shifting information on vehicles with PCM-controlled electronic automatic transaxles. On vehicles so equipped, they can even change the factory-set rev limiter or top-speed limiter. On most applications, your SUV will require a better grade of gas than before, so factor the increased fuel cost in your budget.

Towing is another consideration when chipping an SUV. The octane requirement of a vehicle goes up seriously with increased load. Lighter vehicles require less octane with all other factors being equal. If you tow heavy loads (boat, car trailer, etc.), even occasionally, make sure this is taken into consideration before investing is a new program or chip. You should also tell the chip company if you have changed to a non-stock gear ratio or installed much-taller tires and wheels. The new program can gain back any performance you may have lost with large-diameter wheels or gears and even correct your speedometer readings.

Depending on the year and model of the SUV, a plug-in chip may be available from the aftermarket for your vehicle. In these cases, you don't have to send your PCM to the company, just give them the complete serial number and codes on the decal of your PCM and they'll supply the correct plug-in for you. Another popular method of reprogramming is with an electronic tool. You buy the tool with the programming for your make of SUV, plug it in and download the new program. These tools can even function as a scan tool after that, for reading diagnostic trouble codes.

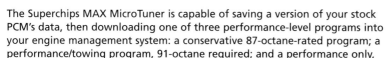

The Superchips MAX MicroTuner is capable of saving a version of your stock PCM's data, then downloading one of three performance-level programs into your engine management system: a conservative 87-octane-rated program; a performance/towing program, 91-octane required; and a performance only, 91-octane program not suited for towing. You can switch programs or go back to stock with the tool. Included are the instructions and the computer cable

01

With the key OFF, plug one end of the cable into the diagnostic connector on your vehicle, in this case a 2004 Chevy being customized at sport-truck shop Aftermarket in Carmichael, California

02

Reprogramming your PCM

Plug the other end of the cable into the MicroTuner and you're ready to go, but make sure you have read the instructions and cautions thoroughly before beginning

03

When first connected to the vehicle (key OFF) the MicroTuner will run a series of diagnostic self-tests, then you will turn the key to ON or RUN and it will save your stock tuning information. It will then instruct you through the steps of downloading the performance program you have chosen – have the instruction book with you during the procedure if you have questions. Your Superchips MicroTuner can be used to tune your specific vehicle; it will not work on another VIN vehicle - however it will still be very useful, as it works as an OBD II code reader for your SUV or another SUV of the same make. If you keep this tool with your vehicle, you can change the program if you decide to tow a heavy load or change to a lower octane gas if 91 isn't available

04

When your engine is being modified for power, mild or wild, it may respond better with an improved ignition system to fire the mix

Engine performance

Ignition system

Higher engine speeds put an increased load on stock ignition systems, but modifications that lead to increased cylinder pressure can really put out the fire. Major power-adders such as nitrous oxide, supercharging or turbocharging create much higher cylinder pressures and require ignition improvements to handle this. The spark plugs need a lot more zap to light off a mixture that is packed tighter than ever. The denser the mixture, the harder it is for a spark to jump the plug's electrodes, like swimming through wet concrete.

For the later-model 4.6L/5.4L overhead-cam Ford engines that do not have a distributor, there are aftermarket coil packs like this one to build increased spark energy

Aftermarket ignition coils

The typical aftermarket coil is capable of making more secondary voltage than the stock coil, so the spark can jump the gap even at extreme cylinder pressures. An aftermarket coil won't add any horsepower and won't improve your fuel economy, but it could eliminate some misfire problems in the upper rpm range, and that will become more important as you add other modifications to your engine.

Most SUVs with a distributor have a very good high-energy coil, but those models can sometimes benefit from an aftermarket performance coil or module for the inside of the distributor, or an external coil to mount on the firewall. Later model Ford (with 4.6L/5.4L modular engines) or Chevy (with Gen III engines) SUVs don't have a conventional distributor to divvy out the sparks to each cylinder, but rather a separate small coil over each spark plug, all controlled and timed by the computer (PCM, as it is usually called). These individual coils add up to very good ignition performance overall. Don't invest in a complete aftermarket ignition system on a late-model SUV unless you are really planning a lot of engine mods or drag racing.

If you've modified your engine for increased performance, you may consider an ignition upgrade like this "ultimate HEI" kit from MSD

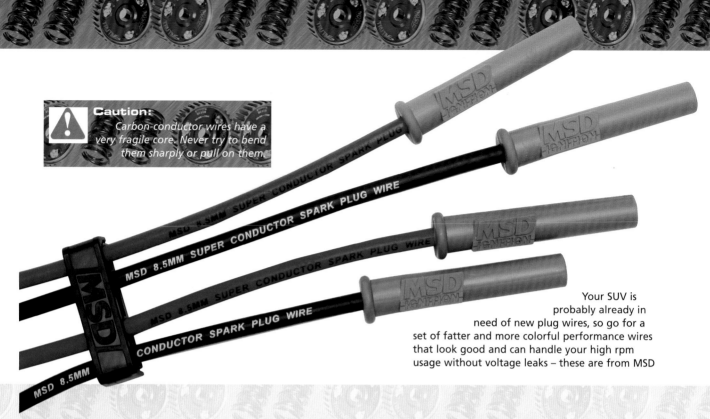

Caution:
Carbon-conductor wires have a very fragile core. Never try to bend them sharply or pull on them.

Your SUV is probably already in need of new plug wires, so go for a set of fatter and more colorful performance wires that look good and can handle your high rpm usage without voltage leaks – these are from MSD

Plug wires

Once you have a decent coil, quality spark plug wires should be next on your ignition agenda. Plug wires are made of a conducting material encased within several layers of shielding. The former carries the current to the plugs, while the latter prevents the high secondary voltage from leaking out. Obviously, if you install a high-voltage coil and keep your stock wires, you are asking for some voltage to leak from the wires at high rpms or boosted (blown or turbocharged) conditions. Voltage will try to seek the path of least resistance and that could be any engine ground that is close to one of your plug wires.

The typical factory plug wire has a core of carbon-impregnated material surrounded by fiberglass and rubber insulation. Solid metal conductor wires are used in racecars and provide a high-capacity, low-resistance transport for high-energy ignition systems. Since most of us are as much into music as we are performance, the metal-core wires are out for street use because they create serious interference with stereo components, not just on your SUV, but on everybody's vehicle around you! They also can interfere with your PCM and cause driveability problems. The carbon-conductor wires are great for suppression of RFI (Radio Frequency Interference) and EMI (Electromagnetic Interference, the kind that affects your PCM) and are inexpensive, but they have a limited lifespan, and aren't capable of handling high-energy ignition components.

Most aftermarket performance wires use a very fine spiral wire wound around a magnetic core, then wrapped in silicone jacketing. Wire sets are available in thicker-than-stock diameters to handle more current flow. Some stock plug wires are as skinny as 5 or 6mm, while aftermarket wires are offered in 8mm, 8.5mm and even 9mm for racing applications. Good aftermarket wires also come with thicker boots, which is important, since the boot-to-plug contact area is a frequent source of voltage leaking to ground. Wires in the 8mm range are big enough to handle the spark of most street-modified SUVs, and the bigger wires are good for racing, but there's no such thing as having too much insulation on your plug wires. There's also the cool factor with plug wires, they come in more exciting colors than the factory black. Look for plug boots that fit tightly to the spark plug. If the boot fits tightly only at the bottom, air can become trapped between the plug and the boot. This air can be heated when the engine is running hard, expanding enough to pop the boot and plug wire off the plug.

An aftermarket coil with more windings and a heavy-duty case can lower resistance and up your secondary voltage to the spark plugs

Caution:
With any boot, remember to use a spark plug boot tool whenever you install or remove the boots from the plugs. Never pull on the plug wire itself. The plug wire's core is fragile and can be broken by careless stretching.

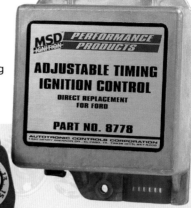

If you do occasional towing of heavy loads like a boat or RV trailer, a timing control box like this will allow you to adjust your ignition timing from inside the cab if your SUV is pinging on the available gasoline

Timing controls

When your spark ignites the cylinder's fuel mix is critical; this is called ignition *timing*. The mix doesn't explode in an instantaneous flash; it actually takes a period of time. The flame front from the point of ignition travels through the mixture, slowly at first and then building speed. This is good, because what is needed is a gradual build of pressure, not a sharp spike, which can be destructive to pistons, rods and crankshafts. Since the mixture takes time to burn, the spark is timed to trigger some time before the piston reaches the top of its stroke (Top Dead Center). So the initial timing is some degrees BTDC, or Before Top Dead Center.

Firing with too much advance (too far before the piston reaches the top) can cause too much pressure to build in the cylinder before the piston reaches TDC, so that the piston and the rising pressure are fighting each other. On the other hand, if the timing is too late (not enough in advance), the engine can't make the most of the gas expansion and power and economy are wasted.

To complicate the timing discussion even further, the spark event must have a different timing at different engine speeds. As engine speed goes up, there is less time available for the combustion event, so the spark must occur sooner. Other factors also influence the correct ignition timing, such as engine load, temperature and fuel mixture. If you map out the amount of ignition advance on a graph related to rpm, you have what's called an advance *curve*, an important factor in performance tuning.

Once you start modifying the engine, you have changed the ignition parameters and you now need to adjust the timing with something other than the factory PCM. Installing a chip or reprogramming your PCM will advance the timing and adjust for other parameters, but usually this means you'll be forced to use higher-octane gas. For older vehicles, a CD (Capacitive Discharge) aftermarket ignition system could be just what you need.

The CD ignition usually consists of an electronic box you mount in the engine compartment, and the wiring harness to connect to your vehicle. In the CD box is a large capacitor, which is an electronic storage device. These ignition systems have been used in performance applications for years and are well proven. Juice usually comes into the coil or coil pack as battery voltage (12V)

and is bumped up from there to 5,000, 10,000 or 40,000 volts of secondary current. In the CD ignition, the capacitor stores incoming juice until there is more like 450 volts to go to the coil. Now the coil has a much easier time of quickly building up to the required voltage for good spark, regardless of the rpm. Some of the better aftermarket ignitions may also provide improved throttle response at lower speeds and keep the spark plugs cleaner in engines that have some mileage on them, though it is by no means a substitute for a properly maintained engine.

There are different models of CD ignitions, with varying "bells & whistles", but one of the most common side benefits is a rev control (later model SUVs already have a rev limiter set in their engine management). Some units are also capable of programming-in an adjustable rate of spark retard at high rpms, which is ideal for supercharged or turbocharged applications. Because of the increased cylinder pressure with boosted engines, it is common to retard the spark progressively as the boost level increases.

A CD electronic ignition control box can provide multi-fire capability as well as user-settable control of rev-limit, plus retard control for boosted engines and nitrous applications – this Holley kit even has a soft-touch handheld programmer for adjustments

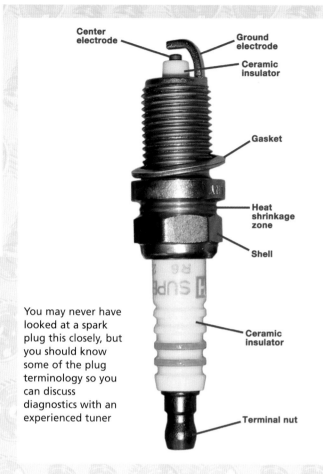

Center electrode

Ground electrode

Ceramic insulator

Gasket

Heat shrinkage zone

Shell

Ceramic insulator

Terminal nut

You may never have looked at a spark plug this closely, but you should know some of the plug terminology so you can discuss diagnostics with an experienced tuner

Spark plugs

The final links in the ignition system's chain-of-command are the spark plugs, the front-line combat troops. We may have mentioned this before but, as with other ignition modifications, don't expect to make any gains in power or mileage by switching spark plugs. Despite the wild claims dreamed up by advertising copywriters over the last fifty years, the only time spark plugs will make much difference on a street-driven engine is when the engine is really in need of a tune-up and you install fresh plugs.

Nonetheless, there are a wide variety of spark plugs out there to choose from. If your engine is only mildly modified, stick with the factory recommended spark plugs, gapped to factory specs. If you add an increasing number of performance modifications to your engine, you may have to reconsider what type of plugs to run, and even what size electrode gap is best. Most engines with above-average level of modifications can utilize a plug that is one heat range colder than stock. Examine your plugs regularly and carefully with a magnifying glass to look for signs of beginning detonation or other problems.

Required reading. . . your spark plugs!

Without a lot of complicated and expensive test equipment, you can tell a great deal about the operating conditions inside your engine just by examining its spark plugs. Of course, scan tools and other electronic gear are very helpful, but they tell you all about the outside conditions and whether there's a problem with your PCM, your TPS, MAP, MAF and other sensors. This is good information, but diagnosis of the true internal operating conditions of an engine, stock or high-performance, begins with a very close look at the spark plugs.

This may seem like a primitive tuning tool, but watch the pit activity at any professional-level race and you'll see the top mechanics looking at spark plugs with a magnifying glass. When a spark plug tells a story, it can save you an entire engine by giving early warning signs of detonation. The color, uniformity, cleanliness and even smell of a freshly-pulled spark plug can tell you reams, if you know what to look for. In the back of the Haynes repair manual for your vehicle (you do have one, don't you?) you'll find a large chart of various spark plug conditions, close-up and in color.

When you pull the plugs on your street-driven SUV, you're looking at long-term conditions - the plugs can tell you if the engine is too rich, too lean, if its burning oil, if the electrodes are worn from too many miles, etc. Whenever you make important changes on your state of tune, like adding more performance equipment, double check the part's influence by doing a plug check like this.

A really good close-up magnifying glass will let you see every tiny detail - compare the results to a Haynes color spark plug chart

Valvetrain
Modifications

When you run fast, you breathe harder - your engine works the same way. To make more power, an engine must inhale more air/fuel and exhale more exhaust. To make this happen, you can open the valves more, leave them open longer and/or enlarge the ports (passages in the cylinder head where the air and exhaust flow).

The modifications discussed here usually come only after all the other bolt-ons have not gained you the power you're after. Most valvetrain modifications require going inside the engine, which is not a place an amateur should go alone. Nevertheless, if you have some engine experience and a copy of the applicable *Haynes repair manual* for your model and year of SUV (see your local auto parts store for a copy), you could tackle a rocker arm, cam or cylinder head swap that could bring you some new-found power.

Much easier than installing a new cam is putting in a set of roller rocker arms with a higher-than-stock ratio for more valve lift

Rocker arms

The camshaft is the mechanical computer inside your engine that times valve events, and has a major influence on both power and driveability, but not everyone is equipped or ready to install one in their SUV. An easy alternative is to install higher-ratio rocker arms. You simply remove the valve covers, remove the stock rocker arms, install the aftermarket ones and reset the valve clearances. The *Haynes Automotive Repair Manual* for your vehicle will detail the whole operation.

If your stock rocker arms have a 1.5 ratio, it means that when the pushrods push up on the rocker at the cam's highest lift, the rocker arm

Camshafts

Installing camshafts is an expensive and precise task. The most important work comes before any tools come out. After consulting with your tuner or a cam manufacturer's tech line, you need to pick out the best cam for your truck and driving style. Stock camshafts are designed as a compromise to consider economy, emissions, low-end torque, good idling and driveability. The performance camshaft lifts the valves higher (lift), keeps them open longer (duration) and is designed mainly to produce more horsepower. A performance camshaft usually makes its gains at mid-to-higher rpm and sacrifices some low-rpm torque. The hotter the cam, the more pronounced these attributes become. A cam design that is advertised for power between 3000 and 8000 rpm won't start feeling really good until that rpm band is reached.

Aftermarket cams are often advertised in Stages of performance. A typical Stage 1 cam might have a little higher lift than stock and a little longer duration. You may even see such cams advertised for SUV applications as an RV or Torque/Towing grind. It would still keep an excellent idle and work from idle or 1000 rpm up. A Stage II cam would be hotter in all specs (with a band from 3000 to 7000 rpm) and have a slightly rough idle (maybe 750 rpm). A Stage III cam would feature serious lift, duration and overlap and make its power from 5000 to 8000 rpm. The hotter the cam specs the worse the idle, low-end performance and fuel economy is going to be, but the more top-end horsepower you'll make. The hotter cams are ordinarily unsuitable for SUVs that spend most of their street life cruising under 4000 rpm or do any heavy towing.

multiplies that movement by one and a half times in relaying the movement to the valves. If your camshaft's lift at the cam lobe is 0.274-inch, then your valve's total lift will be one and a half times that, or 0.411-inch.

Aftermarket rocker arms are available for most popular engines that increase the ratio, so our previous example would achieve .438-inch lift if equipped with 1.6:1 rockers. This will give you some performance gain, but it can't change valve timing or duration as a performance camshaft would. There are other benefits to aftermarket rockers, though. Most are made with roller-tips for reduced drag at the point where rocker and valve stem meet, reducing engine frictional losses a little and thereby helping both performance and economy. A number of aftermarket rocker arms are also available with roller bearings in the center for further friction reduction, and are made of lightweight materials like aluminum. Lighter valvetrain weight allows an engine to rev quicker.

If you decide to upgrade to a performance camshaft later on, you'll have to check that it is compatible with your new rocker-arm ratio. Too much combined lobe and rocker-arm lift could make the valves hit the pistons, so you might have to revert back to the stock rockers arms with the new cam.

Many late-model engines have roller-lifter camshaft designs because they reduce friction losses and make a little more power and save fuel, too – you don't have to give up these advantages to get a hotter aftermarket cam, order a performance roller cam like this set for 4.6L/5.4L Ford modular engines from Comp Cams

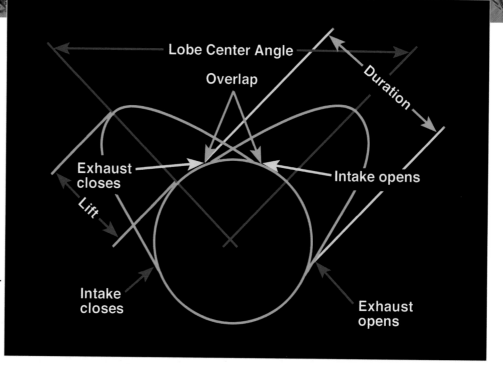

The heartbeat of any performance engine is its camshaft design – you don't need to understand all the science of valvetrain action, just tell the cam manufacturer all your vehicle's specs and the kind of driving you do and they'll pick the right profile

Valve springs

When you install a bigger camshaft, you'll usually want to install better valve springs. High-performance valve springs allow the valves to open further without the springs binding and also are stronger to prevent valve float. Valve float occurs when the engine is at high rpm and the inertia of the valve is too much for the spring to handle. So the valves actually lose contact with the rocker arm or cam follower and can make contact with the piston, bending the valve and/or damaging the piston.

For this reason, high-performance valve springs are recommended whenever you change the camshaft or make other modifications to extend the rpm range beyond stock. Your stock springs will not last long at repeated high-rpm operation, and when springs fail, the valves usually hit the pistons with results that are major-league bad.

Probably no valvetrain modification is as important as good aftermarket valve springs that are strong enough not to float the valves at high engine speeds - these Ultra-Rev springs from REV are designed specifically for high-rpm and high-boost forced-induction engines

The piston top is really part of the combustion chamber and involved with the valvetrain – When you install a bigger cam, you may need pistons with deep valve reliefs (right) – right piston gives 9.8:1 compression to Windsor Ford engines, while the left piston has deep dish to maintain stock late-model compression

Cylinder head work

The most basic of cylinder head work is a valve job, which will assure the valve seats and guides are in good condition. This is very important for an engine running at high rpm, and is essential if your engine has lots of miles on it. If you're planning to install a performance camshaft with new valve springs and lightweight retainers, make sure you get a good valve job at the same time - preferably a three-angle valve job from a performance machine shop. You won't see much performance gain from this work; it's insurance against damage on an engine that will be pushed to the limits.

A popular modification for performance SUVs today is replacing the stock cylinder heads with aftermarket iron or aluminum heads. These heads have improved port size and shape, changes in the combustion chamber, and performance valve springs and often are equipped with stainless-steel valves. The two most important factors for you in choosing such heads are the compression ratio and the legality for your application. Your engine's compression ratio is the biggest factor in the octane it requires, and if you go much above stock in compression ratio, you'll need the middle-grade gas for normal driving and the premium for towing. Consider if the big increase in your fuel costs is going to be worth the extra horsepower gained by raising the compression ratio. Most of our readers have vehicles still subject to emission regulation and testing, and for these we recommend only buying heads that are 50-state legal for emissions. After the expense and labor of installing aftermarket heads, it would ruin your day to fail a state emissions test and have to take them off.

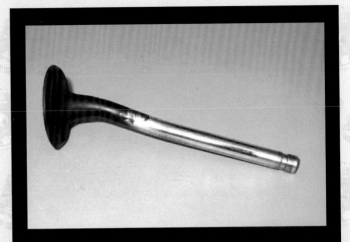

Valve float

Valve float occurs when, at high rpm, the valves are trying to move so fast that they momentarily "float" away from the camshaft or rocker arm lobes. If they float away when the piston is up, damage to something is inevitable. Two factors can keep the valves from floating, the strength of the valve springs and the weight of items in the valvetrain, such as the valves, keepers and retainers. Stronger, aftermarket valve springs are an important upgrade for any high-performance engine. The stronger springs keep the valves following the camshaft, even at high rpm.

Reducing the weight of the valvetrain items (such as with titanium retainers) is another way to lessen the onset of valve float.

Above - A pair of complete aftermarket performance heads is one sure way to add both horsepower and torque – this Edelbrock aluminum Performer head is 50-state-legal for 302/351 Windsor small-blocks and features stainless-steel valves, hardened pushrod plates and maintains your stock compression ratio

Right - The air/fuel mixture enters your engine's combustion chambers through ports in the heads – this is a cutaway of a performance head that has bigger port area than stock for more airflow

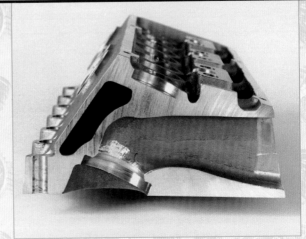

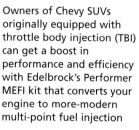

Owners of Chevy SUVs originally equipped with throttle body injection (TBI) can get a boost in performance and efficiency with Edelbrock's Performer MEFI kit that converts your engine to more-modern multi-point fuel injection

Fuel system

Your engine burns fuel and air. When you increase the amount of air it's using, you have to up the fuel, too. The more you modify your engine, the more fuel system modifications you may have to perform.

A performance-type, adjustable fuel pressure regulator will be adequate for all your pressure control needs for now and with any future engine add-ons – this one is made by BBK

Your stock engine management system will adapt to an increase in airflow such as an aftermarket intake pipe and free-flowing air filter, but the physical limitations of the stock fuel delivery system under wide-open throttle (WOT) conditions can hold back the engine's potential when more aggressive mods are made. Since you are modifying the engine to go faster, i.e. spending more time at WOT, you are sort of on your own to develop the fuel combination that works best for your engine and the modifications you've made. The major mods you might make, such as power-adders, cams or head work, have been done by many others before you, and the manufacturer of the components should have plenty of data on what fuel system upgrades go along with their equipment. An important consideration for SUV owners who do any towing is that you definitely don't want the engine to go lean during an uphill tow.

Here's a supercharged engine with two extra fuel injectors for plenty of fuel flow under boost – electronic management of the extra injectors is part of the kit for this Whipple blower installation

An adjustable fuel pressure regulator is probably the first modification for your fuel system. The aftermarket units are a direct bolt-on for the stock regulator, with the same vacuum connection, but feature an adjuster screw on top that changes the fuel system pressure. Once you start playing with your fuel system, you must have a reliable way to measure the fuel pressure, which usually means installing a quality fuel pressure gauge.

When you increase the fuel pressure in your FI system, you are putting a greater load on the injectors themselves. Too much fuel pressure will shorten the life of the injectors. Experts tell us that for street SUVs with mild bolt-on modifications, you shouldn't raise the factory fuel pressure much more than 10%. On a vehicle with 45 psi as the stock pressure, you could safely raise it with an adjustable regulator to 49.5 psi, assuming that your modifications require an increase. Engines with power adders like a supercharger will require extra injectors and a separate electronic control just for the extra injectors, which will add fuel when the engine is under boost.

If you have too much fuel, your engine will be doggy at the bottom end and initial takeoff will be rough unless you're always leaving an intersection at higher rpms. With a minor increase in fuel system pressure, you can have your stock PCM or chip reprogrammed to handle higher fuel pressure, and this is recommended, but there is a finite limit to how much the stock PCM can handle. An exhaust gas analyzer at a tuning shop is a big help, especially if you can run the SUV on a chassis dyno (driven by the rear wheels under load).

An aftermarket high-pressure fuel pump will be needed when you have serious power mods – some replace your in-tank pump like this Holley unit; other types can be added to the system somewhere near the fuel tank

Fuel system volume

For the typical SUV engine modified with bolt-on equipment, your stock fuel pump should be able to handle the fuel supply needs. If you go beyond the simple additions to your engine, you might want to change the fuel rails that hold all your injectors. The aftermarket ones look cool but also can deliver more volume of fuel because their main internal passage is bigger. The larger volume of the aftermarket fuel rail acts like a plenum in an intake manifold, providing all the injectors with a steadier supply of gas, especially if you later on go to larger fuel injectors. Most rails also have extra ports, for attaching a fuel pressure gauge or adding a line to an extra injector for blown or nitrous applications.

With more mods, you may have to have more fuel-pumping capacity. Most tuners in need of increased fuel flow use an extra fuel pump as a booster, leaving the stock pump in the tank. The extra pump may be wired up to either a boost gauge or nitrous solenoid, to just pump when needed.

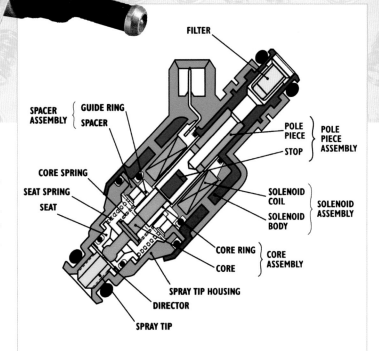

An electronic fuel injector is a complicated piece of engineering – you may not need bigger injectors for your SUV, but you could be losing both power and economy if your stock ones are dirty – have your injectors cleaned at a shop every 60,000 miles

Four-wheel drive?

So what is four-wheel drive, anyway? And do you really need it? The questions seem simple enough, and, if you ask around, you'll likely get some simple answers: "If you drive in the snow, you've got to have it." "It's a waste of money." "It'll give you a cool look, make you ride higher." Unfortunately, no one-liner can provide a good answer.

What is it?

The simplest explanation is that four-wheel drive (4WD) provides engine power to both the front and rear axles of the SUV, theoretically providing rotating force to all four wheels. The result is greatly improved traction on loose or slippery surfaces. To make a two-wheel drive (2WD) SUV into a 4WD SUV, three major components must be added: 1) A transfer case. 2) A second driving axle assembly. 3) A new system of driveshafts to drive both axles from the transfer case. In addition to these components, most modern 4WD systems have electronic systems to shift the transfer case and, on part-time systems, to shift the axle hubs.

Transfer case

You can think of the transfer case as the heart of the 4WD system. Most of the time, the transfer case and transmission are bolted together and appear as one large assembly. The transfer case's job is to take power from the engine, as delivered from the transmission output shaft, and distribute this power to both axles. Many transfer cases also have gearing to provide a low gear range for extra pulling power off-road. Transfer cases come in two flavors: part-time and full-time.

Part-time

Don't worry. The part-time transfer case won't clock-out just when you need it most. The name refers to the

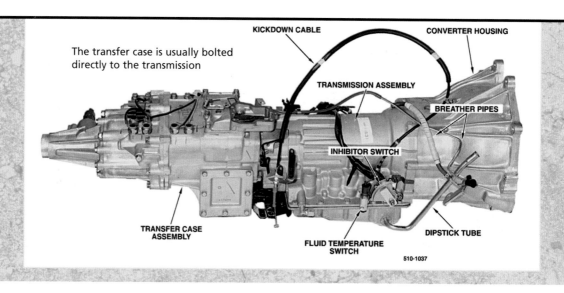

The transfer case is usually bolted directly to the transmission

KICKDOWN CABLE

CONVERTER HOUSING

TRANSMISSION ASSEMBLY

BREATHER PIPES

INHIBITOR SWITCH

TRANSFER CASE ASSEMBLY

FLUID TEMPERATURE SWITCH

DIPSTICK TUBE

510-1037

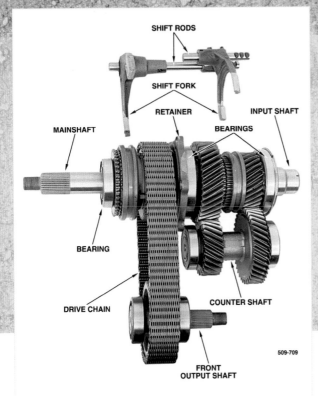

The internal components of a part-time transfer case. The shift rods are for shifting between high and low range, and between 2WD and 4WD

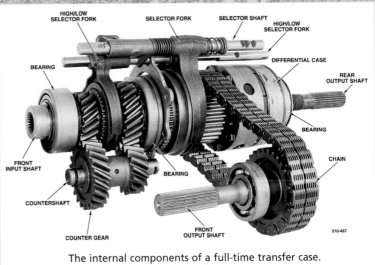

The internal components of a full-time transfer case. Notice the differential assembly

way it is used. The part-time transfer case allows you to shift in and out of 4WD so that you can operate in 4WD off-road, then shift to 2WD when you hit the pavement. And this is not a suggestion – you *must* operate in 2WD mode when you're on hard surfaces. The reason is that the direct-drive mechanism in the part-time transfer case does not allow any slippage between the driveshafts. This works fine on loose surfaces, since the surface itself allows for wheel slippage. But on hard surfaces, there can be no slippage at the wheels, and a phenomenon known as "wind-up" will occur, especially in cornering. Ultimately, a part will break somewhere in the 4WD system – an expensive one!

Part-time systems generally have locking wheel hubs so that the driveshaft that coasts in 2WD mode can be disengaged from the wheels. This prevents the wheels from back-driving the axleshafts and driveshaft, thus saving some fuel. The hubs can be either a manual-locking type or they can use an electric or vacuum-driven shift motor that allows you to shift from the driver's seat.

Part-time 4WD gives excellent performance on loose surfaces and still allows for reasonable fuel economy while driving on pavement (in 2WD mode only – don't forget!)

Full-time

Full-time transfer cases include a differential assembly or viscous coupling that allows the two driveshafts to turn at different speeds. This eliminates the wind-up problem and allows driving on hard surfaces in 4WD mode. Full-time 4WD systems do not require locking hubs at the wheels, since there's no reason to disengage the system. Some full-time transfer cases also have a locking mechanism in the differential that allows you to switch to a fully locked system when off road, like a part-time system.

Many part-time 4WD systems use special wheel hubs that allow you to engage each front wheel manually . . .

. . . but most modern SUVs use remote actuators, like this vacuum-operated one, which allows the driver to keep his feet warm and dry

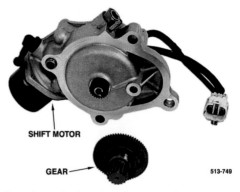

Gone from the interior of most modern 4WD's is the big ol' lever for shifting the transfer case's gear ranges. This electric motor is what does the work now. All the driver needs to do is push a button

513-749

The main advantage of a full-time transfer case is its ease of use. If you're constantly going from hard surfaces to soft surfaces, this system works best, since you don't need to be shifting back and forth. But, since both axles are operating all the time, there tends to be more component wear and slightly lower fuel economy than with a part-time system.

Differentials

The differential assembly in each axle allows the wheels on that axle to rotate at different speeds during turns. Unfortunately, standard differentials also allow the wheels to get stuck more easily off-road. You've probably seen what happens when a vehicle with a standard differential gets stuck in the snow, mud or sand. One wheel will turn as fast as you want, but the other just stays put.

Limited-slip differentials are an improvement over standard differentials. They allow some speed differential between the wheels during turning, but give a relatively solid "lock" between the wheels when traction is needed. Many four-wheel drive vehicles come factory equipped with a limited-slip differential on the rear axle, but limited-slip differentials are not commonly used on front axles.

"Locker" differentials are very popular with off-road enthusiasts. Lockers perform the same basic function as limited-slip differentials, but they use a special ratcheting mechanism to provide the speed differential between the wheels (limited-slip differentials use a less-robust clutch system). Lockers are more precise, transmit more power for traction, and can take more off-road abuse without wearing out.

For maximum traction off road, manual locking systems or "air lockers" are becoming very popular. These systems lock the differential so both wheels turn at the same speed, all the time. Naturally, a system like this cannot be used on roads, and it is only really needed when the vehicle gets stuck. So, air lockers can be easily controlled by the driver, using a compressed-air engagement system.

Axles

Axles for four-wheel drive systems have two basic types: solid and independent. As its name suggests, a solid axle rigidly joins the two wheel hubs, while an independent axle allows each wheel to move up and down independent of the other wheel. Independent axles use Constant Velocity (CV)

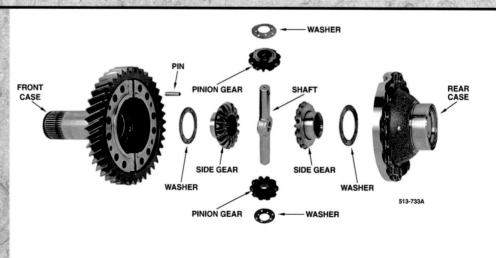

An exploded view of a differential (this one's in a transfer case). The side gears and pinion gears allow the two driveshafts to rotate at different speeds

WASHER

PIN

PINION GEAR

SHAFT

WASHER

FRONT CASE

REAR CASE

SIDE GEAR

SIDE GEAR

WASHER

WASHER

PINION GEAR

WASHER

513-733A

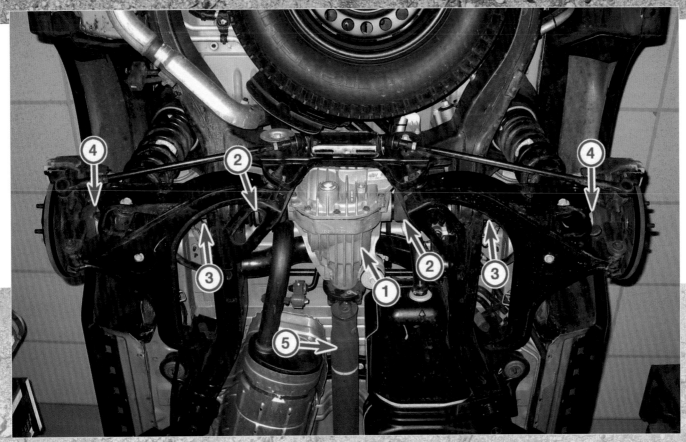

A typical independent axle assembly (rear axle shown)

1 Differential assembly
2 Inner Constant Velocity (CV) joints
3 Driveaxles (difficult to see in this picture)
4 Outer Constant Velocity (CV) joints
5 Driveshaft

joints on their ends to permit this independent movement.

Generally speaking, independent axles provide a smoother ride and more consistent tire-contact on rough roads. However, many off-roaders still prefer the solid axle for its durability and easily altered suspension travel.

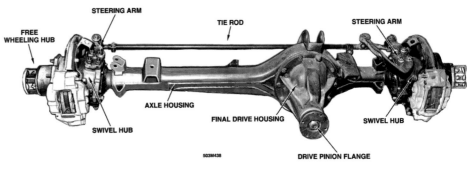

A typical solid axle assembly

Do I really want it?

If you're asking this question, you're probably not convinced that you need 4WD. And if you don't want or need 4WD, you're definitely better off with a money-saving two-wheel drive SUV. If you're not sure you need 4WD, borrow or rent a two-wheel drive SUV and use it during a snowstorm or for your off-road activities – you may find it meets your needs. Limited-slip differentials are commonly available on two-wheel drive SUVs, and they can greatly improve your traction. Remember that four-wheel drive has some drawbacks:

- Higher initial vehicle cost
- Harsher ride
- Extra weight
- Lower fuel economy
- More expensive servicing

So why get four-wheel drive? Well, for many types of driving, it can be a life-saver. And if your weekends are spent camping or on other outdoor activities, you'll be able to get to much more remote locations. Besides, nothing beats the feeling of confidence you get driving a 4WD vehicle. And sometimes, that feeling alone makes up for any down-side!

Off-road driving tips

Don't go out alone. This means you should have a second person traveling with you, but it also means you should travel with another off-road vehicle. Breakdowns happen frequently off-road, especially on rough terrain. If you choose to venture out in a single vehicle, at least choose a time and place to meet with another off-roader. If something goes wrong, they can bring help quickly. And don't rely on your cell-phone; they frequently don't work off-road.

Know the area. Some overconfident off-roaders will make spontaneous decisions to travel into new areas. Many hiking trips have started this way. It's best to review a new area on a map before going in. Some areas have deep sand, mud, holes, vertical caves or abandoned mine-shafts. Many driving areas are subject to flash-flooding. Talk to people who have been in that specific area. Drive slowly in new areas and, when you're not sure what's ahead, get out and walk it first.

Know your SUV. Study your owner's manual and be sure you understand the operation of all systems, especially the four-wheel-drive system (if you have one). Also, familiarize yourself with the SUV's major components and their locations. Pay particular attention to components that could be easily damaged. Make special note of ground-clearance issues.

Bring supplies and equipment. Bring a first-aid kit, fire extinguisher, tools, flashlight, blanket, shovel, food and water. It's also a good idea to bring some common replacement parts and fluids for your SUV. If snakes are in the area, bring a snake-bite kit.

Run lower tire pressures. In soft or muddy terrain, you can increase your traction by lowering your tire pressures a bit. Check your owner's manual for recommendations. Just remember to re-inflate the tires to full pressure before driving on-road.

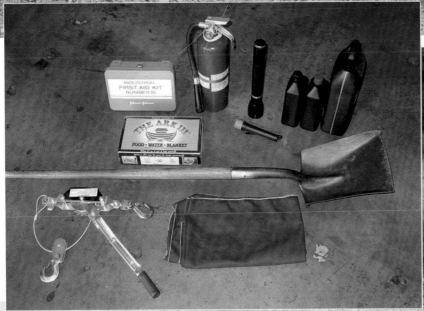

Don't run out of gas! Be sure your tank(s) are full before you head out, and keep track of how far you've gone. Factory fuel gauges are notoriously inaccurate: the last "half" tank always goes much faster than the first half. Many off-roaders bring additional gas cans, just in case the worst happens.

Keep your seatbelts tight. Drivers are often surprised how much they get bounced around when driving off-road. Your seatbelt will save you some bumps and bruises.

Stay relaxed while driving. Sit up straight, but leave your arms, legs and neck relaxed to absorb the inevitable jolts that will come through the suspension.

Don't push yourself. You're more likely to make mistakes if you're rushing to keep to a schedule. Give yourself plenty of time to reach your destination before dark. Which brings us

to another point: you ask for trouble when you drive on unfamiliar terrain at night.

Keep a light grip on the steering wheel. The steering wheel can kick back suddenly when you hit a rock, hole or other obstacle. A light grip will prevent your hands from getting hurt. Also, keep your thumbs and fingers on the outside diameter of the steering wheel, since the spokes can really hurt you on a kick-back.

Don't "gun it." When traversing soft terrain, go easy on the accelerator pedal. Sudden bursts of power can actually get you stuck by digging "ruts" in the dirt or mud. The best approach is to maintain a constant speed. Bumpy terrain can sometimes cause your foot to move involuntarily up and down on the accelerator – to prevent this, press your foot to the right side, against the "hump" in the floorboard.

Conserve your brakes. On long hill descents, select a low gear and use engine braking to keep your speed down. If you have four-wheel drive, use the "Low" range of your transfer case.

Getting unstuck

Nothing can ruin a great day off-road as fast as getting stuck in the mud or sand. Worse still is getting stuck in the middle of a big hill! The best advice we can give is to not get stuck in the first place, but it's bound to happen sooner or later. To minimize the risk of getting stuck, use your four-wheel drive (if you've got it) the entire time you're off-road and don't slow down or stop when you're on soft surfaces. If you're not sure you can make it up a hill, don't try. When you first realize you're stuck, it's best just to get out of the vehicle and take a few minutes to relax and let your anger subside. Don't just sit there and gun the engine – you could get yourself stuck worse or damage the vehicle. Look under the vehicle at the front, rear and on both sides. Most of the time, you'll find that one or more of your wheels have sunk into the soft stuff. But sometimes you'll also find the chassis hung up on a tree stump, rock or other obstruction. It's important to know exactly what the problem is. If you're stuck on an obstruction, you'll have to get the vehicle up above the obstruction before you drive out. If you don't, you're likely to rip a hole through your oil pan or gas tank.

Always carry a tow-rope or tow-strap that's rated to handle the weight of your SUV

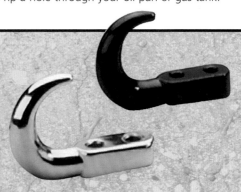

If your SUV doesn't already have tow-hooks, it's a good idea to add them. Again, pick hooks that are rated to handle the weight of your vehicle

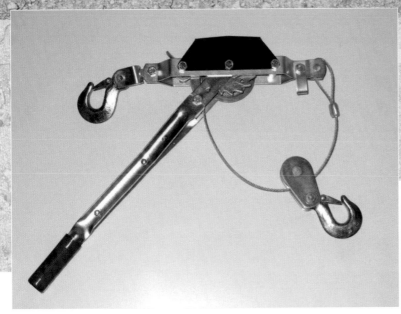

If you don't have a winch, a heavy-duty come-along is good insurance. Be sure to anchor it solidly!

If it's just your wheels that are stuck, and if you're not too deep into the stuff, try "bouncing" the vehicle at the end that's stuck. This approach requires one or two helpers – the bigger the better! While you're in the vehicle, gassing it gently, have your helpers bounce the suspension up and down by pushing on the bumper. The increase in downward pressure can often be just enough for you to regain traction and get unstuck. But be careful – if your helpers are bouncing on the back bumper, only use forward gears. If they're at the front, only use reverse. Don't take a chance that your vehicle will suddenly get traction and run over your friends.

If you can drive a short distance before finally losing traction, you might also try "rocking" the vehicle back and forth. Drive it forward as far as it will go, apply the brakes, drive it in reverse as far as it will go, apply the brakes, then repeat. This way you might build up enough inertia to finally roll out of the rut. If one wheel on an axle is spinning, but the other isn't, try applying the brakes slightly while you're pressing the accelerator. This can stop the free-spinning wheel enough to deliver better traction to the other wheel – sometimes this is enough to get you out.

Still stuck? Try some traction aids. If you're in snow or ice, sand or gravel works very well – just spread it in front of the stuck wheel(s). If you're in mud, use rocks, pieces of tree branches or other non-slippery items. If you're in sand, try to spread the load over a wide area: a large piece of wood or a few large rocks will often do the trick. And with any traction aid, it's going to work best if you level-out the area in front of the wheel first (you did bring your shovel, right?).

If you're stuck in some really big ruts, or if the vehicle is stuck on an obstruction, try jacking it up until the wheel is out of its rut. You can then fill in the rut with gravel, tree branches or similar material. If the chassis is stuck on an obstruction, jack the wheel up as far as possible and put rocks under the tire to effectively raise the vehicle above the obstruction.

If there's another vehicle in the area that's not stuck, you're really in luck. Just take out your tow-strap or tow-rope (don't leave the pavement without one). Hook it between solid, rounded points, such as tow-hooks or a trailer-hitch ball that's rated to handle the load. Don't hook the strap around a bumper or other sharp-edged object that could cut the strap. Stay out of the way while using a tow strap, since it could break suddenly.

When all else fails, it's time to hook up your winch to the nearest solid anchor (if it's a live tree, use a trunk guard to protect it) and pull yourself out. Don't have a winch? Well, you should at least carry a come-along that's rated to handle the weight of your vehicle. Pulling your SUV out with a come-along is a slow, sweaty process, but it usually beats walking.

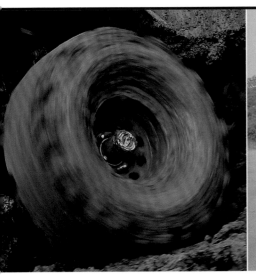

Towing

Towing . . . it's the reason many of us bought our SUV – to get those really big things moved. Many of today's SUVs have truly awesome towing capacity, so why not make use of it? Towing equipment can often be installed at home with simple tools and is not particularly expensive. So let's get to it!

Hitch selection

When selecting a hitch, you need to select a class of hitch that will handle in excess of the maximum weight you're planning to tow. When figuring this out, keep in mind that weight ratings for towing equipment consider the weight of the cargo and the weight of the trailer and associated equipment; this is commonly known as the Gross Towed Weight Rating (GTWR). As a starting point, some trailers, particularly rental trailers, have the weight of the trailer listed on the trailer itself – this weight is referred to as tare weight and does not include the weight of any cargo.

It's best not to economize on a hitch, since it's very possible that you'll want to step up to a bigger trailer in the future. If you're not careful, you'll wind up buying a bigger hitch down the road, negating any previous savings. The following chart shows four common trailer hitch classes and their approximate weight ratings:

Hitch class	Total weight being towed (GTWR)
I	Less than 2000 pounds
II	Less than 3500 pounds
III	Less than 5000 pounds
IV	Less than 10,000 pounds*

*When towing over 5,000 pounds, a weight distributing hitch is recommended

You've probably heard the adage "a chain is only as strong as its weakest link." Well, in the world of towing, every piece of your equipment can be considered a link in the chain. So, again, don't economize on your safety chains, ball-mounts or hitch balls. All towing equipment is rated by the manufacturer as to the amount of weight (GTWR) it will handle. In most cases, the weight rating will be stamped onto the part itself. Always know the weight rating of the equipment and be sure you're safe. The following chart gives some generalized weight ratings for hitch balls, for reference only. This chart should not be used as a substitute for the manufacturer's weight rating, since weight ratings vary by manufacturer:

Ball diameter	Diameter of bolt on ball	Total weight being towed (GTWR)
1-7/8 inch	3/4 to 1-inch	Less than 2000 pounds
2 inch	3/4-inch	Less than 3500 pounds
2 inch	1 to 1-1/4 inch	Less than 5000 pounds
2-5/16 inch	1 inch	Less than 5,000 pounds
2-5/16 inch	1-1/4 inch	Less than 10,000 pounds

For very heavy trailers, such as travel trailers and large boat trailers, a load distributing hitch should be used. These devices use spring bars and other special equipment to distribute the tongue load to both axles of the tow vehicle, which helps to stabilize it during towing. A load-distributing hitch and associated equipment will run the price tag up a bit higher, but if you're towing a heavy trailer, you'll be glad you have it.

And remember: just because you've got a Class IV hitch on your SUV, it doesn't necessarily mean you can tow 10,000 pounds! Your entire SUV must be up to the job, including the engine, cooling system, suspension and brakes. SUV manufacturers rate the towing capacity of each SUV they make. Check your owner's manual for your vehicle's rated towing capacity and don't exceed it!

All towing equipment that carries a load should be clearly marked with its maximum weight rating. Be sure the rating on all your equipment exceeds your GTWR

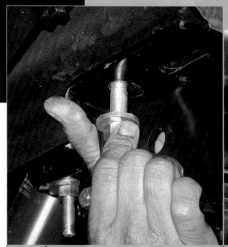

02 First, remove the bumper attachment bolt . . .

01 We chose this nice hitch from Reese. Notice the bent-tube design that allows clearance for the spare tire

Installing a trailer hitch

Many modern trailer hitches are designed to be installed easily, with no cutting or welding required. Before purchase, check with the hitch manufacturer to be sure the hitch can be installed by a do-it-yourselfer. Many hitch manufacturers put their installation instructions on their website for easy download. It's a good idea to become familiar with the procedure in advance so you can have the necessary tools available. The following procedure is typical of many models, but the actual details on your SUV will vary.

06 Install the nut on the front bolt, but leave it loose. Now install the bracket on the other side the same way

07 Lift the hitch cross-bar into position between the brackets and install the bolts on each side. It's helpful to have an assistant hold the cross-bar in place while this is done

08 Tighten the cross-bar bolts to the torque recommended by the hitch manufacturer. Use a back-up wrench to keep the bolt from spinning

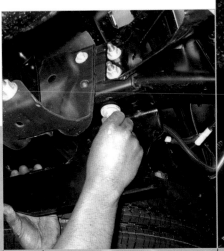

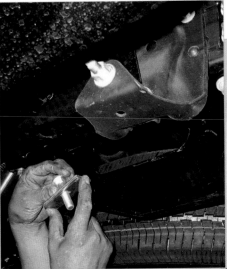

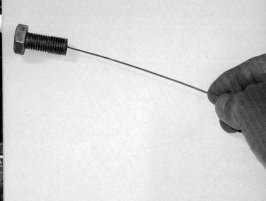

03 . . . put the hitch bracket in place and reinstall the rear mounting bolt. Don't tighten it yet!

04 The front bracket bolt goes through an oversize hole, so this reinforcement plate is necessary. Notice how the flats of the bolt fit into the plate, making it unnecessary to use a back-up wrench when tightening

05 Our SUV has a U-shaped frame rail, so it's easy to install the bolts. On some vehicles you need to install the bolts into a fully enclosed frame rail. This handy tool makes it easy to fish the bolt into the hole. They're available from hitch companies

09 Be sure the hitch receiver is centered at the rear of the vehicle (measure and adjust as necessary), then tighten the bracket bolts to the recommended torque

10 The hitch is installed and you're ready to tow. But wait, what about the trailer lights?

01 Here's the simplest type of trailer connector, with four wires for left stop/turn, right stop/turn, parking lights and ground. When installing, be sure the female end (on left) is connected to the tow vehicle to prevent accidental shorts when the trailer is not connected

02 On larger trailers with electric trailer brakes, you'll need to wire in a brake control box and use a larger connector that has enough wires to operate your brake system. This installation is best left to a professional

Wiring for towing

Although the requirements vary by state, all trailers must have turn signals, brake lights, running lights and a license plate light. In addition to lighting, many larger trailers use electric trailer brakes which must receive an electrical signal from the tow vehicle. There are several types of connectors available for the different types of wiring systems available. When hooking up a wiring connector to your vehicle, it's best to have a wiring diagram available to avoid mistakes. If you're a little uncomfortable working on electrical systems, it's best to let a professional do the job.

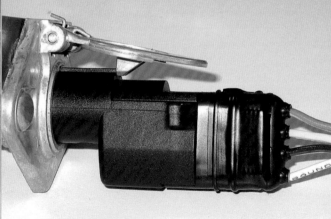

03 Many late-model SUVs have a factory-installed connector that can be plugged straight into the trailer connector. What could be easier than this?

04 It's frustrating when you rent or borrow a trailer, only to discover it uses a different connector design than your SUV. Adapters like this can save a headache

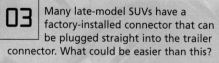

Hooking up a simple trailer connector

01 First, check your SUV's wiring diagram to find the correct wires. The lighting circuits will need three power sources: left stop/turn, right stop/turn and parking lights. A test light will verify you've found each. For example, when probing a stop/turn wire, have the turn signal on and verify the test light flashes

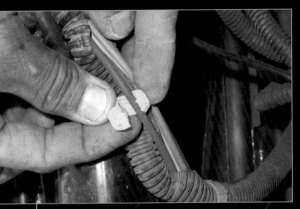

02 Once you've located the correct wires, splice into them. These connectors make it easy and don't damage the wires. Simply fit the connector over the wire . . .

03 . . . press it together with pliers . . . . .

04 . . and plug it into your trailer harness

05 Make a solid ground connection to the chassis on the SUV. The ground on some bolt-on connectors is through the connector itself

01 We're installing this auxiliary cooler from Hayden, which is typical of what you'll find in auto parts stores. It includes an installation kit and instructions. Before beginning, try to park the vehicle so its front end is pointing uphill - this will minimize fluid loss during installation. Read the instructions that come with the kit carefully, since those will be specific for your model and this procedure is typical for all SUVs

Cooling system upgrades

Probably the most important upgrade for a tow vehicle is to make sure its cooling system is up to the job. Generally, SUVs with factory-installed towing packages have bigger radiators, auxiliary trans- mission coolers (automatic only) and heavy-duty cooling fans. Your SUV may not be equipped with these upgrades, and, even if it is, you may want to make further improvements, just to be sure.

Installing an auxiliary transmission cooler

If your SUV has an automatic transmission and you plan to do any towing at all, we consider an auxiliary transmission cooler to be mandatory. Slippage within an automatic transmission generates heat, and heat is the greatest enemy of any automatic transmission. It is often said that a 10-percent reduction in transmission heat can double the life of an automatic transmission. Heat causes fluid to break down, losing its lubricating and heat-transfer properties, and heat also causes the friction material inside the transmission to varnish, causing still more slippage. Since transmission fluid is in contact with virtually all components within an automatic transmission, cooling the fluid will ultimately cool the entire transmission. Original-equipment transmission fluid coolers circulate pressurized fluid through lines (usually steel tubes) to the radiator. A separate transmission fluid chamber within the radiator is in constant contact with engine coolant. Since normal engine coolant temperature is lower than normal transmission fluid temperature, the transmission fluid chamber transfers heat to the engine coolant, cooling the fluid.

This heat exchanger works well under normal conditions, but if the engine overheats, the transmission will likewise overheat. Also, if the transmission is slipping excessively and building up excessive heat, the engine will also overheat. The auxiliary transmission cooler will not only cool the transmission, it will relieve the radiator of the additional duty of cooling the transmission, so the engine can run cooler.

When selecting a cooler, be sure to pick one that's rated to handle the total weight of your SUV and trailer. If you're not sure, remember that bigger is usually better.

REPLACEMENT INSTALLATION

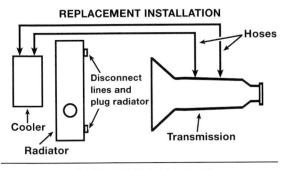

Hoses

Disconnect
lines and
plug radiator

Cooler

Radiator

Transmission

IN-SERIES INSTALLATION

Trans fluid flow direction →

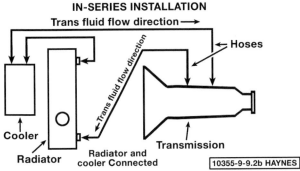

Trans fluid flow direction

Hoses

Cooler

Radiator

Radiator and
cooler Connected

Transmission

10355-9-9.2b HAYNES

03 If you'll be using the existing cooler, you'll need to establish which line is the outlet from the cooler. With the engine cold, have an assistant start the engine and shift the transmission into gear for a moment (no more than 10 seconds, and with the brake pedal firmly depressed). Feel both lines – the warmer line is the inlet, so cut the other line (don't cut it now - it will be done in a later step)

02 Decide if you want to use the cooler in conjunction with the existing cooler in the radiator (bottom) or use it by itself (top). Generally, if you live in a cold climate, incorporating the existing cooler is a good idea, since it will allow the transmission to reach operating temperature faster. In a warm climate, it's best to use the auxiliary cooler by itself

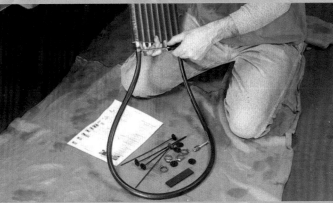

04 Attach the hose provided in the kit to the cooler, but don't cut it (leave it in a loop). The hose clamps should be tightened only to the point where the hose rubber is pressed slightly into the slots in the clamp bands. Do not overtighten to the point where rubber is pressed out above the band slots

05 Find a mounting location for the cooler in front of the radiator or air conditioning condenser. Make sure you've thought out the routing of the hoses so they won't obstruct anything, then mount the cooler with the nylon straps provided. Be sure to stick the adhesive pads to the cooler so they will be sandwiched between the cooler and radiator when the straps are tightened

06 Find a convenient location to cut off the steel cooler line(s), as close to the cooler as possible. The miniature tubing cutter shown here is very useful in tight spaces. When the lines are cut, fluid will leak out, so place a container underneath to catch the leakage. If you'll be using the existing cooler in conjunction with the auxiliary cooler, only the return line will need to be cut

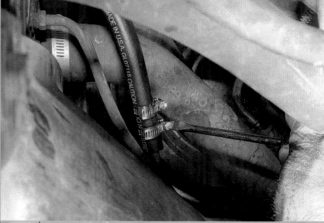

07 Using a flare-nut wrench, unscrew the cut-off ends of the line(s) from the radiator fittings. If you'll be using the existing cooler in conjunction with the auxiliary cooler, install the fitting designed for this purpose – it should be included in the kit

08 Carefully route the hose to the cut-off line(s) (and radiator fitting, if you'll be using the existing cooler). Be careful not to kink the hoses or bend them sharply. Make sure the hoses will not be in contact with any sharp surface or near any hot surfaces that could damage them. If possible, secure the hoses to the chassis or other hoses or lines with nylon tie-straps. Attach the hoses with hose clamps, being careful not to overtighten them. Now start the engine and check carefully for leaks. Check the transmission fluid level and add more, if necessary. After two weeks or so, recheck all hose clamps for tightness

Calculating tongue weight

The tongue weight of a trailer (the downward weight of the trailer at its hitch) should be from 10 to 15 percent of the trailer's overall weight. A 1500-pound trailer, for example, should have a tongue weight from 150 to 225 pounds. A trailer's tongue weight is directly affected by the position of the load's center of gravity: the further forward the center of gravity, the heavier the tongue weight; the further back, the lighter.

For tongue weights up to about 300 pounds or so, you can use a common bathroom scale. Set the scale on a chair or stool high enough to simulate normal ride height of the trailer. This method generally works if the gross weight of the trailer is 2000 pounds or less. For a trailer you suspect may be heavier than this, you can take the trailer to a truck scale and weigh the tongue there, although the accuracy of such scales for light trailer loads is often questionable.

In any case, should your trailer's tongue weight fall outside the 10 to 15-percent range, you should try shifting the weight of the load (to the extent possible) either forward or backward, depending on whether the tongue weight was too high or too low. For example, if your tongue weight was too high, you would want to shift more weight toward the back of the trailer. Conversely, if your tongue weight was too low, try bringing more weight forward until you get the right balance.

If you have a small trailer, you can easily check the tongue weight at home

Trailering safety tips

Check your equipment. Always check your hitch ball, coupler, retaining pins and safety chains every time you tow. Also make regular checks during the trip. Many people with long-time trailer experience use a checklist to be sure all equipment is hooked up and in good condition. Damage can happen quickly when something goes wrong. For example, safety chains can be worn through very quickly if they make contact with the pavement.

No riders! Never allow anyone in or on your trailer while it's being towed.

Observe speed limits. Speed limits for trailers are generally lower than for other vehicles. And for good reason. Trailers present unique safety problems in cornering, rough roads and windy conditions. The first goal for any trip is to arrive alive. Be sure to schedule the extra time needed for slower travel.

Leave extra safety space. Even if you're using trailer brakes, you won't be able to stop nearly as fast as you can without a trailer. A good general rule is to double the old two-second rule, making sure you maintain at least a four second gap between your vehicle and the vehicle in front of you. For heavier trailers, you'll need to leave even more space.

Remember the wide turns! The longer the trailer, the farther you'll have to drive straight into intersections before beginning your turns (especially right turns). Your first time with a particular trailer will be a learning experience. Watch your mirrors carefully and go extra wide, at first, until you get used to it.

Use care when backing. For the inexperienced, backing up a trailer can be a nightmare. To develop your skills, go to a large, empty parking lot and just practice. Basically, the trailer will move in the opposite direction of steering input when backing. Many people find it easier to position their hand at the bottom of the steering wheel; the trailer will go towards the same direction their hand travels. Also, it's best not to rely on your mirrors – turn around and look at the trailer. When there's any chance of damage, use a spotter who can tell you to stop before damage occurs.

Avoid sway. Trailer sway can be a frightening experience, especially if it's a large trailer. If it happens, don't panic. Take your foot off the accelerator and coast to a slower speed, avoiding sudden movements of the steering wheel. Apply the brakes slowly when you're down to a safe speed. Once you're stopped, determine the cause of the sway. Often the problem is insufficient tongue weight. If this is the problem, move some weight forward on the trailer. Remember that some vehicle/trailer combinations require anti-sway devices.

Uphill/downhill. In general, you'll want to keep your speed consistent whether you're going up a hill or down. When ascending a hill, avoid overdrive to keep your transmission from hunting between gears. When descending, be extra careful not to overwork your brakes. Use a lower gear that will keep a consistent speed without constant use of the brakes. Pull off the road occasionally to let your brakes cool and to check your trailer brakes.

Don't forget it's there! If you only use your trailer occasionally, habit can cause you to make mistakes. Stay focused on your driving and don't carry on long conversations or try to perform other tasks. Remember to check your rear-view mirror frequently.

In-car entertainment

DVD, Satellite radio, video screens in every headrest . . . isn't this a great world!

01 Refer to the Haynes manual for your vehicle on how to remove the factory head unit. With this vehicle, we had to remove the dashboard trim panel first . . .

In-dash receivers & players

To give the audio system on your SUV a decent start, you need a good head unit to provide the signal that an amp will beef up, and that the speakers will replay.

If an upgrade of the sound system is what you have in mind, there are plenty of decent head units out there to choose from. Don't be afraid to consult with an expert on which features matter most. The head unit is an important part of a good sound system - always go for the best you can afford.

Head unit installation

06 Since our new head unit is not a DIN-and-1/2-sized unit like the original, we had to fit an adapter bezel to fill the extra space

07 We placed the stereo mounting sleeve into the adapter bezel, then bent the sleeve's mounting tangs to keep it in place. Be sure to bend enough tangs so the sleeve is secure

08 Carefully slide the unit into its mounting sleeve until it snaps into place

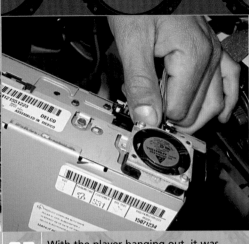

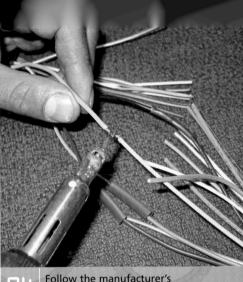

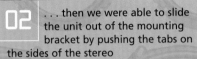

02 . . . then we were able to slide the unit out of the mounting bracket by pushing the tabs on the sides of the stereo

03 With the player hanging out, it was easy to disconnect the harness and antenna

04 Follow the manufacturer's instructions for connecting the wiring to the new unit. In this case we needed to solder an OEM connector to the stereo's wiring harness (which will plug into the existing connector in the dash)

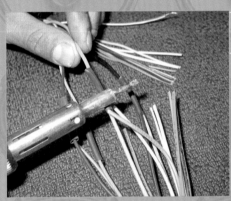

05 We covered each soldered joint with shrink tubing for insulation

The antenna, amplifier signal leads and radio harness are connected to the head unit

09

10 Now it's just a matter of sliding the unit and adapter bezel into place

Once it was clicked in, we added the dashboard trim panel to finish it off. Nice job!

11

Speakers

Most factory speakers are low on power and made with nasty paper cones that disintegrate after a few years - installing *any* aftermarket speakers would be considered an upgrade. But we're going top-shelf with some really first-class speakers courtesy of our friends at Focal.

Crimp connectors

There is a wide variety of crimp-type connectors available at auto parts stores, which will allow you to make virtually any type of connection you need to make. To make the connections properly, you'll need to use a special crimping tool (available at most auto parts stores). Try to get a good-quality tool that presses an indentation into the connector. Some of the cheaper tools simply flatten the connector, which gives an inferior connection. Also, be sure you're using the correct connector type for the gauge of wire you're connecting.

If you don't know the wire gauge, you can figure it out using your crimping tool by inserting the end of the wire into each of the stripping holes in your crimper until you find the one that strips off the wire's insulation.

Crimp connectors are quick and easy to install - simply strip off about 1/4-inch of insulation using the proper-gauge hole on your stripping tool . . .

. . . insert the stripped wire and crimp the connector firmly onto it using the correct crimping jaws of the tool

Note:
When installing spade or bullet connectors, always crimp the female side of the connector to the feed wire. This way, if the connector comes unplugged, the "hot" wire won't short out if it touches a ground (it'll be shielded by the insulation surrounding the female side of the connector).

Wire gauge	Industry standard color on crimp connector
22 to 18	Red
16 to 14	Blue
12 to 10	Yellow

01 We chose to install a set of Focal Utopia component speakers with passive crossovers for the front doors

Speaker installation

Component speakers and crossovers

02 The door panel was pretty straightforward to remove, just be sure you've got all the screws out before you try to yank the panel off. Most door panels are also secured by push-in plastic fasteners around the perimeter of the panel (check your *Haynes Automotive Repair Manual* if necessary)

03 The factory tweeter mounting panel is removed from the back side of the door panel

04 Once the tweeter mounting panel is removed, we use it as a template for the new mount

05 Using a jig-saw, we cut the new mount . . .

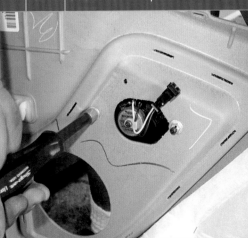

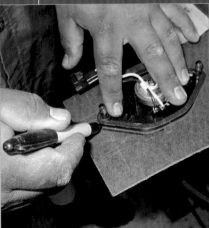

06 . . . then drilled out a hole big enough for the tweeter

07 After applying the matching paint and following the manufacturer's instructions for assembling the tweeter with its mounting clip, we then used a little hot glue and fit the tweeter into its location on the door panel

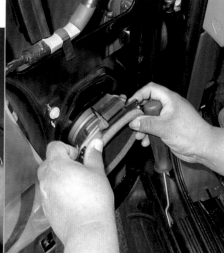

08 We took the factory speaker off the door

12 Back at the door pillar, we fed the tweeter and speaker wires through the harness rubber boot . . .

13 . . . then carefully reinstalled the boot to prevent any water leaks

14 After the door panel was installed, the tweeter wire needed extending to the crossover, so we soldered another length of wire onto the short lead coming from the tweeter. The wire was then fed under the carpet to where the crossovers were to be mounted

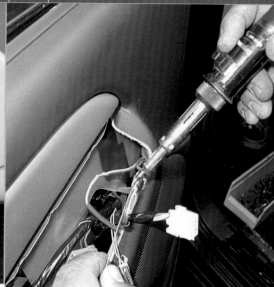

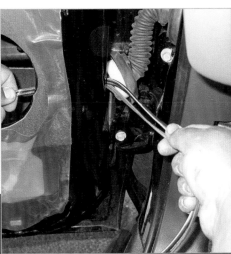

09 New wire for the tweeter and speaker was fed through the inside of the door and later fed through the rubber boot and door pillar

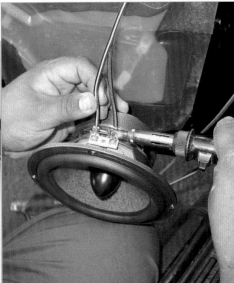

10 Next, the new wire was soldered to the speaker

11 The speaker was then carefully mounted to the door

15 The crossovers were mounted conveniently next to the amplifier, under the seat

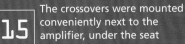

16 We added terminals to the wires . . .

17 . . . then following the manufacturer's instructions, we connected them to the crossovers

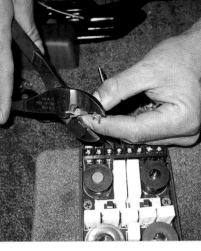

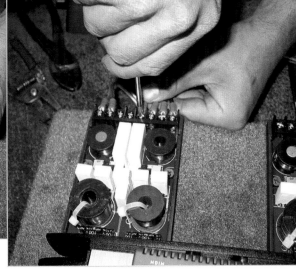

Direct replacement speakers and crossovers

01 A set of Focal Polyglass coaxial speakers and passive crossovers are being installed in the rear doors

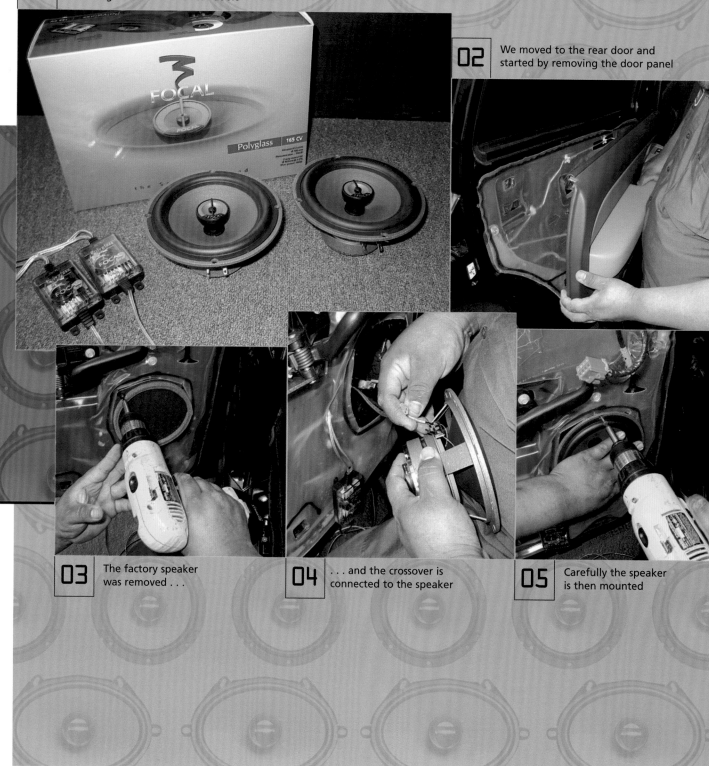

02 We moved to the rear door and started by removing the door panel

03 The factory speaker was removed . . .

04 . . . and the crossover is connected to the speaker

05 Carefully the speaker is then mounted

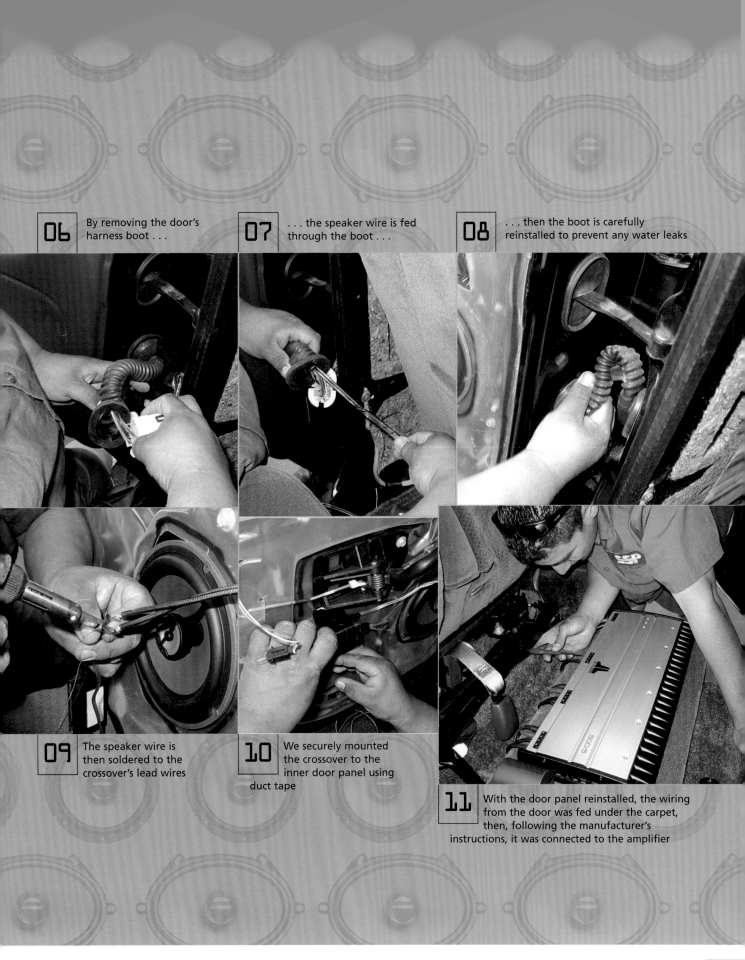

06 By removing the door's harness boot . . .

07 . . . the speaker wire is fed through the boot . . .

08 . . . then the boot is carefully reinstalled to prevent any water leaks

09 The speaker wire is then soldered to the crossover's lead wires

10 We securely mounted the crossover to the inner door panel using duct tape

11 With the door panel reinstalled, the wiring from the door was fed under the carpet, then, following the manufacturer's instructions, it was connected to the amplifier

Amplifiers

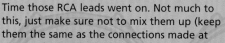
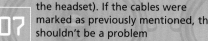

If you really want your sound system to crank, there's no substitute for power. And that means adding an amp.

TIP *Decide where you'll mount the amp carefully. Amps must be adequately cooled - don't cover it up so there's no airflow, and don't hang it upside down. We found ourselves a nice mounting platform under the front passenger's seat.*

01 First we removed the front seat. A simple matter of removing the four bolts securing the seat to the floorpan and lifting the seat from the vehicle. You may also have to disconnect an electrical connector or two. If your vehicle is equipped with side-impact airbags, you'll have to disable the airbag system (refer to the *Haynes Automotive Repair Manual* for your vehicle)

Read the amp's instruction book carefully when connecting any wires, or you might regret it. Identify your speaker positive and negative/left side and right side wires, then make the connections. Securely connect the remote **06** turn on wire, ground wire, and power cable to the amp

Time those RCA leads went on. Not much to this, just make sure not to mix them up (keep them the same as the connections made at **07** the headset). If the cables were marked as previously mentioned, this shouldn't be a problem

With the installation complete it's time to install the fuse and test the amplifier. Carefully follow the manufacturer's instructions for powering up **08** the amp and making any necessary adjustments

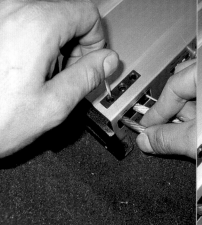

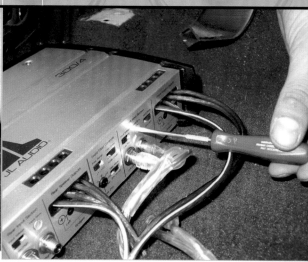

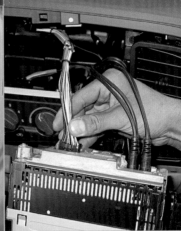
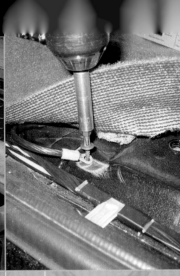

02 Running the amplifier's power wire starts at the battery. The main power wire needs to have a waterproof fuse holder mounted as close to the battery as possible.

03 The power wire needs to be routed to the passenger compartment. How to get the wire through the firewall doesn't have to be a dilemma, just find an existing hole like this one, then remove the grommet, cut a small hole in it and feed the power wire through grommet and firewall. Be sure to refit the grommet to the firewall to prevent water leaks and to protect the wire

04 The amplifier's remote turn on wire and signal patch cable need to be connected at the back of the stereo head. Marking the signal cables left side/right side will assure correct connection at the amplifier

05 Cut a short length of wire for the ground and crimp a ring terminal on one end, then find a spot and mount it to the vehicle chassis. Be sure to sand off any paint so that the connection is made directly to metal

 Note: *Always follow the manufacturer's recommendations for mounting the amplifier. Properly securing an amp is very important so that it's not sliding around. A sliding amplifier that's not properly mounted can damage the unit, or worse, be dangerous in an accident.*

Choosing the right amp

The first step is to determine the needs of your system. If you're just adding an amp to improve your original equipment system, you may need only minimal amplification. Therefore, a small inexpensive amp will suffice. On the other hand, if you're planning on running multiple subwoofers and component speakers, you'll most likely need multiple amplifiers.

Next, you have to figure out if you need an amplifier with a built-in crossover or an amp that is dedicated to playing a full-range signal. A built-in crossover can cross over different frequencies dedicated to a particular speaker, whereas a 12-inch subwoofer will sound best playing 100Hz and down. This will maximize the life of the speaker playing in this frequency range.

How powerful of an amp does your system need? Well, that depends what kind and how many speakers it has to drive. The amp should be capable of putting out 1-1/2 to two times the power (continuous, or RMS power in watts) that the lowest-frequency speaker that it'll be driving is rated. The specifications

you'll find when shopping for an amp will indicate how many watts-per-channel the amp is able to produce continuously. This sounds weird, but an underpowered amp can actually damage your speakers when the volume is turned way up. The waveform it puts out changes from a nice curvy sine wave into more of a square wave, which speakers don't like; this is called clipping, because the top and bottom of the wave gets "clipped" off. The speakers can handle the extra power better than they can this ugly square wave.

Finally, how many channels must the amplifier have in order to interface with the stereo system? Say, for example, you're running four speakers and you want to add amplifiers to enhance the sound. You must decide if you want to retain the use of the fader. If you do, you will need to purchase a four-channel amplifier with four independent RCA inputs. A four-channel amplifier can run four speakers in a stereo fashion without losing fading capability.

Subwoofer

Want to actually *feel* the music pumping through your system?

Subwoofers are usually sold as a stand-alone item, but in just about all applications they will have to be mounted in some type of enclosure. These are big, heavy speakers that just can't be tossed into a door panel or under the dash. There are many types of enclosures, designed to manipulate the acoustics of the subwoofer(s) depending on the type of vehicle in which it is being installed or the type of music that will be listened to. The physics behind these various designs is not easy to understand and is way beyond the scope of this manual, so we won't go there. However, your basic choices are a ready-made cabinet, an enclosure that has been designed to replace a center console or side panel specifically for your model SUV, or a custom built enclosure you construct yourself.

Ready-made cabinet

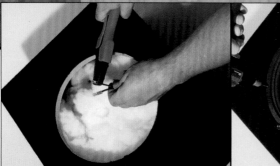  

01 The wiring was already connected to the terminal cup that was fitted on the box, so the ends just needed stripping back and terminating with the correct fittings to join onto the subwoofer. The cable is coded with plus and minus symbols for easy connection. As long as you get the feed wire into the box the right way, everything will be fine

02 After carefully positioning the subwoofer to get the center logo straight, the mounting holes were drilled with pilot holes, and the screws were tightened steadily by hand. You can use a power screwdriver, but be careful not to go too tight and ruin the pilot hole you've just drilled or you'll have to put your speaker in at a funny angle once you've drilled some more holes

03 The sub cable from the amplifier was clamped tightly under these screw terminals. Like the rest of the wiring, the cable was stripped back and the ends were protected with a short piece of heatshrink tube. This neatens the cable ends and makes it more difficult to short out the wiring. Just be sure to leave enough bare cable to connect to the terminal, okay?

01

Handcrafted from fiberglass, the JL Audio Stealthbox will convert our center seat cushion and folding armrest into a sealed, downfiring subwoofer enclosure

Vehicle specific enclosures

Some manufacturers offer ready-made, vehicle-specific sub-box enclosures. These are a convenient alternative for people not willing or able to construct a box, or for those who want a more factory look, sacrificing as little interior space as possible.

02

The first thing to go is the seats. Most of the time, removing the seat is a simple matter of removing the four bolts securing the seat to the floorpan and lifting the seat from the cab. You may also have to disconnect an electrical connector or two. If your SUV is equipped with side-impact airbags and/or seat belt pre-tensioners, you'll have to disable the airbag system (refer to the *Haynes Automotive Repair Manual* for your specific model)

03

With both the driver and passenger seats removed, we lifted the center seat assembly out of the vehicle

04

Following the JL Audio installation guide, we disassembled the factory center-seat cushion and the upper storage tray. We saved all the upper tray's parts for use during reassembly

05

The center seat frame needed a bit of modification. Referring to the illustrations in the installation guide, we drilled each hole, then checked the fit of the frame by placing it on the bottom of the Stealthbox

06

The frame was a perfect fit, so we attached it to the bottom of the Stealthbox with the supplied hardware

07 Before proceeding further, we attached speaker wires to the Stealthbox and tested its operation

08 Following the installation guide, we reassembled the latch, then secured the tray to the Stealthbox with the supplied hardware

09 The Stealthbox was placed in the vehicle and the speaker wires were connected

10 Before installing the driver's seat, we ran the speaker wire under the carpet so it could eventually be connected to the amplifier

11 With the seats back in place, the installation is complete. The finished Stealthbox is a perfect match to the factory interior and sounds great!

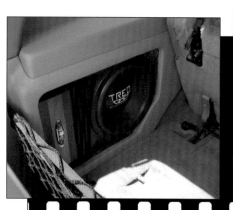

1   36 ▷1A   2   36 ▷2A   3   36 ▷3A

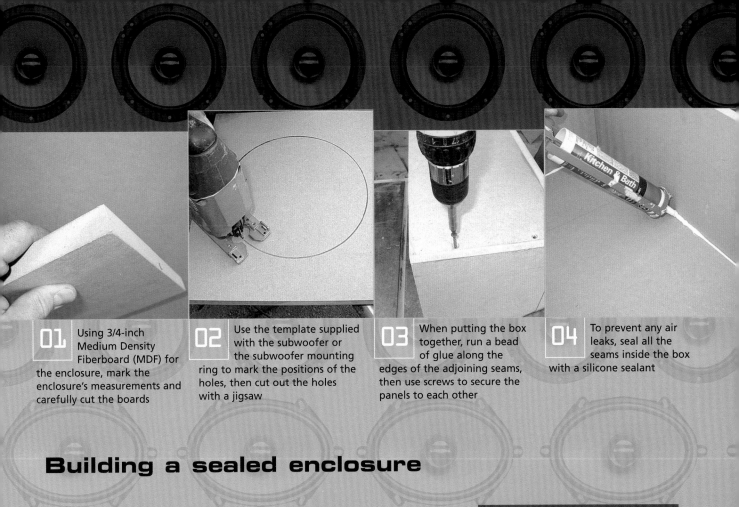

01 Using 3/4-inch Medium Density Fiberboard (MDF) for the enclosure, mark the enclosure's measurements and carefully cut the boards

02 Use the template supplied with the subwoofer or the subwoofer mounting ring to mark the positions of the holes, then cut out the holes with a jigsaw

03 When putting the box together, run a bead of glue along the edges of the adjoining seams, then use screws to secure the panels to each other

04 To prevent any air leaks, seal all the seams inside the box with a silicone sealant

Building a sealed enclosure

> **Warning:**
> Wear a filtering mask before cutting: MDF gives off an extremely fine dust which can be harmful to your health

Using spray glue, cover the box with carpet that'll match your interior, then carefully cut out the holes. You'll also have to drill a hole for **05** the speaker wires

Follow the manufacturer's instructions for connecting the subwoofer wiring, then place them into the enclosure and mount them, also according to the manufacturer's **06** instructions

Be sure to bolt the sub box down so it doesn't roll around. A loose enclosure can be dangerous, particularly in a crash. The last thing you want during an accident is half a ton of unhappy speaker and box bouncing around in the cab to remind **07** you they weren't bolted down!

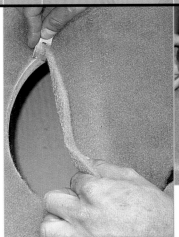

Video

Watch TV. . . pop in a movie on DVD. . . play a video game. . . mobile video now lets you do it all.

The simplest mobile video systems are portable, self-contained units which can be strapped into place between the two front seats. There are other systems similar to these, but they are built into the center console and aren't easily removed like the portable type.

The other kind of system is the component type. All component systems begin at the source unit, which could take the form of a remotely mounted VHS tape deck or DVD player, in-dash DVD player, an overhead flip-down screen with an integral DVD player, a Sony PlayStation, a TV tuner or a combination of these. This source signal is then directed to one or more monitors. Some in-dash DVD players have an integral motorized screen that retracts when not in use. When multiple source units are used, they must be connected to a signal distribution box (switcher) installed between the source units and the monitor(s).

Monitor types include the already-mentioned in-dash motorized screen, sunshade monitors, headrest monitors, flip-down overhead console monitors, center console monitors, and monitors that can be mounted on a pedestal or bracket just about anywhere in the vehicle that there's enough room. Just keep in mind that no screen visible to the driver can be operational when the vehicle is in motion.

Video game consoles can be integrated into the system by the use of a signal distribution box and a power inverter that converts 12 volts DC into 110 volts AC. And, with the use of the proper switchbox, a video game can be played on one monitor while a movie is watched on another.

Another neat option that's available with some systems are infrared headphones that allow passengers to listen to the movie or game audio track without the hassle of cords that could get in the way. The infrared signal on these systems is broadcast from transmitters embedded in the monitor housings or from a remote transmitter, usually mounted on the headliner or at the rear of the overhead console where the line-of-sight between the transmitter and headphone will be uninterrupted.

Audio can also be piped through the vehicle's existing speakers. If you've upgraded your audio system with a surround sound system, your passengers will be able to enjoy a near-theatre experience. Just don't let them spill their drinks on the floor, throw bon-bons at the screen or stick their chewing gum to the underside of the seats!

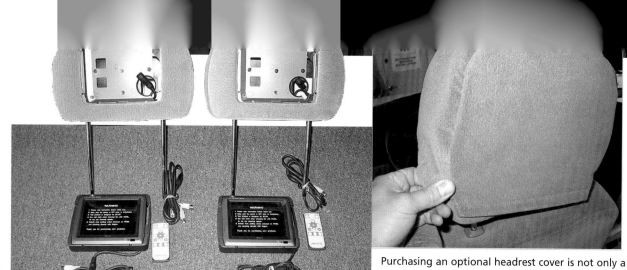

Purchasing an optional headrest cover is not only a good security measure, but it can also protect your monitor from dirt or scratches when not in use

Mobile video system installation
Vehicle-specific headrests

So you've decided to install headrest monitors, but cutting into the factory headrests, scooping out some foam, installing a frame then snapping the monitor into the frame is not what you had in mind. The easy option is installing vehicle-specific headrests like these from savv®. The installation requires no disfiguring headrest modification - the vehicle-specific headrests are designed to replace the factory headrests and after a few easy steps a monitor can be installed.

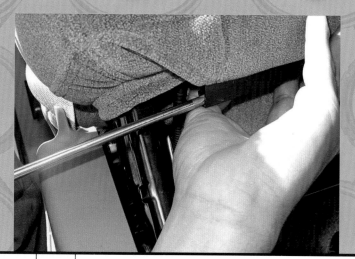

01 After removing the factory headrest, we started by unsnapping the fabric at the bottom of the seat back

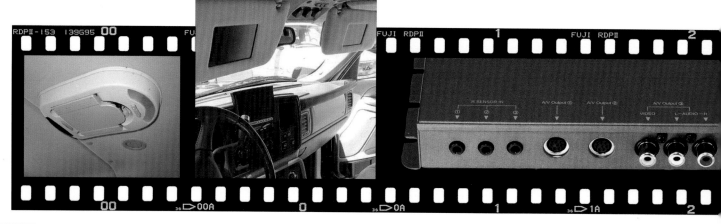

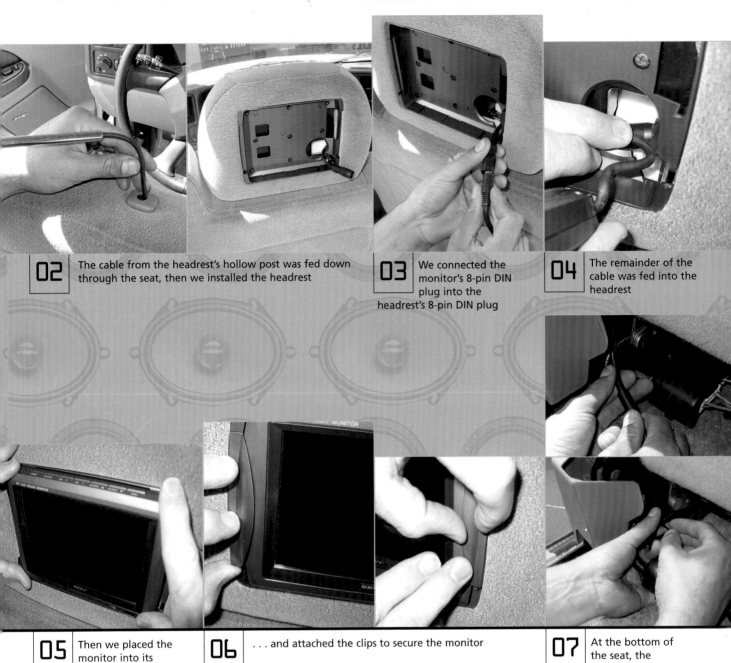

02 The cable from the headrest's hollow post was fed down through the seat, then we installed the headrest

03 We connected the monitor's 8-pin DIN plug into the headrest's 8-pin DIN plug

04 The remainder of the cable was fed into the headrest

05 Then we placed the monitor into its mounting frame . . .

06 . . . and attached the clips to secure the monitor

07 At the bottom of the seat, the monitor's DIN cable is attached to the external A/V power cable (this is the DIN-to-RCA cable which will connect to the A/V selector box). Be sure to use cable ties to prevent the wiring from interfering with the moving parts of the seat

-153 139G95 **00**   FUJI RDPII

Headrest monitor installation

If no vehicle-specific headrests with monitors are available for your vehicle, or for some reason you want to retain your headrests, you can modify them to accept video monitors. If you take your time and work carefully you will wind up with a very clean-looking installation, and save a little cash as well. The only real drawback to choosing this route is that the cable to the monitor will be slightly exposed if the headrest is raised.

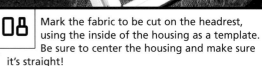

08 Mark the fabric to be cut on the headrest, using the inside of the housing as a template. Be sure to center the housing and make sure it's straight!

09 Carefully cut the fabric, inboard of the marks just made, using a sharp razor blade

10 Cut and remove the foam padding only to the depth required to allow the housing to fit snugly, and flush with the back of the headrest

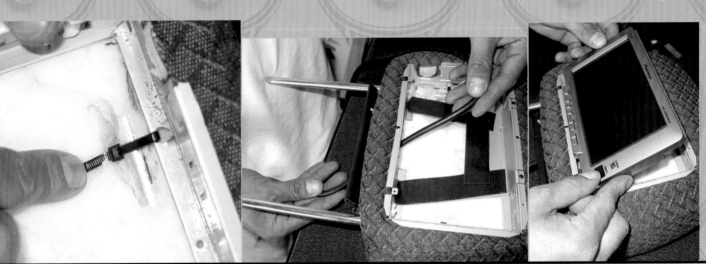

11 Since headrest designs differ between manufacturers, you'll have to figure out a way to mount the housing. With this particular headrest we used a number of zip ties to hold the housing to the headrest support posts

12 The monitor's A/V wire should be fed through the housing then exit at the bottom of the headrest next to one of the support posts

13 Connect the A/V wire, then mount the monitor into the housing following the manufacturer's instructions

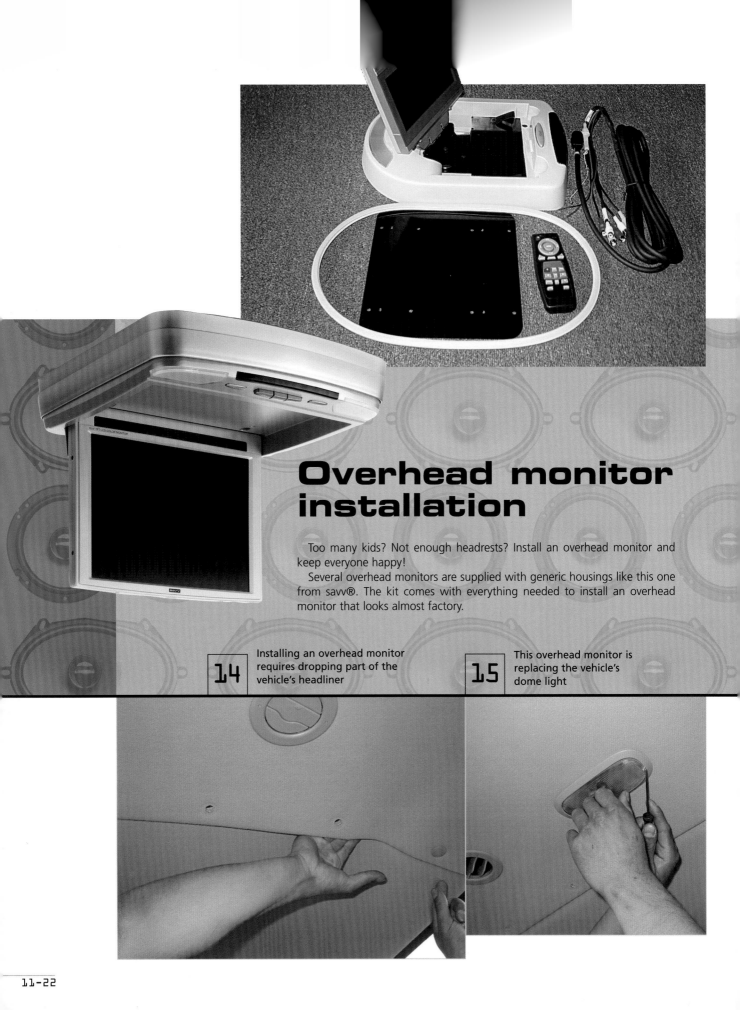

Overhead monitor installation

Too many kids? Not enough headrests? Install an overhead monitor and keep everyone happy!

Several overhead monitors are supplied with generic housings like this one from savv®. The kit comes with everything needed to install an overhead monitor that looks almost factory.

14 Installing an overhead monitor requires dropping part of the vehicle's headliner

15 This overhead monitor is replacing the vehicle's dome light

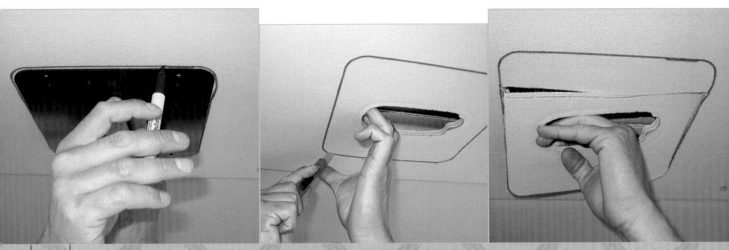

16 A pattern is drawn on the headliner and a hole cut through it for the monitor's mounting bracket and wiring

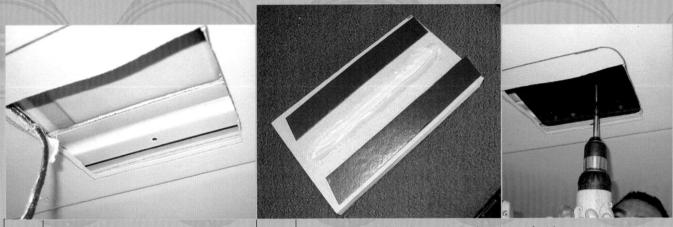

17 The mounting bracket will be secured to the roof's structural support . . .

18 . . . and a board that's been attached to the roof with silicone and double-stick tape

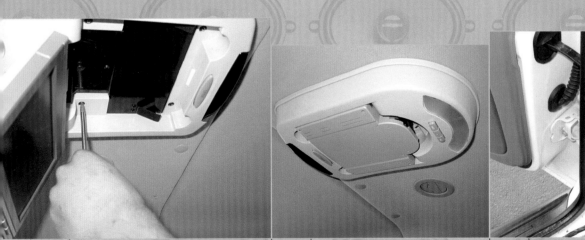

19 The monitor housing is then attached to the mounting bracket

20 Any gaps between the monitor housing and the headliner are taken up by the application of the supplied gasket

21 Some interior panels will require disassembly for the routing of the video cables

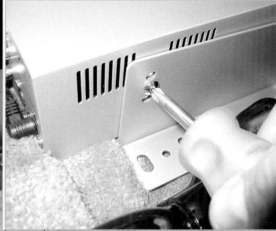

22 A stand-alone DVD player can be mounted in a convenient location like this under the middle seat

23 Using the supplied mounting brackets, the player can be secured to the floor in no time at all

DVD player installation

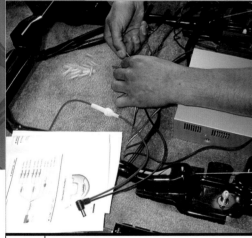

24 Follow the manufacturer's instructions for connecting the power wires

25 A DVD player with accessory inputs, makes it possible to connect a video game console or an alternative video source

26 If the DVD player has a remote sensor, mounting it somewhere on the dash is a smart choice

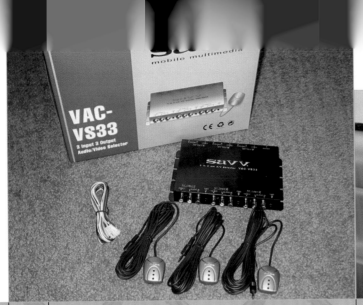

27 This A/V selector is designed to independently control the video source for up to 3 monitors

28 Each remote should be mounted somewhere close to the monitor it controls. The hard-wired remotes control the video source input device to be displayed on the corresponding monitor . . .

3 input - 3 output video selector installation

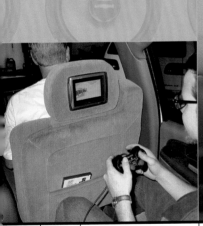

29 . . . so one passenger might be playing video games . . .

30 . . . and another watching a movie on a different screen

31 The A/V selector has a lot of wires connected to it, so mounting it away from foot traffic is definitely a good idea

Navigation system installation

A navigation system is an electronic map, sitting right there in your dashboard. Imagine, no more fumbling with a map spread across the seat as you drive, and no more stopping to ask directions!

There are countless ways to install a navigation system. Accordingly, we do not have the luxury of being able to cover each application. Therefore we will cover the basics. Following are the basics of installing an Eclipse double-DIN size unit that integrates navigation and multi-format entertainment.

01 A few fasteners around the front and a connector or two on the back and this stock radio is out in no time. Resist the urge to just crowbar the thing out of the dash. With most vehicles, radio removal usually involves removing the dashboard trim panel.

02 With this particular model, the factory mounting brackets need to be transferred from the radio to main unit

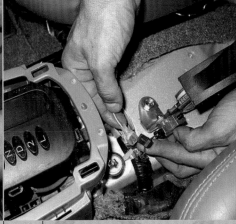

03 Our first connection was made to the back-up light wire; this can be done at the rear taillight housing. Using a supplied splicing connector this was no trouble at all

04 In addition to the back-up light wire, we need to splice into the Vehicle Speed Sensor wire . . .

05 . . . and the parking brake signal wire

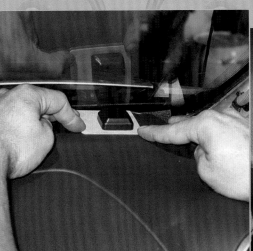

06 We chose to install the ground plate and GPS antenna in a location on the far right side of the dash. Self-adhesive tape secures the antenna

07 With our vehicle being a Toyota, to get power and sound, there's no need for a harness adapter . . .

08 . . . just plug and play. Before buttoning up the dash it's probably a good idea to test the unit

Most vehicles will need a wiring harness adapter for connecting the main unit's harness connector to the vehicles OEM connector

Accessories

Even after tricking out your SUV with vinyl graphics, a trim kit and new rims, there are still a few things you can do to give your ride an extra kick. There are plenty of aftermarket add-ons out there to make your SUV a cut above the rest. Accessories like brushguards and auxiliary lighting not only add function and convenience to your vehicle, they make it look great, too.

01 Mount the auxiliary lights into position. Our lights fit perfectly in the lower valance

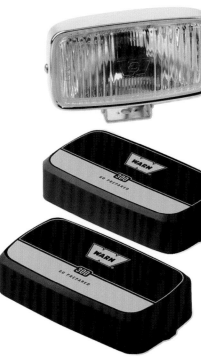

Auxiliary Lighting

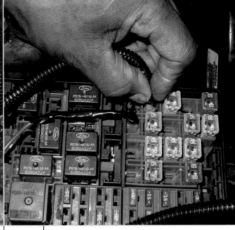

02 Route the power, ground and switch wiring along the side of the engine compartment to the fuse box. Drill a hole in the inner fender panel and mount the relay and the ground wire with self-tapping screws

03 Open the fuse box and find an unused spade terminal that's hot all the time and hook up the power wire to it (you've got a switch, so there's no need to find a switched circuit)

04 Run the switch wire through a grommet in the firewall

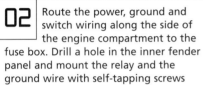

Standard headlights are adequate for nearly all conventional types of driving. But trucks – by their very nature – are often found in some rather unconventional places (in the desert, on the beach, in the woods) and in unpredictable weather (fog, driving rain). Helping your factory headlights with some auxiliary lighting could be the most important modification you make to your SUV.

05 Figure out where you want to locate the switch, then drill a hole just big enough for it to fit. After mounting the switch, splice into a switched 12-volt wire using a quick-splice connector. Start the engine and test out those lights!

In very general terms, there are three types of auxiliary lights; driving lights, fog lights and spot lights. Driving lights are usually rectangular in shape, mounted at the level of the headlights or below and designed to complement your headlight illumination. Fog lights are mounted low on the vehicle and illuminate a wide area immediately in front of your SUV. Spotlights will often be found up high on a light bar and are generally the most powerful of the group, lighting up an entire campground if that's what you want.

Winches

If you routinely venture off the beaten path with your SUV, a winch could very well become your best friend. Sooner or later, you're going to get stuck in the mud or come across a fallen tree, etc. Your winch will save the day.

Types of winches

Power Take Off Drum Winch (PTO)

A PTO incorporates a drum and wire rope system mounted on the front of the vehicle. It can be either mechanically or hydraulically operated by the vehicle engine through the gearbox with the PTO engaged and the transmission in Neutral. If you need a lot of pull power for a long period of time, a PTO is the way to go. It can be operated by one person with little physical effort, but unless you've got one equipped with a hand crank, it's no good if your engine's dead. It's also nearly impossible to use a PTO to move your vehicle backwards or sideways. A PTO is a heavy piece of equipment, and it's the most expensive type of winch available, but it's also the most efficient and powerful.

Electric Drum Winch

The most popular winch, by far. These are similar in appearance to PTO's, but they're electrically driven by your vehicle's battery - which means even if you've got major engine trouble, you'll still be able to pull. Though its single speed often means a slow wind, the remote operation means one person can easily handle any pulling job. Electric drums have a pull power nearly identical to a PTO, but at a lesser cost. But, aggressive use of an electric drum winch quickly drains the battery, so a dual battery setup may be in order.

Portable Hand Winch

This versatile winch is hand operated by a lever and cable system and comes in a range of sizes to suit your needs. Portable hand winches can pull forward, backward, and sideways. They can right overturned vehicles and move trees that have fallen in your path. Though they have decent pulling power, the manual operation can be tedious and slow. But, they are a good value for the money and can accomplish tasks that power-driven winches can't.

Hand Puller

The lightweight and portable hand puller is comprised of a small drum and ratchet enclosed in a metal frame. It's an inexpensive alternative to fancier winches, but it does have limited pull and wind-in distance. Hand pullers have slow operation and no reverse, but they're useful for pulling your ride out of sticky situations.

Grille and Brush guards

Brush guards are really useful if you often find yourself driving through, well, the brush, and they protect your front end from scratches and dings. They are usually made of steel or aluminum tubing and surround the grille as well as the headlights. Some types - usually called grille guards - cover only the grille. Many even sport integrated winch brackets and light mounts. A few brush guards are made to fit virtually any SUV, but there are also model-specific guards available to provide a custom fit. Regardless of the type of guard you're in the market for, a good quality one will always bolt to the bumper and the frame for maximum protection.

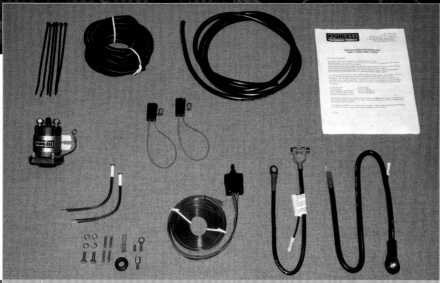

01 We selected a dual-battery kit from Painless Performance Products because it was, well . . . fairly painless to install!

02 Find a convenient location for the isolator near the stock battery, place it in position, mark the location of the mounting bracket holes, drill them out and install the isolator. While you're at it, see that ground wire connected to the isolator? Use one of the mounting bracket bolts to connect the ground wire to the body

Dual-battery setups

The battery on your SUV is more than adequate for starting the engine and running your factory accessories. But add any extras like custom sound, lighting or goodies for off-road or camping, then a second battery is the way to go.

Installing a dual-battery setup

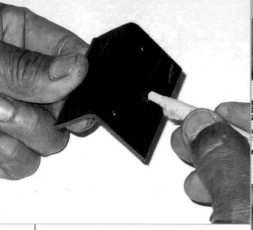

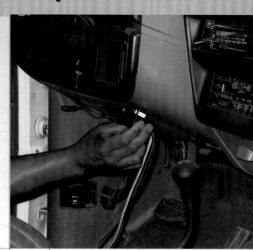

05 Our Painless kit includes a mode switch and a couple of LED indicator lights but not an actual mounting bracket (probably because some people install them in the dash). If you want to keep it simple (and painless!), fabricate a simple L-shaped mounting bracket instead. Bend a small piece of aluminum or steel into an L shape, mark the location of the holes for the LEDS and the switch and drill out the holes (5/16-inch drill bit for the LEDs, 1/2-inch bit for the switch)

06 Install the LEDs and the mode switch on the mounting bracket. To install the LEDs, simply push them through the holes from the backside of the bracket. Small tabs on the LED housings secure the LEDs in their mounting holes. Secure the switch with the locknut provided

07 When the LEDs and the mode switch are installed on the mounting bracket, find a suitable location for the bracket. It should be within easy reach, but not in a spot where it might be accidentally flipped on or off

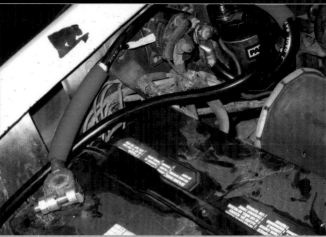

03 With the isolator mounted, install the cable that connects the battery's positive terminal to the isolator and the cable that connects the starter solenoid to the isolator. Refer to the circuit schematic in your kit to ensure that you connect the battery positive terminal and the solenoid to the correct terminal on the isolator

04 Now route the cable that connects the isolator to the auxiliary battery. Keep it away from any hot or moving parts.

So where do I mount the battery?

Your best option may be in the engine compartment, as close as possible to the stock battery. Of course, open space for an additional battery here will depend entirely on the engine and accessories installed on your SUV. If you can carve out the room, you may be able to simply buy a universal battery tray with hold down brackets, bolt it securely in place and add the battery and cables.

Another option is to purchase a battery box, usually made from tough polyethylene or aluminum to mount under the vehicle. Find a spot that is as protected as possible and mount the box and battery. Be careful to secure the thick positive cable along the way back up to the engine compartment and keep it away from exhaust components or moving parts.

08 Connect the LED leads to their corresponding switch leads (refer to the schematic included in your kit), then route the rest of the wiring harness under the dash. Connect the power wire to a circuit that's switched on by the ignition key and the ground wire to a good grounding nut or bolt

Finally, find a grommet in the firewall and run **09** the remaining two wires through the firewall and route them to the isolator solenoid (again, refer to the schematic in your kit)

Regardless of how enthusiastic you may be about getting on with the job at hand, take the time to ensure that your safety is not jeopardized. A moment's lack of attention can result in an accident, as can failure to observe certain simple safety precautions. The possibility of an accident will always exist, and the following points should not be considered a comprehensive list of all dangers. Rather, they are intended to make you aware of the risks and to encourage a safety conscious approach to all work you carry out on your vehicle.

Safety First

Essential DOs and DON'Ts

DON'T rely on a jack when working under the vehicle. Always use approved jackstands to support the weight of the vehicle and place them under the recommended lift or support points.

DON'T attempt to loosen extremely tight fasteners (i.e. wheel lug nuts) while the vehicle is on a jack - it may fall.

DON'T start the engine without first making sure that the transmission is in Neutral (or Park where applicable) and the parking brake is set.

DON'T remove the cooling system pressure cap from a hot cooling system - let it cool or cover it with a cloth and release the pressure gradually.

DON'T attempt to drain the engine oil until you are sure it has cooled to the point that it will not burn you.

DON'T touch any part of the engine or exhaust system until it has cooled sufficiently to avoid burns.

DON'T siphon toxic liquids such as gasoline, antifreeze and brake fluid by mouth, or allow them to remain on your skin.

DON'T inhale brake lining dust - it is potentially hazardous (see **Asbestos**).

DON'T allow spilled oil or grease to remain on the floor - wipe it up before someone slips on it.

DON'T use loose fitting wrenches or other tools which may slip and cause injury.

DON'T push on wrenches when loosening or tightening nuts or bolts. Always try to pull the wrench toward you. If the situation calls for pushing the wrench away, push with an open hand to avoid scraped knuckles if the wrench should slip.

DON'T attempt to lift a heavy component alone - get someone to help you.

DON'T rush or take unsafe shortcuts to finish a job.

DON'T allow children or animals in or around the vehicle while you are working on it.

DO wear eye protection when using power tools such as a drill, sander, bench grinder, etc. and when working under a vehicle.

DO keep loose clothing and long hair well out of the way of moving parts.

DO make sure that any hoist used has a safe working load rating adequate for the job.

DO get someone to check on you periodically when working alone on a vehicle.

DO carry out work in a logical sequence and make sure that everything is correctly assembled and tightened.

DO keep chemicals and fluids tightly capped and out of the reach of children and pets.

DO remember that your vehicle's safety affects that of yourself and others. If in doubt on any point, get professional advice.

Steering, suspension and brakes

These systems are essential to driving safety, so make sure you have a qualified shop or individual check your work. Also, compressed suspension springs can cause injury if released suddenly - be sure to use a spring compressor.

Airbag

Airbags are explosive devices that can cause injury if they deploy while you're working on the car. Follow the manufacturer's instructions,to disable the airbag whenever you're working in the vicinity of airbag components. Never use airbag system wiring when installing electronic components. When in doubt, check your vehicle's wiring diagram.

Asbestos

Certain friction, insulating, sealing, and other products - such as brake linings, brake bands, clutch linings, torque converters, gaskets, etc. - may contain asbestos or other hazardous friction material. Extreme care must be taken to avoid inhalation of dust from such products, since it is hazardous to health. If in doubt, assume that they are harmful.

Fire

Remember at all times that gasoline is highly flammable. Never smoke or have any kind of open flame around when working on a vehicle. But the risk does not end there. A spark caused by an electrical short circuit, by two metal surfaces contacting each other, by a tool falling on concrete, or even by static electricity built up in your body under certain conditions, can ignite gasoline vapors, which in a confined space are highly explosive. Do not, under any circumstances, use gasoline for cleaning parts. Use an approved safety solvent.

Always disconnect the battery ground (-) cable at the battery before working on any part of the fuel system or electrical system. Never risk spilling fuel on a hot engine or exhaust component. It is strongly recommended that a fire extinguisher suitable for use on fuel and electrical fires be kept handy in the garage or workshop at all times. Never try to extinguish a fuel or electrical fire with water.

Fumes

Certain fumes are highly toxic and can quickly cause unconsciousness and even death if inhaled to any extent. Gasoline vapor falls into this category, as do the vapors from some cleaning solvents. Any draining or pouring of such volatile fluids should be done in a well ventilated area.

When using cleaning fluids and solvents, read the instructions on the container carefully. Never use materials from unmarked containers.

Never run the engine in an enclosed space, such as a garage. Exhaust fumes contain carbon monoxide, which is extremely poisonous. If you need to run the engine, always do so in the open air, or at least have the rear of the vehicle outside the work area.

The battery

Never create a spark or allow a bare light bulb near a battery. They normally give off a certain amount of hydrogen gas, which is highly explosive.

Always disconnect the battery ground (-) cable at the battery before working on the fuel or electrical systems.

If possible, loosen the filler caps or cover when charging the battery from an external source (this does not apply to sealed or maintenance-free batteries). Do not charge at an excessive rate or the battery may burst.

Take care when adding water to a non maintenance-free battery and when carrying a battery. The electrolyte, even when diluted, is very corrosive and should not be allowed to contact clothing or skin.

Always wear eye protection when cleaning the battery to prevent the caustic deposits from entering your eyes.

Household current

When using an electric power tool, inspection light, etc., which operates on household current, always make sure that the tool is correctly connected to its plug and that, where necessary, it is properly grounded. Do not use such items in damp conditions and, again, do not create a spark or apply excessive heat in the vicinity of fuel or fuel vapor.

Secondary ignition system voltage

A severe electric shock can result from touching certain parts of the ignition system (such as the spark plug wires) when the engine is running or being cranked, particularly if components are damp or the insulation is defective. In the case of an electronic ignition system, the secondary system voltage is much higher and could prove fatal.

Glossary of terms

A

A-arm - A suspension locating link shaped like the letter "A." An A-arm can be used as an upper arm, a lower arm or for both locating links.

AC (Alternating Current) - Energy that alternates back and forth at a certain frequency. The frequency is measured in hertz. In automobiles, AC is produced by the alternator and then rectified to DC.

Acoustical energy - Energy consisting of fluctuating waves of pressure called sound waves.

Acoustics - A science dealing with the production, effects, and transmission of sound waves through various mediums.

Adjustable shock absorbers - Shocks with adjustable *jounce* and *rebound* characteristics can be stiffened to fine tune a suspension for a particular application such as rough roads, heavy loads or racing.

Adjusting sleeve - A device on the steering linkage which changes *toe-in* or *toe-out*.

A-frame - See *A-arm*.

Air-fuel ratio - The ratio of air to the *weight* of the fuel supplied to the mixture for combustion. See *stoichiometric*.

Air shock - A shock absorber utilizing an air chamber, that when pressurized with compressed air, increases the shock absorber resistance.

Air spring - A bladder of compressed air which is used instead of a coil spring in an air suspension system. See *air suspension*.

Air suspension - A suspension system that uses air instead of metal or composite springs to support the vehicle and control ride motions. Air springs can be made very soft for lightly loaded conditions and the pressure can be automatically increased to match any increase in load, thus maintaining a constant spring vibration period for any load.

Alignment - An adjustment to bring related components into a line. For example, the correct adjustment of a vehicle's front or rear suspension for camber, toe, caster and ride height.

Alloy wheel - A generic term used to describe any non-steel road wheel. The alloys are usually aluminum or magnesium (hence the term *mag wheel,* which refers to any non-steel wheel).

Alternator - A mechanically driven automotive device that generates DC power; it is the primary source of vehicle power.

Amplification - An increase in signal level, amplitude or magnitude.

Antenna - A mechanical device, such as a rod or wire, that picks up a received signal or radiates a transmitted signal.

Anti-lock brake system (ABS) - A system, usually electronically controlled, that senses incipient wheel lockup during braking and relieves hydraulic pressure at wheels that are about to skid. An anti-lock brake system prevents wheel lock-up, improves steering control and reduces stopping distances, especially on wet or icy surfaces.

Anti-roll bar - See *stabilizer bar*.

Anti-seize compound - A coating that reduces the risk of seizing on fasteners that are subjected to high temperatures, such as exhaust manifold bolts and nuts.

Anti-skid - See *anti-lock brake system*.

Anti-sway bar - See *stabilizer bar*.

Aspect ratio - The ratio of section height to section width on a tire.

Asymmetrical tread - A tread grooved in an irregular pattern shape and size. Asymmetrical treads are designed to provide an optimum combination of braking, ride, handling and wet-dry road characteristics.

Audio frequency spectrum - The band of frequencies extending roughly from 20 Hz to 20 kHz.

Audio signal - An electrical representation of a sound wave in the form of alternating current (AC) or voltage.

Automatic level control - A suspension system that compensates for variations in load at the front, rear or both ends of the vehicle, positioning the vehicle at a pre-designed level regardless of load.

Auxiliary springs - Extra springs on a vehicle, usually at the rear, to support heavier loads.

Axle - A shaft on which a wheel revolves, or which revolves with a wheel. Also, a solid beam that connects the two wheels at one end of the vehicle. An axle is *live* if it transmits power, as in, for example, a front-engine, rear-wheel-drive vehicle. It's called a *beam axle* or a *dead axle* if it does nothing but support the wheels, as at the rear of a front-wheel-drive vehicle.

Axle bearing - A bearing which supports a rotating axle in an axle housing.

Axle boot - See *CV joint boot*.

Axle flange - Flange to which a road wheel attaches at the end of an axleshaft.

Axleshaft - A rotating shaft, splined to the differential, which delivers power from the final drive assembly to the drive wheels.

Axle wind-up - Also known as *axle tramp, axle hop* or *wheel tramp*. The tendency of an axle housing on a vehicle to rotate with the wheels as high torque is applied (as under acceleration), then quickly return to its original location.

B

Backing plate - The flat, round metal plate to which the brake shoes and wheel cylinders are attached.

Backpressure - Any resistance to free flow in the exhaust system. For example, catalytic converters and mufflers cause backpressure.

Balljoints - The ball-and-socket connecting links used to attach the steering knuckles to the upper and/or lower control arms and the tie-rod ends to the steering arms.

Banjo fitting - A type of hydraulic fitting, shaped like a banjo, through which a hollow bolt passes, allowing fluid transfer from a hydraulic line to a hydraulic component.

Bass - The low audio frequency range, normally considered to be below 500 Hz.

Battery - A device that stores electrical energy. A battery makes direct current through a collection of cells.

Belt - A reinforcing band, usually fabric, fiberglass or steel, running around the circumference of a tire and strengthening the tread area.

Bleeder valve - A valve on a wheel cylinder, caliper or other hydraulic component that is opened to purge the hydraulic system of air.

Blower - A pump-like device which forces air into the cylinders at higher-than-atmospheric pressure. Because of this higher pressure, the cylinder gets more air per intake stroke, which means it can burn more fuel, which means more horsepower. There are two types of blowers - A turbocharger uses the exhaust gases to drive a compressor and pump the air; a belt-driven supercharger uses engine power to pump air. See *turbocharger* and *supercharger*.

Blow-off valve - A control valve on a turbocharged engine, installed on the intake side of the system, which relieves pressure if it exceeds a predetermined value.

Brake bleeding - Procedure for removing air from lines of a hydraulic brake system.

Brake caliper - The component of a disc brake that converts hydraulic pressure into mechanical energy.

Brake cylinder - A cylinder in which a movable piston converts pressure to mechanical force to move brake shoes against the braking surface of the drum or rotor.

Brake disc - The component of a disc brake that rotates with the wheels and is squeezed by the brake caliper and pads, which creates friction and converts the energy of the moving vehicle into heat. Also referred to as a brake rotor.

Brake drum - The component of a drum brake that rotates with the wheel and is acted upon by the expanding brake shoes, which creates friction and converts the energy of the moving vehicle into heat.

Brake fade - A condition in which repeated severe applications of brakes cause expansion of brake drum or loss of frictional ability or both, which results in impaired braking efficiency.

Brake fluid - A compounded liquid for use in hydraulic brake systems, which must meet exacting conditions (impervious to heat, freezing, thickening, bubbling, etc.).

Brake hose - A flexible conductor for transmission of fluid pressure in brake system.

Brake lines - The rigid metal tubing connecting the master cylinder to the brake calipers and/or wheel cylinders in a hydraulic brake system. Flexible brake hoses usually bridge the gap between the rigid metal lines and calipers/wheel cylinders to allow for the up-and-down motion of the suspension.

Brake linings - The replaceable friction material which contacts the brake drum to retard the vehicle's speed. The linings are bonded or riveted to the brake shoes. See *brake shoe*.

Brake pads - On disc-brake systems, the replaceable friction pads that pinch the brake disc when the brakes are applied. Brake pads consist of an organic or metallic friction material bonded or riveted to a rigid backing plate.

Brake shoe - The crescent-shaped carrier to which the friction linings are mounted and which force the lining against the rotating drum during braking.

Bump - The upward movement of the wheels and suspension; also called *jounce*.

Bump steer - The slight turning or steering of a wheel away from its normal direction of travel as it moves through its suspension travel.

Bump stop - A cushioning device, usually rubber, that limits the upward movement of the wheels and suspension to prevent metal-to-metal contact that could lead to suspension damage or failure. Also referred to as *jounce bumpers*.

Burr - A rough edge or area remaining on metal after it has been cast, cut or drilled.

Bushing - A one-piece sleeve placed in a bore to serve as a bearing surface for shaft, piston pin, etc. Usually replaceable.

C

Caliper - The non-rotating part of a disc-brake assembly that straddles the disc and contains the hydraulic components that pinch the disc when the brakes are applied.

Caliper mounting plate - The component that connects a brake caliper to the steering knuckle, hub carrier or rear axle.

Camber - In wheel alignment, it is the outward or inward tilt of a wheel at it's top.

Camshaft - A rotating shaft on which a series of *cam lobes* operate the valve mechanisms. The camshaft is driven by gears or sprockets and a timing chain. Usually referred to simply as the *cam*.

Carcass - Tire structure except for sidewall and tread.

Cardan joint - A universal joint with corresponding yokes at a right angle with each other. It's named after a 16th century Italian who developed the concept. Over a century later, Robert Hooke of England developed and patented the conventional universal joint, or U-joint, which is sometimes referred to as a Cardan or Hooke universal.

Castellated - Resembling the parapets along the top of a castle wall. For example, a castellated balljoint stud nut.

Caster - In wheel alignment, the backward or forward tilt of the steering axis. The angle between the steering axis and the vertical plane, as viewed from the side. Caster is considered positive when the steering axis is inclined rearward at the top.

Catalytic converter - A muffler-like device in the exhaust system that catalyzes a chemical reaction which converts certain air pollutants in the exhaust gases into less harmful substances.

Center of gravity - Point of a body from which it could be suspended, or on which it could be supported, and be in balance. For example, the center of gravity of a wheel is the center of the wheel hub.

Centrifugal force - A force which tends to move a body away from its center of rotation. For example, a whirling weight attached to a string.

Chase - To repair or clean up damaged threads with a tap or die.

Chassis - A French word meaning framework of a vehicle without a body and fenders. Generally speaking, the suspension, steering, and braking components of a vehicle are all regarded as part of the chassis.

Clevis - A U-shaped metal piece with holes in each end through which a pin or bolt is run, used for attaching the brake pedal to the power brake booster pushrod, the clutch pedal to the clutch cable or master cylinder pushrod and for various other connections on an automobile.

Clipping - Distortion that occurs when a power amplifier is overdriven. This can be seen visually on an oscilloscope, when the peaks of a waveform are flattened, or "clipped-off" at the signal's ceiling.

Coaxial speaker - A coaxial speaker has a large cone for the low range and a smaller tweeter for the high spectrum. There is a crossover network that divides and routes the signal to the correct driver. Named for two speakers sharing a single axis.

Coil spring - A spiral of elastic steel found in various sizes throughout a vehicle, most importantly as a springing medium in the suspension and in the valve train.

Constant velocity (CV) joint - A universal joint whose output shaft travels at the same velocity as the input shaft, through 360-degrees, with no fluctuations in speed.

Contact patch - The area of a tire's tread in contact with the ground.

Cord - Textile or steel-wire strands which form the plies of a tire.

Countersink - To cut or form a depression to allow the head of a screw to go below surface.

Crossover - A device that separates the different frequency bands and redirects them to different components.

Crossover frequencies - The frequencies at which a passive or electronic crossover network divides the audio signals, which are then routed to the appropriate speakers.

CV joint boot - The flexible, accordion-plated rubber dust boot which encloses the constant velocity joint and the end of the axleshaft attached to it. The CV joint boot prevents dirt, dust, mud and moisture from entering the CV joint.

D

Damper - See *shock absorber.*

Dead axle - See *axle.*

Deceleration - Negative acceleration. The rate of change in velocity as a vehicle slows down during braking.

Detonation - The uncontrolled spontaneous explosion of air/fuel mixture in the combustion chamber - after the spark occurs at the spark plug - which spontaneously combusts the remaining air/fuel mixture, resulting in a "pinging" noise, and causing a loss of power and possible engine damage. Commonly referred to as spark knock or ping.

Detonation-activated ignition retard - A system which retards the ignition timing when the detonation

knock sensor picks up vibration at frequencies typical of detonation.

Differential - A device with an arrangement of gears designed to permit the division of power to two shafts. For example, the differential permits one drive wheel to turn faster than the other.

DIN - Deutscher Industrie Normen. German industrial standards that are used in many European countries. DIN size refers to the stereo size that fits most European cars.

Disc - See *Brake disc.*

Disc brake - A brake design incorporating a flat, disc-like rotor onto which brake pads containing lining material are squeezed, generating friction and converting the energy of a moving vehicle into heat.

Distortion - A warpage or change in form from the original shape.

Dog clutch - Mating collars, flanges or lugs which can be moved as desired to engage or disengage similar collars, flanges or lugs in order to transmit rotary motion.

Double-wishbone suspension - Another name for a double-A-arm suspension. A suspension system using two wishbones, or A-arms to connect the chassis to the spindle or knuckle.

Dowel pin - A steel pin pressed into matching shallow holes in two adjacent parts to provide proper alignment of the two parts.

Drag link - A connecting rod or link between steering gear Pitman arm and steering control linkage .

Driveline - Universal joints, driveshaft and other parts connecting transmission with driving axles.

Driveshaft - The long hollow tube with universal joints at both ends that carries power from the transmission to the differential.

Drum brake - A type of brake using a drum-shaped metal cylinder that attaches to the inner surface of the wheel and rotates with it. When the brake pedal is pressed, curved brake shoes with friction linings press against the inner circumference of the drum to slow or stop the vehicle.

Duo-servo drum brake - A type of self-energizing drum brake that has servo action in both forward and reverse.

Dust boot - A rubber diaphragm-like seal that fits over the end of a hydraulic component and around a pushrod or end of a piston, not used for sealing fluid in but keeping dust out.

E

Electronic Control Module (ECM) - A generic term referring to the computer. The ECM is the brain of the engine control systems receiving information from various sensors in the engine compartment. The ECM calculates what is required for proper engine operation and controls the different actuators to achieve it.

Endplay - The amount of lengthwise movement between two parts. As applied to a crankshaft, the distance that the crankshaft can move forward and back in the cylinder block.

Exhaust manifold - Attached to the cylinder head, the exhaust manifold collects the exhaust from all engine exhaust ports and routes the exhaust gasses into a single exhaust pipe.

Exhaust oxygen sensor - Also known as an *oxygen sensor* or an *02 sensor.* Device that detects the amount of oxygen in the exhaust stream, and sends that information to the ECM.

Exhaust system - The pipes, resonators and mufflers that carry the exhaust gases from the exhaust manifold out into the atmosphere.

F

Fade - A condition brought about by repeated or protracted application of the brakes, resulting in a reduction or fading of brake effectiveness. Heat is the primary culprit, causing expansion of the brake drums/discs and lowering the friction coefficient of the brake shoe linings and/or disc brake pads.

Fatigue - A breakdown of material through a large number of loading and unloading cycles. The first signs are cracks followed shortly by breaks.

Feeler gauge - A thin strip or blade of hardened steel, ground to an exact thickness, used to check and/or measure clearances between parts. Feeler gauges are graduated in thickness by increments of .001 inch.

Final drive ratio - The ratio between the driveshaft or transmission output shaft rpm and the drive-wheel axleshaft rpm. It's determined by the ring and pinion gearing inside the differential. For example, if the ratio is 4:1, the driveshaft

Flange - A rib or rim used to provide strength to a panel or a means of attachment for another panel.

Flare-nut wrench - A wrench designed for loosening hydraulic fitting tube nuts (flare-nuts) without damaging them. Flare-nut wrenches are kind of like a six-point box-end wrench with one of the flats missing, which allows the wrench to pass over the tubing but still maintain a maximum amount of contact with the nut.

Flywheel - A heavy, usually metal, spinning wheel in which energy is absorbed and stored by means of momentum. On cars, this heavy metal wheel that's attached to the crankshaft to smooth out firing impulses. It provides inertia to keep the crankshaft turning smoothly during periods when no power is being applied. It also serves as part of the clutch and engine cranking systems.

Flywheel ring gear - A large gear pressed onto the circumference of the flywheel. When the starter gear engages the ring gear, the starter cranks the engine.

Foot-pound - A unit of measurement for work, equal to lifting one pound one foot.

Foot-pound (tightening) - A unit of measurement for torque, equal to one pound of pull one foot from the center of the object being tightened.

Four-wheel ABS - An anti-lock brake system that operates on all four wheels.

Four-wheel drive - A type of drive system in which both the front and rear wheels are connected through drivelines and driving axles to the transmission, usually via a transfer case. Four-wheel drive can be either full-time, with power delivered to both axles at all times, or part time, where the driver can select either rear-wheel drive only or four-wheel drive for marginal traction conditions.

Frame - The structural load-carrying members of a vehicle that support the engine and body and are in turn supported by the wheels.

Free height - The unloaded length or height of a spring.

Freeplay - The amount of travel before any action takes place. The looseness in a linkage, or an assembly of parts, between the initial application of force and actual movement. Usually perceived as "slop" or slight delay. For example, In a brake pedal it is the distance the pedal moves before the pistons in the master cylinder are actuated.

Frequency - The term in physics that refers to a number of vibrations or cycles that occur within a given time.

Friction - Surface resistance to relative motion.

Full-floating axle - A driveaxle design in which the axleshaft does not carry the vehicle's weight. Two roller bearings support the weight of the vehicle, so the axle can be removed without disturbing the wheel.

Fully-independent rear suspension - A suspension system that uses driveaxles and a series of links to allow each wheel to rise and fall independently of the other wheel. Also known as a fully-articulated independent rear suspension system.

Fuse - A device designed to provide protection for a given circuit or device by physically opening the circuit. Fuses are rated by their amperage and are designed to blow or open when the current being drawn through it exceeds its design rating.

Fusible link - Designed to perform the same task as a fuse, but resembles a wire. Fusible links are commonly used in ignition switches and other high-current circuits.

G

Gear puller - A tool that's specially designed for removing press-fitted gears from their respective shafts.

Gear ratio - Number of revolutions made by a driving gear as compared to number of revolutions made by a driven gear of different size. For example, if one gear makes three revolutions while the other gear makes one revolution, the gear ratio is 3 to 1.

Grommet - A round rubber seal which fits into a hole or recess, intended to seal or insulate the component passing through it. A donut-shaped rubber or plastic part used to protect wiring that passes through a panel, firewall or bulkhead.

Groove - The space between two adjacent tire tread ribs.

Ground - The term given to anything that has an electrical potential of zero. Most modern vehicles are designed around a negative ground system, with the metal frame being the vehicle's ground.

Guide pin - A caliper mounting bolt used for fastening a floating caliper to its mounting plate.

H

Halfshaft - A rotating shaft that transmits power from the final drive unit to the drive wheels, but usually refers to the two shafts that connect the wheels to the final drive with independent rear suspension or front-wheel drive rather than the axleshafts of a live rear axle.

Harness - The universal name for a bundle or loom of wires that compose the wiring for a system.

Hat - The portion of a detachable brake disc that comes in contact with the wheel hub.

Header - A high-performance exhaust manifold that replaces the stock exhaust manifold. Designed with smooth flowing lines to prevent back pressure caused by sharp bends, rough castings, etc. See *Exhaust manifold*.

Helical gear - A gear design where gear teeth cut at an angle to shaft.

Heli-Coil - A rethreading device used when threads are worn or damaged. The device is installed in a retapped hole to reduce the thread size to the original size.

Hooke joint - See *Cardan joint*.

Horsepower - A measure of mechanical power, or the rate at which work is done. One horsepower is the amount of power required to lift 550 pounds one foot per second. One horsepower equals 33,000 ft-lbs of work per minute. It's the amount of power necessary to raise 33,000 pounds a distance of one foot in one minute.

Hotchkiss drive - A live axle rear suspension design in which the axle is located by semi-elliptic leaf springs. The springs, mounted longitudinally, connect to the chassis at their ends and the axle is hung from them. Thus they not only spring the axle but also determine its freedom to move and transmit all cornering, braking and driving forces from the axle to the body.

Hydraulically operated power booster - A power booster that uses hydraulic pressure to assist the driver in the application of the brakes. This hydraulic pressure usually comes from the power steering pump or an electro-hydraulic pump.

Hydraulic brake system - System in which brake operation and control utilizes hydraulic brake fluid.

Hydraulic control unit - The portion of an anti-lock brake system that houses the solenoid valves and electro-hydraulic pump.

Hypoid gears - A design of pinion and ring gear in which the centerline of the pinion is offset from the centerline of the ring gear.

I

Ideal air/fuel mixture, or ideal mixture - The air/fuel ratio which provides the best performance while maintaining maximum conversion of exhaust emissions, typically 14.7:1. See *stoichiometric*.

Idle - Rotational speed of an engine with vehicle at rest and accelerator pedal not depressed.

Idler arm - One of the connecting levers in a parallel, relay-type steering linkage. The steering gearbox is attached to a Pitman arm which converts rotary motion to lateral motion. The Pitman arm usually connects to a transverse center link which in turn is connected to the idler arm attached to the frame rail on the opposite side of the vehicle. The ends of the center link connect to two adjustable tie-rods that transmit the lateral movement of the center link to the steering arms at each steering knuckle.

Idler gear - A gear interposed between two other gears to reverse the direction of rotation of the output gear.

Ignition timing - The moment at which the spark plug fires, usually expressed in the number of crankshaft degrees before the piston reaches the top of its stroke.

Independent suspension - A suspension design in which the wheel on one side of the vehicle may rise or fall independently of the wheel on the other side. Thus, a disturbance affecting one wheel has no effect on the other wheel.

Input (Audio) - The high-level (speaker) or line level (RCA) signal connections that run into one component from another system component.

Input shaft - Transmission shaft which receives power from engine and transmits it to transmission gears.

Intake manifold - A tube or housing with passages through which flows the air-fuel mixture (carbureted vehicles and vehicles with throttle body injection) or air only (port fuel-injected vehicles) to the port openings in the cylinder head.

Intercooler - A radiator used to reduce the temperature of the compressed air or air/fuel mixture before it enters the combustion chamber. Either air-to-water or, more commonly, air-to-air.

J

Jam nut - A nut used to lock an adjustment nut, or other threaded component, in place. For example, a jam nut is employed to keep the adjusting nut on the rocker arm in position.

Jounce - See *bump*.

K

Knock - The sharp, metallic sound produced when two pressure fronts collide in the combustion chamber of an engine, usually because of *detonation*. Also, a general term used to describe various noises occurring in an engine; can be used to describe noises made by loose or worn mechanical parts, such as a bad bearing. Connecting rod or main bearing knocks are created by too much oil clearance or insufficient lubrication. Also referred to as *detonation, pinging* and *spark knock*.

L

Ladder frame - A type of frame construction consisting of two heavy-section longitudinal members connected together step-ladder fashion by smaller transverse crossmembers. This design is no longer used much anymore because it's heavy and lacks torsional rigidity.

Lash - The amount of free motion in a gear train, between gears, or in a mechanical assembly, that occurs before movement can begin. Usually refers to the lash in a valve train.

Lateral acceleration - Sideways acceleration created when a vehicle corners.

Lateral runout - The amount of side-to-side movement of a rotating wheel, tire or brake disc from the vertical.

Leading/trailing drum brake - A drum brake design in which both brake shoes are attached to an anchor plate, and only one of the shoes is self-energized.

Leaf spring - A slightly curved steel plate, usually mounted in multiples of two or more plates of varying lengths, installed on top of each other. When used with a live rear axle, the ends of the springs are attached to the vehicle frame and the center is fixed to the axle.

Lean - A term used to describe an air/fuel mixture that's got either too much air or too little fuel.

LED - Light Emitting Diode. A form of diode that sheds light. Used in many systems for indicator purposes.

Limited slip differential - A differential that uses cone or disc clutches to lock the two independent axleshafts together, forcing both wheels to transmit their respective drive torque regardless of the available traction. It allows a limited amount of slip between the two axleshafts to accommodate the differential action.

Live axle - A shaft through which power travels from the driveaxle gears to the driving wheels. See *axle*.

Load range - Tire designation, with a letter (A, B, C, etc.), used to identify a given size tire with its load and inflation limits. Replaced the old term, *ply rating*.

Load Sensing Proportioning Valve (LSPV) - A hydraulic system control valve that works like a proportioning valve, but also takes into consideration the amount of weight carried by the rear axle.

Lock washer - A form of washer designed to prevent attaching nut from working loose.

Lower arm - The suspension arm which connects the vehicle chassis to the bottom of the steering knuckle.

Low frequency - Refers to radio frequencies within the 30-300 kHz band. In audio it usually refers to frequencies in the 40-160 Hz band.

Lubricant - Any substance, usually oil or grease, applied to moving parts to reduce friction between them.

Lug nuts - The nuts used to secure the wheels to a vehicle.

M

MacPherson strut - A type of suspension system devised by Earle MacPherson at Ford of England. In its original form, this layout used a simple lateral link with the stabilizer bar to create the lower control arm. A long *strut* - an integral coil spring and shock absorber, which also serves to support the steering knuckle - was mounted between the body and the steering knuckle. Many modern MacPherson strut systems use a conventional lower A-arm and don't rely on the stabilizer bar for location.

Mag wheel - See *alloy wheel*.

Manifold Absolute Pressure (MAP) sensor - A pressure-sensitive disk capacitor used to measure air pressure inside the intake manifold. The MAP sensor sends a signal to the computer which uses this information to determine load conditions so it can adjust spark timing and fuel mixture.

Master cylinder - In brake systems, a cylinder containing a movable piston actuated by foot pressure, producing hydraulic pressure to push fluid through the lines and wheel cylinders and force the brake linings or pads against a drum or disc. In hydraulic clutch systems, a similar device is used to push hydraulic fluid into a slave cylinder which activates the clutch release arm with a rod.

Multimeter - A common term used to describe a Volt-Ohm-Meter, or VOM. A multimeter usually can measure volts, ohms and amperes or milliamperes.

Multiple disc clutch - A clutch having a number of driving and driven discs as compared to a single-plate clutch.

N

Needle bearing - An anti-friction bearing using a great number of rollers of small diameter in relation to their length.

Neutral - A handling characteristic where the slip angles are equal at the front and at the rear. The vehicle exhibits neither oversteer or understeer characteristics and is described as "balanced."

Normally aspirated - An engine which draws its air/fuel mixture into its cylinders solely by piston-created vacuum, i.e. not supercharged or turbocharged.

Normally closed - Refers to the electrical state in which a switch may rest. Its contacts are held together or closed so that current is allowed to flow through its contacts.

Normally open - Refers to the electrical state in which a switch may rest. Its contacts are held apart or open so that no current flows through its contacts.

O

OEM (Original Equipment Manufacturer) - A designation used to describe the equipment and parts installed on a vehicle by the manufacturer, or those available from the vehicle manufacturer as replacement parts.

Out-of-round - The condition of a brake drum when it has become distorted and is no longer perfectly round. In many cases an out-of-round brake drum can be salvaged by resurfacing on a brake lathe.

Output (Audio) - The high-level (speaker) or line-level (RCA) signals sent from one system component to another, or the high-level signal from an amplifier to the system speakers.

Output shaft - Shaft which receives power from transmission and transmits it to vehicle drive shaft.

Oversteer - A handling characteristic where the slip angles are larger at the rear than at the front. During hard cornering, the rear tires slip while the front tires maintain traction. An oversteering vehicle breaks away at the rear, so the driver must countersteer with the front wheels and possibly apply opposite lock to keep the vehicle from spinning. When a vehicle exhibits oversteer it is described as "loose."

Oxygen sensor - A device installed in the engine exhaust system, which senses the oxygen content in the exhaust and converts this information into an electric current.

P

Pad - Disc brake friction material generally molded to metal backing, or shoe.

Panhard rod - A locating link running laterally across the vehicle, with its upper end attached to the body and its lower end attached to a live axle, beam axle or DeDion axle. The Panhard rod provides lateral location of the axle. Also known as a *track bar*.

Park/Neutral - The selected nondrive modes of the transmission.

Passive crossover - An electrical circuit consisting of capacitors, inductors, and resistors designed to separate an audio signal into specific speaker groups.

Penetrating oil - Special oil used to free rusted parts so they can be moved.

Pilot bearing - A small bearing installed in the center of the flywheel (or the rear end of the crankshaft) to support the front end of the input shaft of the transmission.

Pinion - A small gear which engages a larger geared wheel or rack. Pinions are used in rack-and-pinion steering gearboxes and in the differential ring-and-pinion set.

Pinion carrier - Mounting or bracket which retains bearings supporting a pinion shaft.

Pitman arm - The large lever, pressed onto the splined end of the steering gearbox Pitman shaft, which connects the steering gearbox with the steering linkage.

Pivot - A pin or short shaft upon which another part rests or turns, or about which another part rotates or oscillates.

Ply - The layer of rubber-coated parallel cords forming a tire body, or carcass, on a bias tire. See *load range*.

Ply rating - An index of tire strength. See *load range*.

Polyurethane - A chemical used in the production of resins.

Positive lead - The lead or line connected to the positive terminal of a current, voltage or power source.

Pre-amp - A circuit that takes a small signal and amplifies it sufficiently to be fed into the power amplifier for further amplification. A pre-amp includes all of the controls for regulating tone, volume and channel balance.

Preignition - Short for *premature ignition*. The premature burning of the air/fuel mixture in the combustion chamber, caused by combustion chamber heat and/or fuel instability. Preignition begins before the spark plug fires.

Preload - The amount of load placed on a bearing before actual operating loads are imposed. Proper preloading requires bearing adjustment and ensures alignment and minimum looseness in the system.

Press-fit - A tight fit between two parts that requires pressure to force the parts together. Also referred to as drive, or force, fit.

Propeller shaft - Another name for the driveshaft connecting the transmission or transfer case to the axle.

Proportioning valve - A hydraulic control valve located in the circuit to the rear wheels which limits the amount of pressure to the rear brakes during panic stops to prevent wheel lock-up.

Puller - A special tool designed to remove a bearing, bushing, hub, sleeve, etc. There are many, many types of pullers.

R

Race (bearing) - The highly-finished inner or outer ring that provides a contact surface for ball or roller bearings.

Rack-and-pinion steering - A steering system with a pinion gear on the end of the steering shaft that mates with a rack (think of a geared wheel opened up and laid flat). When the steering wheel is turned, the pinion turns, moving the rack to the left or right. This movement is transmitted through the tie-rods to the steering arms at the wheels.

Radius rods - Rods attached to the axle and to the frame to prevent fore-and-aft motion of the axle, yet permit vertical motion.

Range (Audio) - Usually described as frequency range, this is a system's frequency transmission limit, beyond which the frequency is attenuated below a specified tolerance. Also, the frequency band or bands within which a receiver or component is designed to operate.

Ratio - Relation or proportion that one number bears to another.

Ream - To size, enlarge or smooth a hole by using a round cutting tool with fluted edges.

Receiver - A device designed to receive a signal or command from a source such as a transmitter.

Recirculating-ball steering - A steering system in which the turning forces are transmitted through the ball bearings from a worm gear on the steering shaft to a sector gear on the Pitman arm shaft.

Relay - An electromagnet switch that allows small, relatively low-level signals to operate higher amperage devices. Also used when polarity reversal is necessary.

Resistance - The electrical term used to describe the property that various materials possess to restrict or inhibit the flow of electricity. Electrical resistance is relatively low in most metals and relatively high in most nonmetallic substances. Electrical resistance is measured in ohms.

Retread - Used tire with new rubber bonded to worn surface from shoulder to shoulder.

Ring and pinion - A term used to describe the differential drive pinion and ring gear. See *final drive ratio*.

Ring gear - The outer gear within which the other gears revolve in a planetary system. Term also refers to driven gear which mates with drive pinion in a differential assembly.

Rivet - To attach with rivets or to batter or upset end of a pin.

Riveted linings - Brake linings that are riveted to the pad backing plate or brake shoe.

Roll - A rotating motion about a longitudinal center line through the vehicle that causes the springs on one side of the vehicle to compress and those on the other side to extend.

Roll center - That point about which the body rolls when cornering.

Rolling radius - The distance from the center of the tire's ground contact patch to the center of the wheel rim.

Rotor - Another name for a brake disc in a disc brake system. Also, the rotating assembly of a turbocharger, including the compressor wheel, shaft and turbine wheel.

Runout - The amount of wobble (in-and-out movement) of a gear or wheel as it's rotated. The amount a shaft rotates "out-of-true." The out-of-round condition of a rotating part.

S

SAE - Society of Automotive Engineers.

SAE thread - Refers to a table of threads set up by Society of Automotive Engineers and determines number of threads per inch. Example: a quarter inch diameter rod with an SAE thread would have 28 threads per inch.

Schrader valve - A spring-loaded, one-way valve installed on all road wheels, for putting air into the tire. Also installed on the throttle body or the fuel rail on fuel injection systems, for attaching fuel pressure gauges and/or relieving system fuel pressure. Also located inside the service valve fitting on air conditioning systems, to hold refrigerant in the system. Special adapters with built-in depressors must be used to attach service hoses to Schrader valves.

Section height - The height of an inflated tire from the bottom of the bead to the top of the tread.

Section width - The width between the exterior surfaces of the sidewalls of an inflated tire at its widest point.

Self-leveling suspension - See *automatic level control*.

Semi-elliptic spring - A type of leaf spring that takes its name from the shape which is part of an ellipse. See *leaf spring*.

Semi-floating axle - A driveaxle construction in which the axleshafts support the weight of the vehicle.

Semi-independent rear suspension - A rear suspension system that allows up-and-down movement of the wheels.

Sensitivity - The rating of a loudspeaker that indicates the level of sound intensity the speaker produces (in dB) at a distance of one meter when it receives one watt of input power.

Sensor - The generic name for a device that senses either the absolute value or a change in a physical quantity such as temperature, pressure, or flow rate, and converts that change into an electrical signal which is monitored by a computer.

Servo action - A brake design in which a primary shoe pushes a secondary shoe to generate higher braking force.

Servo-action drum brake - See *Duo-servo drum brake*.

Shackle - A swinging support by which one end of a leaf spring is attached to the vehicle frame. The shackle is needed to take care of the changes in length of the spring as it moves up and down.

Shackle bolt - A link for connecting one end of a chassis spring to the frame, which allows the spring end to extend during compression.

Shim - Thin sheet used as a spacer between two parts. For example, alignment shims between the control arm pivot shaft and the frame serve to adjust caster and camber.

Shock absorber - A hydraulic and/or pneumatic device which provides friction to control the excessive deflection of the vehicle's springs. Also referred to as a *damper*.

Short circuit - The condition that occurs when a circuit path is created between the positive and negative poles of a battery, power supply or circuit. A short circuit will bypass any resistance in a circuit and cause it not to operate.

Sidewall - The portion of the tire between the tread and the bead.

Slip angle - In cornering, the angle formed by the direction the tire is pointed and the direction the vehicle is moving.

Slip joint - A variable-length connection that permits the driveshaft or axleshaft to change its length as the shaft moves up and down.

Snap-ring - A ring-shaped clip used to prevent endwise movement of the cylindrical parts and shafts. An internal snap-ring is installed in a groove in a housing; an external snap-ring fits into a groove cut out the outside of a cylindrical piece such as a shaft.

Sound - A type of physical kinetic energy called acoustical energy. See *Acoustical energy*.

Sound Pressure Level (SPL) - An acoustic measurement for the ratios of sound energy. Rated in decibels (SPL, dBA, SPL dBC).

Spider gear - One of two to four small gears in the differential that mesh with the bevel gears on the ends of the axles. See *pinion*.

Spiral bevel gear - A ring gear and pinion in which the mating teeth are curved and placed at an angle to the pinion shaft.

Spring - An elastic device that yields under stress or pressure but returns to its original state or position when the stress or pressure is removed. The three most common types of automotive springs are leaf springs, coil springs and torsion bars.

Sprung weight - A term used to describe all parts of an automobile that are supported by car springs. Example: frame, engine, body, etc.

Stabilizer bar - A transverse bar linking both sides (either front or rear) of the suspension, used to reduce body roll when cornering. Also referred to as an *anti-sway bar*, an *anti-roll bar* or simply a *roll bar*.

Standard thread - Refers to the U.S.S. table of the number of threads per inch. For example, a quarter-inch diameter standard thread is 20 threads per inch.

Steering arm - The arm attached to the steering knuckle that turns the knuckle and wheel for steering.

Steering axis inclination - The angle formed by the centerline of the suspension balljoints and the true vertical centerline.

Steering column - A shaft connecting the steering wheel with the steering gear assembly. Also called the *steering shaft*.

Steering gear - A steering unit, whether it's recirculating ball, rack-and-pinion, etc.

Steering geometry - The various angles between the front wheels, the frame and the attachment points. Includes camber, caster, *steering axis inclination* and *toe-in and toe-out*. See *toe-out on turns*.

Steering linkage - The rods, arms and other links that carry movement of the Pitman arm to the steering knuckles. See *idler arm*.

Steering ratio - The ratio of the gearing within a steering system such as the rack to the pinion, or the worm gear to the recirculating nut.

Stoichiometric - The ideal ratio of air to fuel, in terms of mass; results in the most complete and efficient combustion, converting the carbon and hydrogen content of the fuel into (mainly) water and carbon dioxide. The stoichiometric ratio varies with the heating value of the fuel: For example, it's around 15.1:1 by weight for 100-octane gasoline, 14.6:1 for regular, 9.0:1 to ethanol, 6.45:1 for methanol and so on.

Subframe - A partial frame that is sometimes bolted to the chassis of unit-body vehicles. It can be used to support the engine, transmission and/or suspension instead of having these components bolted directly to the main body structure. This more expensive design generally results in better road isolation and less harshness.

Subwoofer - A loudspeaker made specifically to reproduce frequencies below 125 Hz.

Supercharger - A mechanically-driven device that pressurizes the intake air, thereby increasing the density of charge air and the consequent power output from a given engine displacement. Superchargers are usually belt-driven by the engine crankshaft pulley. See *blower*.

Suspension - Refers to the various springs, shock absorbers and linkages used to suspend a vehicle's frame, body, engine and drivetrain above the wheels.

Sway bar - See *stabilizer bar*.

T

Tang - A lip on the end of a plain bearing used to align the bearing during assembly.

Tap - To cut threads in a hole. Also refers to the fluted tool used to cut threads.

Tapered roller bearing - A bearing utilizing a series of tapered, hardened steel rollers operating between an outer and inner hardened steel race.

Threaded insert - A threaded coil that's used to restore the original thread size to a hole with damaged threads; the hole is drilled oversize and tapped, and the insert is threaded into the tapped hole.

Throttle Body Injection (TBI) - Any of several injection systems which have the fuel injector(s) mounted in a centrally located throttle body, as opposed to positioning the injectors close to the intake ports.

Throttle Position Sensor (TPS) - A potentiometric sensor that tells the computer the position (angle) of the throttle plate. The sensor wiper position is proportional to throttle position. The computer uses this information to control fuel flow.

Thrust washer - A bronze or hardened steel washer placed between two moving parts. The washer prevents longitudinal movement and provides a bearing surface for thrust surfaces of parts.

Tie-rod - A balljoint connecting the steering linkage (on recirculating ball type steering gearboxes) or the rack (on rack-and-pinion type steering gearboxes) to the steering arm or steering knuckle. The tie-rod end (the balljoint part) is threaded so that it can be moved in or out in relation to the inner tie-rod to allow toe adjustments.

Toe-in - The amount the front wheels are closer together in front than at the rear when viewed from the front of the vehicle. A slight amount of toe-in is usually specified to keep the front wheels running parallel on the road by offsetting other forces that tend to spread the wheels apart.

Toe-out on turns - The related angles assumed by the front wheels of a vehicle when turning.

Torque - A turning or twisting force, such as the force imparted on a fastener by a torque wrench. Usually expressed in foot-pounds (ft-lbs).

Torque converter - A fluid coupling that transmits power from a driving to a driven member

Torque wrench - A special wrench which can accurately measure and indicate the tightening force applied to a fastener.

Torsion bar - A long straight bar fastened to the frame at one end and to a suspension part at the other. In effect, a torsion bar is merely an uncoiled coil spring and spring action is produced when the bar is twisted. the main advantage of the torsion bar over the coil spring in the front suspension is the ease of adjusting the front suspension height.

Track - The distance from the center of one front (or rear) tire (or wheel) to the other front (or rear) tire (or wheel) with the vehicle set to its normal ride height and wheel alignment specifications.

Track rod - See *panhard rod*.

Traction - The amount of adhesion between the tire and ground.

Transfer case - An auxiliary device in a four-wheel-drive vehicle that allows power to be delivered to both axles. Normally, the transfer case incorporates a shifting device so that the front drive can be disconnected for running on pavement.

Tread - The portion of the tire that comes in contact with the road. Also, the distance between the center of the tires at the points where they contact the road surface.

Turbocharger - A centrifugal device, driven by exhaust gases, that pressurizes the intake air, thereby increasing the density of the charge air, and therefore the resulting power output, from a given engine displacement.

Turning circle or turning radius - The diameter of a circle within which a vehicle can be turned around.

Tweeter - A small loudspeaker or driver meant to reproduce high frequencies.

Two-wheel ABS - An anti-lock brake system that only operates on the rear wheels.

U

Understeer - A handling characteristic where the slip angles are larger at the front than at the rear. During hard cornering, the front tires slip while the rear tires maintain traction. The vehicle will tend to travel in a straight line, requiring more steering input to negotiate the turn. When a vehicle exhibits understeer it is said to "push."

Unfused wire - Any section of wire between the power supply and a load that does not include the protection of a fuse or circuit breaker.

Universal joint or U-joint - A double-pivoted connection for transmitting power from a driving to a driven shaft through an angle.

Unsprung weight - The parts of the vehicle - wheels, axles, etc. - that isn't supported by the springs.

Upper and lower A-arms - A suspension system utilizing a pair of A-arms. See *double-wishbone suspension*.

V

Vacuum gauge - An instrument used to measure the amount of intake vacuum.

Vacuum-operated power booster - A power booster that uses engine manifold vacuum to assist the driver in the application of the brakes.

Volt - The term used to refer to the property of electrical pressure through a circuit.

Voltage - The electrical pressure produced to do work.

Voltage drop - The amount of energy consumed when a device has resistance in its circuit. The voltage (E) measured across a resistance (R) carrying a current (I). E=IR (see also *Volt*).

W

Wastegate - A device which bleeds off exhaust gases before they reach the turbocharger when boost pressure reaches a set limit.

Watt - The basic practical unit of measure for electrical or acoustical power.

Wattage - Electrical power.

Wave - A single oscillation in matter (e.g., a sound wave). Waves move outward from a point of disturbance, propagate through a medium, and grow weaker as they travel farther. Wave motion is associated with mechanical vibration, sound, heat, light, etc.

Waveform - The shape of a wave.

Wavelength - The length of distance a single cycle or complete sound wave travels.

Weight transfer effect - Because the center of gravity of a vehicle is located above the centers of wheel rotation, a sudden stoppage of the vehicle tends to cause the center of gravity to move forward, thus throwing more weight onto the front wheels.

Wheel alignment - See *alignment*.

Wheelbase - The longitudinal distance between the centerlines of the front and rear axles.

Wheel cylinder - A small cylinder with one or two pistons that's fitted inside each brake drum. When brake fluid is forced from the master cylinder, it flows through the brake lines into the wheel cylinder, pushing the pistons apart. This pushes the brake shoes out, forcing the brake shoes tightly against the rotating brake drums. See *backing plate*.

Wheel hub and bearing assembly - The precision made assembly which houses the wheel bearings and to which the brake disc and/or wheel are bolted.

Wheel speed sensor - The component of an anti-lock brake system that picks up the impulses of the toothed signal rotor, sending these impulses to the ABS ECU.

Wishbone - See *A-arm*.

Woofer - A large dynamic loudspeaker that is well suited for reproducing bass frequencies.

Source List

Allen Engine
(Ford truck and SUV supercharger kits)
2521-B Palma Drive
Ventura, CA 93003
(805) 658-8262
www.allenengine.com

Airaid/Poweraid
(Intake products)
14840 N. 74th Street
Scottsdale, AZ 85260
1-800-498-6951
www.airaid.com

American Products Company (APC)
(Truck and SUV accessories)
22324 Temescal Canyon Rd.
Corona, CA 92883
(909) 898-9840
www.4apc.net

Applied Products Group
Orange, CA 92867
(714) 906-1639
www.getapplied.com

ATS Design
(Light-truck and SUV styling products,
fender flares, running boards and fender
flares)
11110 Business Circle
Cerritos, CA 90703
1-866-213-2873
www.atsdesign.com

BBH Luxury Motorsports
(Luxury automotive and SUV customizing)
390 Camarillo Ranch Rd.
Camarillo, CA 93012
1-866-541-5412
www.blingzwheels.com

BBK Performance Parts
(Intake and exhaust products)
1871 Delilah Street
Corona, CA 92879
(909) 735-2400
www.bbkperformance.com

Blingz, Inc.
(Collector edition wheels)
390 Camarillo Ranch Rd.
Camarillo, CA 93012
1-866-541-5412
www.blingzwheels.com

Bridgestone/Firestone
(Tires)
535 Marriott Dr.
Nashville, TN 37214-2428
(615) 937-1000
www.bridgestone-firestone.com

Competition Cams
(Cams, valvetrain parts, ZEX nitrous kits)
3406 Democrat Road
Memphis, TN 38118
(888) 817-1008
www.zex.com

Eclipse
by Fujitsu Ten
(mobile electronics)
19600 S. Vermont Ave.
Torrance, CA 90502
1-800-233-2216
www.eclipse-web.com

Edelbrock Corp.
(Engine and suspension products)
2700 California Street
Torrance, CA 90503
(310) 781-2222
www.edelbrock.com

Eibach Springs Inc.
(Suspension parts)
264 Mariah Cir.
Corona, CA 92879-1751
(909) 256-8300
www.eibach.com

Empire Motor Sports
(Billet accessories, suspension systems and
spray in bedliners)
9261 Bally Ct.
Rancho Cucamonga, CA 91730
(909) 980-8922
www.empiremotorsports.com

Focal America, Inc.
ORCA Design and Manufacturing Corp.
(Amplifiers, speakers, subwoofers)
1531 Lookout Dr.
Agoura, CA 91310
(818) 707-1629
www.focal-america.com

Full-Force Suspension, Inc.
(Suspension parts)
1914 Bon View Ave., #8
Ontario, CA 91761
(909) 673-0000
www.fullforceinc.com

Gale Banks Engineering
(exhaust, intakes, diesel tuners,
turbocharging)
546 Duggan Avenue
Azusa, CA 91702
1-800-601-8072
www.bankspower.com

Genera Corporation
(Aftermarket automotive lamps)
26 Centerpointe Dr. Suite 100
La Palma, CA 90623
(888) 963-9888
www.elegantebytyc.com

GM Performance Parts
1-800-468-7387
www.goodwrench.com

Grant Products
(Custom steering wheels and steering
wheel covers)
700 Allen Ave.
Glendale, CA 91201
(818) 247-2910
www.grantproducts.com

Source List

Grillcraft Custom Products
(Custom grilles)
11651 Prairie Ave.
Hawthorne, CA 90250
(310) 970-0300
www.grillcraft.com

Hellwig Suspension Accessories
(load- and sway-control systems)
16237 Ave. 296
Visalia, CA 93292
(559) 734-7451
www.hellwigproducts.com

Holley Performance Products
(Airmass Exhaust, Holley Ignition, NOS, Earl's)
1801 Russellville Road, P.O. Box 10360
Bowling Green, KY 42102-7360
1-800-Holley-1
www.holley.com

J.C. Whitney & CO.
(Mail-order company)
225 N. Michigan Ave.
Chicago, IL 60601-7601
(312) 431-6000
www.jcwhitney.com

Jet Performance
(Computer upgrades)
17491 Apex Circle
Huntington Beach, CA 92647
1-800-736-9578
www.jetchip.com

JL Audio, Inc.
(Amplifiers, speakers, subwoofers)
10369 N. Commerce Parkway
Miramar, FL 33025
(954) 443-1100
www.jlaudio.com

K&N Engineering
(air filters, intake kits)
P.O. Box 1329
Riverside, CA 92502
(888) 949-1832
www.knfilters.com

Katzkin Leather Inc.
(Ready-to-install leather car and truck interiors)
6868 Acco St.
Montebello, CA 90640
1-800-842-0590
www.katzkin.com

Lokar Inc.
10924 Murdock Dr.
Knoxville, TN 37932
(865) 966-2269
www.lokar.com
www.lokarmotorsports.com

Lund International
(Running boards, bedcovers, spoilers and styling accessories)
911 Lund Blvd. Suite 100
Anoka, MN 55303
(763) 576-4200
www.lundinternational.com

Magnuson Products, Inc.
(Magnacharger superchargers and kits)
3172 Bunsen Avenue
Ventura, CA 93003
(805) 289-0044
www.magnacharger.com

Mattracks
(Track wheel conversion)
202 Cleveland Ave. E.
P.O. Box 214
Karlstad, MN 56732-0214
(218) 436-6500
www.mattracks.com

Mike McGaughys Classic Chevy Car Parts, Inc.
(Suspension parts)
5680 W. Barstow
Fresno, CA 93722
(559) 226-8196
www.mcgaughys.com

MSD
(Ignition products)
1490 Henry Brennan Drive
El Paso, TX 79936
(915) 857-5200
www.msdignition.com

Painless Performance
(Complete automotive electrical systems and components)
2501 Ludelle St.
Fort Worth, TX 76105-1036
(817) 244-6212
www.painlessperformance.com

Powerdyne
104-C East Avenue K-4
Lancaster, CA 93535
(661) 723-2800
www.powerdyne.com

Race Car Dynamics Inc. (RCD)
(Suspension systems for trucks and SUVs)
11433 Woodside Ave.
Santee, Ca 92071
(619)588-4723
www.rcdsuspension
www.racecardynamics.com

Scosche
(Car audio equipment and accessories)
1550 Pacific Ave.
Oxnard, CA 93033
1-800-621-3695
www.scosche.com

Smeding Performance
(Performance crate engines)
3340 Sunrise Blvd., Unit #E
Rancho Cordova, CA 95742
(916) 638-0899
www.smedingperformance.com

Smittybilt
Automotive Group, Inc.
(Tubular side bars, front guards, and accessories)
1550 Magnolia Ave. Suite 101
Corona, Ca 92879
1-888-717-5797
www.smittybiltinc.com

SSP Street Sound Plus
(Custom stereo installation)
2751 Thousand Oaks Blvd.
Thousand Oaks, CA 91362
(805) 557-1054

Street Scene Equipment, Inc.
(Truck and SUV accessories)
365 McCormick Ave.
Costa Mesa, CA 92626
1-888-477-0707
www.streetsceneeq.com

Superchips
(Computer reprogramming tools)
1790 E. Airport Blvd.
Sanford, FL 32773
(407) 585-7000
www.superchips.com

Trail Master Suspension
Div. of Smittybilt
(Truck and SUV systems)
1550 Magnolia Ave. #101
Corona, CA 92879-2073
(909) 736-8686
www.trailmastersuspension.com

Universal Products, Inc.
(Vinyl graphic packages, striping and decals)
521 Industrial St.
Goddard, KS 67052
(316) 794-8601
www.u-p.com

Warn Industries, Inc.
(Off-road accessories, winches, bumpers and 4WD hubs)
12900 S.E. Capps Road
Clackamas, OR 97015-8903
1-800-543-9276
www.warn.com

Wheel Concepts
(Wheels)
1103 Lawrence Dr.
Newbury Park, CA 91320
(805) 376-2113

Whipple Superchargers
3292 N. Weber
Fresno, CA 93722
(559) 442-1261

Woodview
(Interior trim kits)
5670 Timberlea Blvd.
Mississauga, Ontario, Canada
L4W 4M6
1-800-797-DASH (3274)
www.woodcorp.com

A special thanks to:

- APC (American Products Company), Bridgestone/Firestone, Grillcraft, Grant Products, MSD, JL Audio, Focal America, Genera Corp., Scosche, Woodview, Katzkin, Lokar, Lund, a brand of Lund International, Painless Performance, Street Scene, Empire Motor Sports and Universal Products for supplying many of the custom and performance parts seen throughout this book.
- Jeff Yoder (RCD Suspensions)
- Robin Girard (Woodview)
- Stan Rodgers (Universal Products)
- Rick Craze (Lokar)
- Ivan Diaz and Ron Leslie (Katzkin)
- Shari McCullough-Arfons (McCullough Public Relations)
- Susan Anz Carpenter (ATS Design)
- Danny Treptow (Street Scene)
- Jerry Loaiza (Grillcraft)
- Jay Lusignan (Lund)
- Gary Rubin (Warn)
- Tom Terry (Grant Products)
- Mike Deschenes and Larry Ashley (APC)
- Dennis Overholser (Painless Performance)
- Nathan Perkins (Scosche)
- Don and Ernie Boehm (Blingz of Beverly Hills)
- Lucette Nicoll (Nicoll Public Relations) for arranging much of the Mobile entertainment.
- Michael West (Eclipse)
- Aftermarket, Carmichael, CA
- Marco Muffler, Sacramento, CA
- California Truck Works, Rancho Cordova, CA
- Jaime (Dracula) Palafox and Hector Galvan at SSP (Street Sound Plus), Thousand Oaks for all of the Mobile Entertainment installations.

HAYNES REPAIR MANUALS

ACURA
- 12020 **Integra** '86 thru '89 & **Legend** '86 thru '90
- 12021 **Integra** '90 thru '93 & **Legend** '91 thru '95

AMC
- **Jeep CJ** - see JEEP (50020)
- 14020 **Mid-size models** '70 thru '83
- 14025 **(Renault) Alliance & Encore** '83 thru '87

AUDI
- 15020 **4000** all models '80 thru '87
- 15025 **5000** all models '77 thru '83
- 15026 **5000** all models '84 thru '88

AUSTIN-HEALEY
- **Sprite** - see MG Midget (66015)

BMW
- *18020 **3/5 Series** not including diesel or all-wheel drive models '82 thru '92
- 18021 **3-Series** incl. Z3 models '92 thru '98
- 18025 **320i** all 4 cyl models '75 thru '83
- 18050 **1500 thru 2002** except Turbo '59 thru '77

BUICK
- *19010 **Buick Century** '97 thru '02
  - **Century** (front-wheel drive) - see GM (38005)
- *19020 **Buick, Oldsmobile & Pontiac Full-size** (Front-wheel drive) '85 thru '02
  - **Buick** Electra, LeSabre and Park Avenue; **Oldsmobile** Delta 88 Royale, Ninety Eight and Regency; **Pontiac** Bonneville
- 19025 **Buick Oldsmobile & Pontiac Full-size** (Rear wheel drive)
  - **Buick** Estate '70 thru '90, Electra '70 thru '84, LeSabre '70 thru '85, Limited '74 thru '79 **Oldsmobile** Custom Cruiser '70 thru '90, Delta 88 '70 thru '85, Ninety-eight '70 thru '84 **Pontiac** Bonneville '70 thru '81, Catalina '70 thru '81, Grandville '70 thru '75, Parisienne '83 thru '86
- 19030 **Mid-size Regal & Century** all rear-drive models with V6, V8 and Turbo '74 thru '87
  - **Regal** - see GENERAL MOTORS (38010)
  - **Riviera** - see GENERAL MOTORS (38030)
  - **Roadmaster** - see CHEVROLET (24046)
  - **Skyhawk** - see GENERAL MOTORS (38015)
  - **Skylark** - see GM (38020, 38025)
  - **Somerset** - see GENERAL MOTORS (38025)

CADILLAC
- 21030 **Cadillac Rear Wheel Drive** all gasoline models '70 thru '93
  - **Cimarron** - see GENERAL MOTORS (38015)
  - **DeVille** - see GM (38031 & 38032)
  - **Eldorado** - see GM (38030 & 38031)
  - **Fleetwood** - see GM (38031)
  - **Seville** - see GM (38030, 38031 & 38032)

CHEVROLET
- *24010 **Astro & GMC Safari Mini-vans** '85 thru '02
- 24015 **Camaro V8** all models '70 thru '81
- 24016 **Camaro** all models '82 thru '92
- 24017 **Camaro & Firebird** '93 thru '00
  - **Cavalier** - see GENERAL MOTORS (38016)
  - **Celebrity** - see GENERAL MOTORS (38005)
- 24020 **Chevelle, Malibu & El Camino** '69 thru '87
- 24024 **Chevette & Pontiac T1000** '76 thru '87
  - **Citation** - see GENERAL MOTORS (38020)
- 24032 **Corsica/Beretta** all models '87 thru '96
- 24040 **Corvette** all V8 models '68 thru '82
- 24041 **Corvette** all models '84 thru '96
- 10305 **Chevrolet Engine Overhaul Manual**
- 24045 **Full-size Sedans** Caprice, Impala, Biscayne, Bel Air & Wagons '69 thru '90
- 24046 **Impala SS & Caprice** and **Buick Roadmaster** '91 thru '96
  - **Impala** - see LUMINA (24048)
  - **Lumina** '90 thru '94 - see GM (38010)
- *24048 **Lumina & Monte Carlo** '95 thru '01
  - **Lumina APV** - see GM (38035)
- 24050 **Luv Pick-up** all 2WD & 4WD '72 thru '82
  - **Malibu** '97 thru '00 - see GM (38026)
- 24055 **Monte Carlo** all models '70 thru '88
  - **Monte Carlo** '95 thru '01 - see LUMINA (24048)
- 24059 **Nova** all V8 models '69 thru '79
- 24060 **Nova and Geo Prizm** '85 thru '92
- 24064 **Pick-ups** '67 thru '87 - Chevrolet & GMC, all V8 & in-line 6 cyl, 2WD & 4WD '67 thru '87; Suburbans, Blazers & Jimmys '67 thru '91

- 24065 **Pick-ups** '88 thru '98 - Chevrolet & GMC, full-size pick-ups '88 thru '98, C/K Classic '99 & '00, Blazer & Jimmy '92 thru '94; Suburban '92 thru '99; Tahoe & Yukon '95 thru '99
- *24066 **Pick-ups** '99 thru '03 - Chevrolet Silverado & GMC Sierra full-size pick-ups '99 thru '02, Suburban/Tahoe/Yukon/Yukon XL '00 thru '02
- 24070 **S-10 & S-15 Pick-ups** '82 thru '93, **Blazer & Jimmy** '83 thru '94,
- *24071 **S-10 & S-15 Pick-ups** '94 thru '01, **Blazer & Jimmy** '95 thru '01, **Hombre** '96 thru '01
- *24072 **Chevrolet TrailBlazer & TrailBlazer EXT, GMC Envoy & Envoy XL, Oldsmobile Bravada** '02 and '03
- 24075 **Sprint** '85 thru '88 & **Geo Metro** '89 thru '01
- 24080 **Vans** - Chevrolet & GMC '68 thru '96

CHRYSLER
- 25015 **Chrysler Cirrus, Dodge Stratus, Plymouth Breeze** '95 thru '00
- 10310 **Chrysler Engine Overhaul Manual**
- 25020 **Full-size Front-Wheel Drive** '88 thru '93
  - **K-Cars** - see DODGE Aries (30008)
  - **Laser** - see DODGE Daytona (30030)
- 25025 **Chrysler LHS, Concorde, New Yorker, Dodge Intrepid, Eagle Vision,** '93 thru '97
- *25026 **Chrysler LHS, Concorde, 300M, Dodge Intrepid,** '98 thru '03
- 25030 **Chrysler & Plymouth Mid-size** front wheel drive '82 thru '95
  - **Rear-wheel Drive** - see Dodge (30050)
- *25035 **PT Cruiser** all models '01 thru '03
- *25040 **Chrysler** Sebring, **Dodge** Avenger '95 thru '02

DATSUN
- 28005 **200SX** all models '80 thru '83
- 28007 **B-210** all models '73 thru '78
- 28009 **210** all models '79 thru '82
- 28012 **240Z, 260Z & 280Z** Coupe '70 thru '78
- 28014 **280ZX** Coupe & 2+2 '79 thru '83
  - **300ZX** - see NISSAN (72010)
- 28016 **310** all models '78 thru '82
- 28018 **510 & PL521 Pick-up** '68 thru '73
- 28020 **510** all models '78 thru '81
- 28022 **620 Series Pick-up** all models '73 thru '79
  - **720 Series Pick-up** - see NISSAN (72030)
- 28025 **810/Maxima** all gasoline models '77 thru '84

DODGE
- **400 & 600** - see CHRYSLER (25030)
- 30008 **Aries & Plymouth Reliant** '81 thru '89
- 30010 **Caravan & Plymouth Voyager** '84 thru '95
- *30011 **Caravan & Plymouth Voyager** '96 thru '02
- 30012 **Challenger/Plymouth Saporro** '78 thru '83
- 30016 **Colt & Plymouth Champ** '78 thru '87
- 30020 **Dakota Pick-ups** all models '87 thru '96
- *30021 **Durango** '98 & '99, **Dakota** '97 thru '99
- 30025 **Dart, Demon, Plymouth Barracuda, Duster & Valiant** 6 cyl models '67 thru '76
- 30030 **Daytona & Chrysler Laser** '84 thru '89
  - **Intrepid** - see CHRYSLER (25025, 25026)
- *30034 **Neon** all models '95 thru '99
- 30035 **Omni & Plymouth Horizon** '78 thru '90
- 30040 **Pick-ups** all full-size models '74 thru '93
- *30041 **Pick-ups** all full-size models '94 thru '01
- 30045 **Ram 50/D50 Pick-ups & Raider and Plymouth Arrow Pick-ups** '79 thru '93
- 30050 **Dodge/Plymouth/Chrysler** RWD '71 thru '89
- 30055 **Shadow & Plymouth Sundance** '87 thru '94
- 30060 **Spirit & Plymouth Acclaim** '89 thru '95
- *30065 **Vans** - Dodge & Plymouth '71 thru '03

EAGLE
- **Talon** - see MITSUBISHI (68030, 68031)
- **Vision** - see CHRYSLER (25025)

FIAT
- 34010 **124 Sport Coupe & Spider** '68 thru '78
- 34025 **X1/9** all models '74 thru '80

FORD
- 10355 **Ford Automatic Transmission Overhaul**
- 36004 **Aerostar Mini-vans** all models '86 thru '97
- 36006 **Contour & Mercury Mystique** '95 thru '00
- 36008 **Courier Pick-up** all models '72 thru '82
- *36012 **Crown Victoria & Mercury Grand Marquis** '88 thru '00

- 10320 **Ford Engine Overhaul Manual**
- 36016 **Escort/Mercury Lynx** all models '81 thru '90
- 36020 **Escort/Mercury Tracer** '91 thru '00
- 36022 **Ford Escape & Mazda Tribute** '01 thru '03
- 36024 **Explorer & Mazda Navajo** '91 thru '01
- 36025 **Ford Explorer & Mercury Mountaineer** '02 and '03
- 36028 **Fairmont & Mercury Zephyr** '78 thru '83
- 36030 **Festiva & Aspire** '88 thru '97
- 36032 **Fiesta** all models '77 thru '80
- *36034 **Focus** all models '00 and '01
- 36036 **Ford & Mercury Full-size** '75 thru '87
- 36044 **Ford & Mercury Mid-size** '75 thru '86
- 36048 **Mustang V8** all models '64-1/2 thru '73
- 36049 **Mustang II** 4 cyl, V6 & V8 models '74 thru '78
- 36050 **Mustang & Mercury Capri** all models Mustang, '79 thru '93; Capri, '79 thru '86
- *36051 **Mustang** all models '94 thru '03
- 36054 **Pick-ups & Bronco** '73 thru '79
- 36058 **Pick-ups & Bronco** '80 thru '96
- *36059 **F-150 & Expedition** '97 thru '02, **F-250** '97 thru '99 & **Lincoln Navigator** '98 thru '02
- *36060 **Super Duty Pick-ups, Excursion** '97 thru '02
- 36062 **Pinto & Mercury Bobcat** '75 thru '80
- 36066 **Probe** all models '89 thru '92
- 36070 **Ranger/Bronco II** gasoline models '83 thru '92
- *36071 **Ranger** '93 thru '00 & **Mazda Pick-ups** '94 thru '00
- 36074 **Taurus & Mercury Sable** '86 thru '95
- *36075 **Taurus & Mercury Sable** '96 thru '01
- 36078 **Tempo & Mercury Topaz** '84 thru '94
- 36082 **Thunderbird/Mercury Cougar** '83 thru '88
- 36086 **Thunderbird/Mercury Cougar** '89 and '97
- 36090 **Vans** all V8 Econoline models '69 thru '91
- *36094 **Vans** full size '92 thru '01
- *36097 **Windstar Mini-van** '95 thru '03

GENERAL MOTORS
- 10360 **GM Automatic Transmission Overhaul**
- 38005 **Buick Century, Chevrolet Celebrity, Oldsmobile Cutlass Ciera & Pontiac 6000** all models '82 thru '96
- *38010 **Buick Regal, Chevrolet Lumina, Oldsmobile Cutlass Supreme & Pontiac Grand Prix** (FWD) '88 thru '02
- 38015 **Buick Skyhawk, Cadillac Cimarron, Chevrolet Cavalier, Oldsmobile Firenza & Pontiac J-2000 & Sunbird** '82 thru '94
- *38016 **Chevrolet Cavalier & Pontiac Sunfire** '95 thru '01
- 38020 **Buick Skylark, Chevrolet Citation, Olds Omega, Pontiac Phoenix** '80 thru '85
- 38025 **Buick Skylark & Somerset, Oldsmobile Achieva & Calais and Pontiac Grand Am** all models '85 thru '98
- *38026 **Chevrolet Malibu, Olds Alero & Cutlass, Pontiac Grand Am** '97 thru '00
- 38030 **Cadillac Eldorado** '71 thru '85, **Seville** '80 thru '85, **Oldsmobile Toronado** '71 thru '85, **Buick Riviera** '79 thru '85
- *38031 **Cadillac Eldorado & Seville** '86 thru '91, **DeVille** '86 thru '93, **Fleetwood & Olds Toronado** '86 thru '92, **Buick Riviera** '86 thru '93
- 38032 **Cadillac DeVille** '94 thru '02 & **Seville** - '92 thru '02
- 38035 **Chevrolet Lumina APV, Olds Silhouette & Pontiac Trans Sport** all models '90 thru '96
- *38036 **Chevrolet Venture, Olds Silhouette, Pontiac Trans Sport & Montana** '97 thru '01
  - **General Motors Full-size Rear-wheel Drive** - see BUICK (19025)

GEO
- **Metro** - see CHEVROLET Sprint (24075)
- **Prizm** - '85 thru '92 see CHEVY (24060), '93 thru '02 see TOYOTA Corolla (92036)
- 40030 **Storm** all models '90 thru '93
  - **Tracker** - see SUZUKI Samurai (90010)

GMC
- **Vans & Pick-ups** - see CHEVROLET

HONDA
- 42010 **Accord CVCC** all models '76 thru '83
- 42011 **Accord** all models '84 thru '89
- 42012 **Accord** all models '90 thru '93
- 42013 **Accord** all models '94 thru '97
- *42014 **Accord** all models '98 and '99

42020	**Civic 1200** all models '73 thru '79
42021	**Civic 1300 & 1500 CVCC** '80 thru '83
42022	**Civic 1500 CVCC** all models '75 thru '79
42023	**Civic** all models '84 thru '91
42024	**Civic & del Sol** '92 thru '95
*42025	**Civic** '96 thru '00, **CR-V** '97 thru '00, **Acura Integra** '94 thru '00
42040	**Prelude CVCC** all models '79 thru '89

HYUNDAI

*43010	**Elantra** all models '96 thru '01
43015	**Excel & Accent** all models '86 thru '98

ISUZU

	Hombre - see CHEVROLET S-10 (24071)
*47017	**Rodeo** '91 thru '02; **Amigo** '89 thru '94 and '98 thru '02; **Honda Passport** '95 thru '02
47020	**Trooper & Pick-up** '81 thru '93

JAGUAR

49010	**XJ6** all 6 cyl models '68 thru '86
49011	**XJ6** all models '88 thru '94
49015	**XJ12 & XJS** all 12 cyl models '72 thru '85

JEEP

50010	**Cherokee, Comanche & Wagoneer Limited** all models '84 thru '00
50020	**CJ** all models '49 thru '86
*50025	**Grand Cherokee** all models '93 thru '00
50029	**Grand Wagoneer & Pick-up** '72 thru '91 Grand Wagoneer '84 thru '91, Cherokee & Wagoneer '72 thru '83, Pick-up '72 thru '88
*50030	**Wrangler** all models '87 thru '00

LEXUS

	ES 300 - see TOYOTA Camry (92007)

LINCOLN

	Navigator - see FORD Pick-up (36059)
*59010	**Rear-Wheel Drive** all models '70 thru '01

MAZDA

61010	**GLC Hatchback** (rear-wheel drive) '77 thru '83
61011	**GLC** (front-wheel drive) '81 thru '85
61015	**323 & Protegé** '90 thru '00
*61016	**MX-5 Miata** '90 thru '97
61020	**MPV** all models '89 thru '94
	Navajo - see Ford Explorer (36024)
61030	**Pick-ups** '72 thru '93 Pick-ups '94 thru '00 - see Ford Ranger (36071)
61035	**RX-7** all models '79 thru '85
61036	**RX-7** all models '86 thru '91
61040	**626** (rear-wheel drive) all models '79 thru '82
61041	**626/MX-6** (front-wheel drive) '83 thru '91
61042	**626** '93 thru '01, **MX-6/Ford Probe** '93 thru '97

MERCEDES-BENZ

63012	**123 Series Diesel** '76 thru '85
63015	**190 Series** four-cyl gas models '84 thru '88
63020	**230/250/280** 6 cyl sohc models '68 thru '72
63025	**280 123 Series** gasoline models '77 thru '81
63030	**350 & 450** all models '71 thru '80

MERCURY

64200	**Villager & Nissan Quest** '93 thru '01 All other titles, see FORD Listing.

MG

66010	**MGB** Roadster & GT Coupe '62 thru '80
66015	**MG Midget, Austin Healey Sprite** '58 thru '80

MITSUBISHI

68020	**Cordia, Tredia, Galant, Precis & Mirage** '83 thru '93
68030	**Eclipse, Eagle Talon & Ply. Laser** '90 thru '94
*68031	**Eclipse** '95 thru '01, **Eagle Talon** '95 thru '98
68035	**Mitsubishi Galant** '94 thru '03
68040	**Pick-up** '83 thru '96 & **Montero** '83 thru '93

NISSAN

72010	**300ZX** all models including Turbo '84 thru '89
72015	**Altima** all models '93 thru '01
72020	**Maxima** all models '85 thru '92
*72021	**Maxima** all models '93 thru '01
72030	**Pick-ups** '80 thru '97 **Pathfinder** '87 thru '95
*72031	**Frontier Pick-up** '98 thru '01, **Xterra** '00 & '01, **Pathfinder** '96 thru '01
72040	**Pulsar** all models '83 thru '86
	Quest - see MERCURY Villager (64200)
72050	**Sentra** all models '82 thru '94
72051	**Sentra & 200SX** all models '95 thru '99
72060	**Stanza** all models '82 thru '90

OLDSMOBILE

73015	**Cutlass** V6 & V8 gas models '74 thru '88
	For other OLDSMOBILE titles, see BUICK, CHEVROLET or GENERAL MOTORS listing.

PLYMOUTH

	For PLYMOUTH titles, see DODGE listing.

PONTIAC

79008	**Fiero** all models '84 thru '88
79018	**Firebird** V8 models except Turbo '70 thru '81
79019	**Firebird** all models '82 thru '92
79040	**Mid-size Rear-wheel Drive** '70 thru '87
	For other PONTIAC titles, see BUICK, CHEVROLET or GENERAL MOTORS listing.

PORSCHE

80020	**911** except Turbo & Carrera 4 '65 thru '89
80025	**914** all 4 cyl models '69 thru '76
80030	**924** all models including Turbo '76 thru '82
80035	**944** all models including Turbo '83 thru '89

RENAULT

	Alliance & Encore - see AMC (14020)

SAAB

*84010	**900** all models including Turbo '79 thru '88

SATURN

*87010	**Saturn** all models '91 thru '02
87020	**Saturn** all L-series models '00 thru '04

SUBARU

89002	**1100, 1300, 1400 & 1600** '71 thru '79
89003	**1600 & 1800** 2WD & 4WD '80 thru '94

SUZUKI

90010	**Samurai/Sidekick & Geo Tracker** '86 thru '01

TOYOTA

92005	**Camry** all models '83 thru '91
92006	**Camry** all models '92 thru '96
*92007	**Camry, Avalon, Solara, Lexus ES 300** '97 thru '01
92015	**Celica Rear Wheel Drive** '71 thru '85
92020	**Celica Front Wheel Drive** '86 thru '99
92025	**Celica Supra** all models '79 thru '92
92030	**Corolla** all models '75 thru '79
92032	**Corolla** all rear wheel drive models '80 thru '87
92035	**Corolla** all front wheel drive models '84 thru '92
92036	**Corolla & Geo Prizm** '93 thru '02
92040	**Corolla Tercel** all models '80 thru '82
92045	**Corona** all models '74 thru '82
92050	**Cressida** all models '78 thru '82
92055	**Land Cruiser** FJ40, 43, 45, 55 '68 thru '82
92056	**Land Cruiser** FJ60, 62, 80, FZJ80 '80 thru '96
92065	**MR2** all models '85 thru '87
92070	**Pick-up** all models '69 thru '78
92075	**Pick-up** all models '79 thru '95
*92076	**Tacoma** '95 thru '00, **4Runner** '96 thru '00, & **T100** '93 thru '98
*92078	**Tundra** '00 thru '02 & **Sequoia** '01 thru '02
92080	**Previa** all models '91 thru '95
*92082	**RAV4** all models '96 thru '02
92085	**Tercel** all models '87 thru '94

TRIUMPH

94007	**Spitfire** all models '62 thru '81
94010	**TR7** all models '75 thru '81

VW

96008	**Beetle & Karmann Ghia** '54 thru '79
*96009	**New Beetle** '98 thru '00
96016	**Rabbit, Jetta, Scirocco & Pick-up** gas models '74 thru '91 & Convertible '80 thru '92
96017	**Golf, GTI & Jetta** '93 thru '98 & **Cabrio** '95 thru '98
*96018	**Golf, GTI, Jetta & Cabrio** '99 thru '02
96020	**Rabbit, Jetta & Pick-up** diesel '77 thru '84
96023	**Passat** '98 thru '01, **Audi A4** '96 thru '01
96030	**Transporter 1600** all models '68 thru '79
96035	**Transporter 1700, 1800 & 2000** '72 thru '79
96040	**Type 3 1500 & 1600** all models '63 thru '73
96045	**Vanagon** all air-cooled models '80 thru '83

VOLVO

97010	**120, 130 Series & 1800 Sports** '61 thru '73
97015	**140 Series** all models '66 thru '74
97020	**240 Series** all models '76 thru '93
97040	**740 & 760 Series** all models '82 thru '88
97050	**850 Series** all models '93 thru '97

TECHBOOK MANUALS

10205	**Automotive Computer Codes**
10210	**Automotive Emissions Control Manual**
10215	**Fuel Injection Manual, 1978 thru 1985**
10220	**Fuel Injection Manual, 1986 thru 1999**
10225	**Holley Carburetor Manual**
10230	**Rochester Carburetor Manual**
10240	**Weber/Zenith/Stromberg/SU Carburetors**
10305	**Chevrolet Engine Overhaul Manual**
10310	**Chrysler Engine Overhaul Manual**
10320	**Ford Engine Overhaul Manual**
10330	**GM and Ford Diesel Engine Repair Manual**
10340	**Small Engine Repair Manual, 5 HP & Less**
10341	**Small Engine Repair Manual, 5.5 - 20 HP**
10345	**Suspension, Steering & Driveline Manual**
10355	**Ford Automatic Transmission Overhaul**
10360	**GM Automatic Transmission Overhaul**
10405	**Automotive Body Repair & Painting**
10410	**Automotive Brake Manual**
10411	**Automotive Anti-lock Brake (ABS) Systems**
10415	**Automotive Detaiing Manual**
10420	**Automotive Eelectrical Manual**
10425	**Automotive Heating & Air Conditioning**
10430	**Automotive Reference Manual & Dictionary**
10435	**Automotive Tools Manual**
10440	**Used Car Buying Guide**
10445	**Welding Manual**
10450	**ATV Basics**

SPANISH MANUALS

98903	**Reparación de Carrocería & Pintura**
98905	**Códigos Automotrices de la Computadora**
98910	**Frenos Automotriz**
98915	**Inyección de Combustible 1986 al 1999**
99040	**Chevrolet & GMC Camionetas** '67 al '87 Incluye Suburban, Blazer & Jimmy '67 al '91
99041	**Chevrolet & GMC Camionetas** '88 al '98 Incluye Suburban '92 al '98, Blazer & Jimmy '92 al '94, Tahoe y Yukon '95 al '98
99042	**Chevrolet & GMC Camionetas Cerradas** '68 al '95
99055	**Dodge Caravan & Plymouth Voyager** '84 al '95
99075	**Ford Camionetas y Bronco** '80 al '94
99077	**Ford Camionetas Cerradas** '69 al '91
99088	**Ford Modelos de Tamaño Mediano** '75 al '86
99091	**Ford Taurus & Mercury Sable** '86 al '95
99095	**GM Modelos de Tamaño Grande** '70 al '90
99100	**GM Modelos de Tamaño Mediano** '70 al '88
99110	**Nissan Camioneta** '80 al '96, **Pathfinder** '87 al '95
99118	**Nissan Sentra** '82 al '94
99125	**Toyota Camionetas y 4Runner** '79 al '95

Listings shown with an asterisk (*) indicate model coverage as of this printing. These titles will be periodically updated to include later model years - consult your Haynes dealer for more information.

Haynes North America, Inc., 861 Lawrence Drive, Newbury Park, CA 91320-1514 • (805) 498-6703